OBSERVING THE NIXON YEARS

OBSERVING THE NIXON YEARS

"Notes and Comment"
from *The New Yorker* on
the Vietnam War
and the Watergate Crisis,
1969–1975

JONATHAN SCHELL

With a preface by William Shawn

PANTHEON BOOKS   NEW YORK

Copyright © 1989 by Jonathan Schell

Preface Copyright © 1989 by William Shawn

All rights reserved under International and Pan-American Copyright Conventions. Published in the United States by Pantheon Books, a division of Random House, Inc., New York, and simultaneously in Canada by Random House of Canada Limited, Toronto.

The "Notes and Comment" columns in this book originally appeared in *The New Yorker* magazine from 1969 to 1975.

LIBRARY OF CONGRESS CATALOGING-IN-PUBLICATION DATA

Schell, Jonathan, 1943–
  Observing the Nixon Years.

  1. United States—Politics and government—1969–1974.
2. Nixon, Richard M. (Richard Milhous), 1913–
3. Vietnamese Conflict, 1961–1975—United States.
4. Watergate Affair, 1972–1974.   5. United States—
Politics and government—1974–1977.   I. Title.
E855.S356   1989   973.924   88-43134
ISBN 0-394-57495-8

Book design by Anne Scatto

Manufactured in the United States of America

First Edition

For Matthew, for Phoebe,
and for Thomas with love.

CONTENTS

PREFACE

On Thursday, January 23, 1969, when Jonathan Schell was a staff writer for *The New Yorker* and I was the magazine's editor-in-chief, he handed me his first piece of editorial comment on the Vietnam war. It was written for, and appeared in, the "Notes and Comment" section of the February 1, 1969 issue. Schell could not have known, and I could not have guessed, that he was embarking on a monumental project that he would sustain over a period of six years: more than a hundred Comment pieces, as we called them, on the tragically interrelated subjects of Vietnam, President Richard Nixon, and Watergate. Those are the pieces that now constitute this book.

I know of no journalist or thinker who saw more clearly or more deeply or more consistently than Jonathan Schell into the truth of the part we Americans played in Vietnam. From the outset, he thought that our presence in Vietnam was a mistake and morally wrong, and in his first, prophetic Comment piece he introduced a theme to which he would return again and again: that the government of South Vietnam did not have, and never would have, the support of the Vietnamese people, and that its very existence and the existence of its military forces were totally dependent on American advisers, American weapons, American uniforms, American planes, and American funds: that the South Vietnam government and its military forces were phantoms, figments of the American imagination, and with our departure would simply vanish. He soon saw, too, that we were devastating the country we were supposedly defending, that the war we were fighting, with its successive "aims"—to save South Vietnam from Communist North Vietnam, to stop the spread of World Communism, to thwart China, to thwart Russia, to show our "resolve" and "credibility" to the rest of the world—was misbegotten and doomed. In April of 1973, after the last of our troops had been

withdrawn, Schell, in another piece of Comment, described the details of
the disintegration of the South Vietnam government and its military forces:
precisely the ending he had foreseen. In the intervening period, as he watched
the anguished story unfold, he pounded away tirelessly with his protests.
When the public appeared to be benumbed by events, and many commentators, perhaps out of fatigue, fell silent, Schell remained wide-awake and
alert and vocal. His voice carried. He spoke for all of us then at *The New
Yorker*, but he also spoke for thousands beyond our walls. His passionate,
eloquent writings entered the history of our time. They in themselves became
history.

Political events at home, of course, were intimately bound up with Vietnam:
the anti-war demonstrations, the campus unrest, the attempts to intimidate
the press, the Administration's fear of insurrection, the beginnings of repression, the direct threats to the Constitution and to the survival of the Republic
by President Nixon, Vice-President Spiro Agnew, and Attorney General John
Mitchell, and, finally, Watergate and the President's resignation. Schell followed all these developments closely and understood them profoundly. The
Constitution was his touchstone; he went back to it for inspiration time after
time. He approached each new situation with his historical perspective and
his particular political vision intact. However intense his feelings may have
been, his prose was always measured, beautifully controlled, lucid. The cast
of his mind was, and is, original without ever becoming bizarre or eccentric.
His writing is marked by a rock-solid sanity and a strict logic.

I will quote three passages, in order to give some hint, at least, of how
his extraordinary mind works. In the June 12, 1971 issue, referring to President
Nixon, he wrote, "A disturbing interpretation of the law itself emerges from
the President's remarks. The ordinary way of dealing with people who break
the law is to invoke the law against them. The President seems to want to
replace law enforcement with retaliation in kind—to deal with lawbreakers
by suspending the law. The police are, after all, an arm of the law. In earlier
times, they were called 'the law.' But if the law breaks the law, there is no
law." In the issue of July 29, 1972, referring to Vietnam, he wrote, "The war
has inertia on its side. In a strange reversal of the usual order of things, it
requires inaction to fight the war and action to stop fighting it. And because
it takes so little for us to go on with the war, we sometimes get the feeling
that someone else is waging it—as though the computers and the B-52s could
wage it by themselves. Yet in fact it is no one who is killing the Vietnamese
but we ourselves. If we are not killing them, who is?" On December 17, 1973,
he wrote, " 'Credibility' is the modern version of candor. Candor entails

truthfulness, but credibility does not. Credibility is the public-relations version of truthfulness. It is the truth's 'image.' "

What to me is most characteristic of Schell's writing is the unexpectedness of his turn of thought. He is constantly saying what has not been said before. So what we have here, in these hundred or so pieces, is not only an incomparable political document but also a literary work that will endure.

WILLIAM SHAWN

NEW YORK, SEPTEMBER 1988

I. THE WAR

IN the years when the Vietnam war was still escalating, it often seemed that Washington was enlarging our official war goals to match and justify the escalation of our military commitment. At first, when the commitment was small, it was enough to believe that we were protecting democracy in Vietnam. Later, as our forces grew, the domino theory was advanced, to show that the real stake was the future of freedom in all Southeast Asia. And in the final days, when the present level of half a million men had been reached, we were told that the true enemy was China and "Asian Communism." Likewise, the growing commitment, and the growing losses, seemed to require increasingly optimistic reports on the progress of the war. Then, as the gap between the official optimism and the reality widened, it began to seem that we were fighting as much to vindicate our past pronouncements as to achieve any concrete objective in Vietnam. It was as though by continuing and widening the war we could transform it into the kind of war we'd thought we were going to be fighting in the first place. Thus it has happened that, along with a tragic, unhopeful position within Vietnam, the Nixon Administration has inherited a ponderous baggage of grandiose war aims and dogmatically optimistic appraisals of our achievement.

Now that President Nixon's own people have opened the substantive phase of the negotiations in Paris, it may prove that the inflated war aims we have built up will turn out to be our most serious obstacle to reaching a settlement. Success in the negotiations may depend in large part on our finding a way to back down gracefully from the war aims that were devised to support the policy of escalation. No issue reveals our predicament more clearly than the issue of a coalition government, on which we are now taking the stand, in support of the regime in Saigon, that there can be no coalition that would include the National Liberation Front. The present Saigon government is probably unique in the history of government. About a year ago, John Kenneth Galbraith estimated that it would collapse within a month if American support were to be completely withdrawn. Actually, it had already collapsed—not just once but again and again, as it was driven from the countryside by the enemy and repeatedly overturned by coups d'état. Its continued existence depends on American support more heavily than any government has ever relied on foreign support before. Over ninety per cent of the government's revenue is donated by the United States. Every one of its officials, down to the level of district chief, has been assigned a full-time American adviser of equal military rank, so the entire administration is paralleled by an American structure. Every unit of its Army is advised by a team of Americans, and its Army is equipped entirely with American weapons. Since almost all transportation in Vietnam, whether of people or of things, is by air, most of it is American. A Vietnamese province chief receives a salary that derives ultimately from American sources, he commands an army that is clothed, armed, and advised by Americans, he gives his people food and housing that arrive on American planes, and he receives the full-time advice of an American colonel. What makes this condition of total dependence difficult to perceive is that although the Saigon regime owes its existence to us, it does not appear to give us its allegiance. No doubt because American policymakers have genuinely wished—however abortive their efforts to make the wish come true—the Saigon regime to become a strong democratic government, our style has been to let its leaders go on making bitter anti-American remarks in their public speeches. Many observers have seen Saigon's freedom to criticize us as a sign that it must have a base of support apart from us. But the whole question of whether Saigon behaves as we would like it to or not is a side issue. The fundamental issue is whether the Saigon regime exists at all as a government—not in relation to us but in relation to its own people—and whether it has any chance of continuing to exist if we leave. Measured by this standard, the regime, which has been unable to set up effective administration or get visible popular support for any of its many projects of construction, and, in fact, has overseen the destruction, mostly by allied bombing, of roughly half of its villages and some of its cities, too, may not deserve the name "government" at all. It would be more accurate to call it a conscripted army and leave it at that—or, insofar as it exists in other ways for its people, to call it a public-relations firm. Even to call it a corrupt dictatorship is, in a sense, too complimentary, because to speak of corruption is to imply that what is corrupt was once healthy, and to speak of a dictatorship implies a degree of control that Saigon does not exercise over its people. Its one talent is for destruction, and this is borrowed from us.

The question of a coalition government is, therefore, one of whether we can assure the Saigon regime's participation in a future South Vietnamese government, not of whether we should let the National Liberation Front—which is now certainly the most powerful political force in South Vietnam—participate. When one considers how little the Saigon regime has achieved with the help of half a million Americans, one can hardly imagine that, in the long run, it can survive without us. The idea that we could afford to demand a settlement without a coalition had been an integral part of the set of views on Vietnam that led the Johnson Administration to believe year after year that the feeble Saigon government was about to gain the allegiance of the South Vietnamese and that we were about to win the war. To persist in that demand now, at the negotiating table, is to place our negotiators in the impossible position of being unable even to consider the solution that is the most favorable one we can conceivably hope for, and the one that may offer us our only way of getting our troops home soon.

SEPTEMBER 27, 1969

WHEN we heard last week that President Nixon planned to reduce our forces in Vietnam by thirty-five thousand men, we recalled some thoughts we had had during the previous reduction of troops there. Early in July, a month after President Nixon announced the withdrawal of twenty-five thousand troops from Vietnam, we saw television news coverage of a parade in Seattle of troops who were identified by the Army as one contingent of the troops being withdrawn. Watching the parade, we began to have the feeling, not for the first time in the course of this war, that something was false and wrong. For some reason we couldn't quite put our finger on, the parade seemed like the kind of thing that can't be taken at face value—perhaps like the year-round American flags that so many people are flying outside their houses these days, and that seem to be saying something as simple as "I love America" but are actually saying something more complicated, such as "I hate hippies and am in favor of wiretapping." At first, as we tried to analyze our mistrustful reaction, it occurred to us that the problem might be just that we were naturally uneasy about a parade celebrating a war we opposed. But on second thought we decided that, however much we disliked what our soldiers had been doing in Vietnam, it was quite fitting for the country that had sent them there to show them some gratitude on their return. Thinking it over some more, we remembered that the parade was celebrating not only the courage of our soldiers but also, more specifically, the troop withdrawal, and we began to wonder if what we doubted might not be the authenticity of the withdrawal. From the start, there had been a number of suspicious signs. Most of the soldiers to be withdrawn, we had learned, were at the end of their one-year tours of duty anyway, and there had been reports that men in the units to be withdrawn whose tours of duty were not up were being shifted to other units. Then, after the parade was over, one paper reported that the man who had led the parade got on a plane and went back to Vietnam the next day. A few weeks later, Senators Albert Gore and J. W. Fulbright discovered that during the period in which the twenty-five thousand men were supposed to have been withdrawn the number of servicemen in Vietnam had actually risen by several thousand. The Pentagon denied this, pointing out that because the number of men in Vietnam is controlled by a rotation system in which each man has, on the average, a one-year tour of duty, the size of our force is always fluctuating. Pentagon officials issued a graph showing that at the time of President Nixon's announcement the total had been at a seasonal low, and explained that the "withdrawal" had taken the form of a cancellation of a scheduled seasonal increase. Whether or not the cancellation of a seasonal increase can properly be called a "withdrawal," this information put the Seattle parade in a strange light. The idea had been that the men in it constituted part of the twenty-five thousand being "withdrawn," but since the twenty-five thousand, if they can be said to exist at all, were men who had got out of being sent in the first place, the Army, in order to be strictly honest, would have had to make up its parade of men who had never been to Vietnam.

For a while, we thought we had got to the heart of the matter. But as we read more reports of the fanfare connected with the withdrawal, we had a feeling that part of the problem was still eluding us. We read that as the men departed, dozens of South Vietnamese girls had been recruited to give them flowers and presents of desk sets decorated with South Vietnamese and American flags, and that President Thieu had made a speech thanking them for coming to Vietnam. In New York, the mayoral candidate Mario Procaccino went to the airport to congratulate the New Yorkers who were returning, and the press ran articles on how the men felt to be back. A story in the *Post* reported that the returning men "had their sights fixed on Mom's cooking." It seemed to us that the government and the press were mesmerized by the word "withdrawal," and were treating the event as though it were something like the end of the Second World War, when men who had spent years on the battlefields were being returned home because the war was over. Actually, of course, unless the number of troops in Vietnam is reduced to zero in less than a year any withdrawal will inevitably take the form of sending fewer troops over and bringing back the troops already there as their tours of duty expire.

The importance of the point is not that this method of withdrawal is more false than some more dramatic method but only that the men returning home during a period of withdrawal are no different from the millions of men who for years have been returning from exactly the same duties. We wondered why this latest group was being accorded the special fanfare. We recalled the homecoming of some of the millions before them. There had been no desk sets, no parades and speeches, no pretty girls giving them flowers, and no mayoral candidates meeting them at the airport. Were they less brave than the men who paraded in Seattle? Were their sacrifices less? Did they look forward to their mothers' cooking less? Where was Mario Procaccino when they arrived? Why did the parades and the speeches of gratitude start up only when the men were being "withdrawn," rather than when they were simply being sent home? In part, we reflected, the answer probably was that the government wanted to make the reduction of our troops "more real" to the public through tangible events like parades, instead of merely giving out an explanation of the complexities of the rotation system. But it also undoubtedly wanted to drum up support for the current twists and turns of policy, and to persuade people that the war was nearing its close by making the withdrawal look like the end of other wars we have been in. If showing appreciation of our Army was the only aim of the fanfare, why did the government wait until now to show it? By using an appeal to the public's patriotism and the public's gratitude to its soldiers for narrow purposes of public relations, it insulted the public and insulted the millions of soldiers who have returned home without any fanfare. We support the policy of getting our men out of Vietnam. Bring them home, by all means—but quietly, please. Quietly.

OCTOBER 4, 1969

M ANY people here have commented that events in Vietnam have an unreal, dreamlike quality. This may be partly because Vietnam is the first war to be shown on television, but we believe that there are more important reasons. A man dreaming is caught up in a reality that is entirely his own creation. Although he is in fact the author of everything that occurs, he may feel shock and surprise, just as though events were part of a reality outside him and beyond his control, as in his waking hours. We believe that the confusion engendered by our government and our military in Vietnam has been like the confusion of a dreamer. In some matters they have mistaken their own actions and the results of their actions for external events and conditions beyond their control, and in other matters they have suffered from the delusion that they were able to control circumstances that were given in the situation and actually were beyond their control. Although the United States is in fact, of course, only one actor among many powerful actors in Vietnam, we have often behaved as though we believed we were the omnipotent author of the situation, with the power to decide what parts all the actors were to play, and to determine how the plot—or "scenario," to use the current Defense Department jargon—was to develop. The tendency to think in this way has been shown most clearly at the times when other actors have deviated most dramatically from the roles we thought we had assigned them, as they did during the Tet offensive. Our military officers reacted then with a stunned, amazed anger that seemed more like the reaction of the director of a play whose actors have suddenly gone berserk on the stage and started speaking the wrong lines than like the response of Army officers to an attack by the enemy. It was perhaps some such feeling that prompted General Westmoreland to characterize the offensive to newsmen as "deception" and "treachery"—as though he had expected the enemy to submit a proposal for their attack before they carried it out.

The definitions of the war which our government has sought to impose upon the world have changed over the years. In the early years—up until about 1965—officials used terminology from the scenario of economic de-velopment to describe bloody military campaigns. It was then that defoliation was named "natural-resource control" and that the forced evacuation and bombing of villages was named "population control." Some economists vis-iting Vietnam for the government referred to the flight of the peasants from the villages we were bombing as the "war-induced generation of an urban labor force," as though it were one step in a plan we had for the industrial development of South Vietnam. Using terms devised by economic, social, and military theorists as the names of our projects and campaigns has played an important part in the complex process of our self-deception. These terms have tended to take on a life of their own. By seeing everything we do as part of a grand socio-economic-cultural-military plan—which may or may not actually be working—we have fallen into the habit of judging events that involve the Vietnamese as well as ourselves only in the light of our own intentions. Also, by the enormous weight of our technology and military strength we have been able to change the appearance of certain things enough so that they at least superficially resemble our scenarios. This procedure can be seen as falling into three stages. In the first stage, Army decision-makers may decide, for example, to call someone they have deported from his village "a V.C. suspect." They tie his hands behind his back and put a meal sack over his head, and he comes to resemble an imprisoned enemy soldier. Or they may decide that an area is hostile, and bomb it, so to the next pilot who flies over the area it *looks* hostile *because* it has been bombed. Thus, in the second stage they come to judge a person by something they have done to him. "If the man isn't an enemy, then why are his hands tied?" they ask themselves. Using the results of their own actions as evidence, they convince themselves that they made a correct judgment in the first place. In the third stage, the man, because he has been abused, comes to hate the United States, and joins the enemy. And even though he then fires unmistakably real bullets at our troops, we are still boxing with one of our own shadows.

But if in some cases arbitrarily treating people according to our precon-ception of them causes them eventually to fulfill our expectations, in other cases the opposite occurs. If we decide to fight the war as though it were a campaign against the Japanese during the Second World War, the enemy doesn't oblige us by fighting like the Japanese. (False analogies with the Second World War have bedevilled the Vietnam war at all levels, from the analogy between the Munich conference of 1938 and "making a stand" in Vietnam down to the details of battle strategy. No matter how many times the military has repeated the slogans "This is not a war for territory" and "There is no front line in this war," once it is on the battlefield it is unable to resist measuring its progress in terms of hilltops taken, and the like.) And our habit of deciding the nature of the situation we face by taking notice only of our own intentions and our own actions has led us into a habit that is still odder and still more frightening. We have started to take actions—even to wage battles—not to gain concrete objectives, whether they are noble or ignoble, well advised or ill advised, but to vindicate our past mis-judgments by trying to force reality to conform to them. Usually, one thinks of propaganda as a technique by which men in back rooms try to mold public opinion through giving out false information about things that have already happened. But in Vietnam the propagandists have got themselves into the planning stage of things, and it is not the reports of the events but the events themselves that are, in a sense, false. One tragic example of this is the siege of Khe San.

A striking fact about the siege of Khe San is that the position held there by the Marines had no strategic importance. That was demonstrated in the clearest possible way by the Marines' quitting the position as soon as the siege was over. During the siege, two main explanations were made of why the base wasn't evacuated. The first was that the base blocked an important enemy infiltration route, but even at the time it was clear that it did nothing of the sort, since the enemy had already found it possible not merely to infiltrate men through the valley leading to Khe San but to encircle the base. The second was that the encirclement of the base gave our planes a wonderful opportunity to bomb enemy troops. But this argument assumed that the Marines at Khe San were being used as bait to lure the enemy into a trap, and that the whole siege, including the extreme vulnerability of the base to enemy shelling, had been planned by the Marines in the first place—an extremely unlikely assumption. The question remains: Why did we fight at Khe San rather than withdraw the men? Part of the answer probably is that, for all their eager study of Mao Tse-tung on guerrilla warfare, our military men found that his advice about "withdrawing when the enemy attacks" went against their proud instinct to hold on to a position in the face of heavy odds. But a stranger rationale also seems to have been at work. As the siege— or "battle," to use the term the military preferred—continued, the government, the military, and a good part of the press began to attach greater and greater importance to it, until some people were saying that it was an American Dien Bien Phu, and that the whole outcome of the war depended on it. The fact is that the evacuation of Khe San would have had almost no strategic effect and that someone had decided to invest it with an imaginary importance. But although an army can determine what the outcome of a battle will be, it is beyond the power of any army to determine the *importance* of the outcome. At Khe San, it was as though, having failed for years to make progress toward our initial objectives in Vietnam—toward "winning the hearts and minds of the people," building a strong government, and breaking the power of the enemy—the Army had set up a new and perhaps attainable surrogate objective of holding on to an unimportant base, and now pursued this objective as though it had been the real objective all along. Perhaps because of the painful confusion of fighting a war and trying to win the hearts and minds of the people at the same time, many officers had been muttering for years that this was not a "real" war, and perhaps it was almost a relief to them to find in Khe San an unambiguously military conflict—one that they felt they could fully understand. But Khe San was far from being more understandable than other battles; instead, it seemed as though in Khe San the Marines had superimposed an irrelevant drama upon a real war, and that even as they battled a real enemy they were fighting in a dream world. This unreal crisis received unexpected support when President Johnson, taking a step that was unprecedented in American military history, had the Chairman of the Joint Chiefs of Staff sign a statement on behalf of the Joint Chiefs saying that "Khe San could and should be" defended. For a moment, it seemed as though the entire government, from top to bottom, were in headlong flight from reality. And even this flight was made to seem somewhat unreal by the fact that nobody appeared to have cynical intentions. The evidence seemed to be that the government was deceiving itself at least as much as it was deceiving the public—and probably more. But then, again and again, the story of Vietnam has been a story of good intentions with hideous consequences. In fact, there is a direct parallel between the escalation of a false sense of urgency around the siege of Khe San and the escalation of the whole war. In both cases, once blood had been shed, perhaps for a mistaken objective, more and more blood was shed to justify it, until the issue of self-justification and national prestige—or "face," as it is sometimes called—completely overshadowed the initial objectives of the campaign.

Whatever our intentions may have been, it is a measure of how deeply we are enmeshed in our illusions that now, as we attempt to disengage ourselves from the war, we do so in the name of new illusions. President Nixon refers to our troop withdrawals as "troop replacements," as though a South Vietnamese soldier were going to materialize for every one of ours who is pulled out. But it is hard to believe that a government that couldn't win with our help is going to win, or even survive, without it. Of course, behind all the shadows and fantasies of our policies in Vietnam there are realities. They are the death of our men and their men and the gradual destruction of South Vietnamese society. These realities are the reason America must awaken from her terrible dream.

DECEMBER 6, 1969

SOME events of the last few weeks indicate that the Nixon Administration may have come to view the issue of the war in Vietnam as a problem more of ending dissent against the war than of ending the war itself. When, near the end of his November 3rd address to the nation on Vietnam— at the point where Presidents, in their speeches, often make an appeal to all the citizens of the country to support Administration policies—President Nixon said, "So tonight, to you, the great silent majority of my fellow-Americans, I ask for your support," we felt that although the Administration's policy toward the war seemed to be unchanged, a new tone had been set in its policy toward the American people. Never before in our democracy has silence had such a high reputation. This Administration's praise and encouragement of the "silent majority," together with its campaign to silence the "vocal minority," suggest a new vision of America—as the Silent Nation. But we found the Presidential appeal to one segment of the population disturbing, in part because it seemed to add authority to an idea that had been expressed in much more intemperate and frightening language by the Vice-President shortly before. The Vice-President had referred to protest against the war as "sick and rancid" and to the protesters—millions of American citizens—as "vultures," "ideological eunuchs," and "parasites," and had said that "we can afford to separate them from our society with no more regret than we should feel over discarding rotten apples from a barrel." He had given no explanation of what he meant by "separate them from our society," and, with our imagination left free to wander, we could not help thinking of the prisons and concentration camps employed by other men in our century who have spoken of separating parasites from society. The President has himself remained silent since his Vietnam address, except to give public approval to speeches made by the Vice-President, but a number of Administration officials have made moves and stated opinions that, taken together, constitute a trend that poses the gravest threat in our memory to the rights guaranteed by the Constitution to all citizens.

One of the most telling signs of this danger was the position that the Justice Department took toward the New Mobilization march in Washington on November 15th. Before the march, Justice Department officials attempted to discourage citizens from attending it by spreading alarms of violence; troops were called into the city on the basis of Justice Department "intelligence reports" stating that the march was organized by Communists. After the march, a number of Administration officials made baseless and inflammatory allegations about the people who had marched. Transportation Secretary John Volpe declared that most of the organizers of the march were "Communist or Communist-inspired," and Postmaster General Winton M. Blount said that dissent in America was "killing American boys." And—most significant of all—Attorney General Mitchell claimed that the march had been characterized by violence and that the Mobilization leaders had wanted violence to occur. Anyone who saw the march or has read reports of it knows that there were only two infinitesimal incidents of violence in a vast peaceful event and that the Attorney General's statements are not just distortions of the truth but are simply false. Nonetheless, Deputy Attorney General Richard G. Kleindienst announced shortly after he made them that the Justice Department had embarked on investigations that could lead to indictments against a number of the Mobilization leaders. If the organizers of this peaceful march, who, whatever their other political beliefs may be, are nearly all fervent advocates of non-violence, and who attempted, through the deployment of their marshals, to prevent violence wherever it threatened, can be brought to trial on the basis of Mitchell's charges, then the right of free assembly in this country is seriously imperilled. And while the Justice Department was threatening the leaders of the march with indictments, Vice-President Agnew gave two speeches, one attacking television and the other attacking the nation's newspapers, which, in combination with several moves made by other Administration officials, pose a parallel threat to the freedom of the press.

Of course, there is no reason a Vice-President, or even a President, should not defend his Administration and his policies against criticism by the press. Government officials are as free as any newspaper or any television commentator to enter into press debates on government policies. It is when the government sets out not only to disagree with the press but to threaten or coerce it that the danger line is crossed. Several officials of the present Administration have crossed that line. Federal Communications Commission Chairman Dean Burch crossed the line when—in a gesture that, in its timing and in its context, was intimidating—he called up several television stations after Nixon's Vietnam speech and asked for transcripts of their editorial comments on it. The Vice-President crossed the line when he pointedly asserted, in his attack on television news coverage, that commentators enjoy a "monopoly sanctioned and licensed by government." (It is precisely *because* television stations are federally licensed that officials of the federal government, when they choose to engage in political debate with television commentators, have a special duty to debate the issues, and not to brandish the government's power to revoke licenses.) Communications Director Herbert

G. Klein crossed the line in a particularly threatening way when he said, "If you [people in the television industry] look at the problems you have today and you fail to continue to examine them, you do invite the government to come in. I would not like to see that happen." The Vice-President crossed it again when he took it upon himself, in his speech attacking television, to inaugurate a public write-in campaign against the networks. Indeed, the burden of Agnew's two speeches was not the defense of Administration policies against criticism—in fact, he hardly mentioned any questions of Administration policy in either of his speeches about the news media—but the setting in motion of forces that would bring about concrete changes in the news media, in the form of greater support for the President's policies. Although the Vice-President certainly sees himself as a defender of our system of government and no doubt believes that the actions of the Administration he belongs to pose no threat to it, the content of his two speeches—and also his decision, as Vice-President, to give them—rests on several fundamental misunderstandings of democracy and of the Constitution, and these same misunderstandings may underlie the Administration's entire ill-advised campaign.

The Bill of Rights was added to the Constitution in order to protect the people against the government, because of the government's great power. After Thomas Jefferson had seen a draft of the Constitution which did not contain a bill of rights, he wrote in a letter to a friend, "What I disapproved from the first moment also, was the want of a bill of rights, to guard liberty against the legislative as well as the executive branches of the government." In a letter to James Madison, again urging the inclusion of a bill of rights, he wrote, "The tyranny of the legislatures is the most formidable dread at present, and will be for many years," and then he added, "That of the executive will come in its turn; but it will be at a remote period." The freedom of the press was not intended for the benefit of the press. Like the rest of the Bill of Rights, it was intended as a protection for the people against the enormous power of the government. As for protecting the people against the press, we have libel laws to do that. In Vice-President Agnew's speeches, the relationships between the people, the press, and the government are muddled and reversed. He does seem to have had some idea that his thinking represented a departure from the Constitution, for, in one of the more ominous passages in his first speech, he said of the influence exercised by the networks, "We cannot measure this power and influence by the traditional democratic standards." What, then, are the new standards? At several points, he spoke as though the right of free speech had been established to protect the government against censorship by the press or by the people. In his speech attacking the press, he said, "My political and journalistic adversaries seem to be asking . . . that I circumscribe my rhetorical freedom while they place no restriction on theirs," and at the beginning of that speech he had referred to his speech attacking the networks as an exercise of "my right to dissent." But his "right to dissent" (if one can even speak of the government as having a "right to dissent," since in our democracy the term "dissent" refers to the citizens' right to criticize their government) is not a *right* at all but simply a *fact*, since there is no power great enough to threaten its exercise. In both his speeches, the Vice-President consistently portrayed the press and the government as foes that were equally powerful, except that one of them—the government—had been unfairly shackled until the moment when he decided to speak out. In an article in the *Times*, he was quoted as carrying this idea to an absurd extreme by saying, "The Vice-President has a right to dissent, too. If anybody is intimidated, it should be me. I don't have the resources the networks have." But, as the framers of the Constitution well knew, the press and the government are not two adversaries with equal powers and equal rights. There is no comparison between the power of the government and the power of the press. Whereas the government has virtually unchallengeable power in the form of, among other things, the Army, the Air Force, the Navy, the Marines, and the various police forces, the press has only its rights, and can survive only as long as the government continues to honor them.

The Vice-President's concept of censorship is like his concept of rights. In a democracy, the word "censorship" refers specifically to official government interference with the press. When the Vice-President told us in his speech attacking television that he opposed censorship, he said that he was "not asking for government censorship" but was "asking whether a form of censorship already exists when the news that forty million Americans receive each night is determined by a handful of men responsible only to their corporate employers." But, like his idea of his rights and the Constitution's idea of the people's rights, the two kinds of "censorship" are not comparable; one, by definition, is censorship and the other is not. The presentation of a consistently biassed interpretation of the news by the networks, if that were possible, would result in an extremely regrettable state of public misinformation, but government censorship would interfere with the public's right to know and would mean the loss of liberty. Because of the inescapability of federal licensing, what must be devised is a set of guarantees that protects the public against any political misuse of the air and also—what is far more important—protects the stations and networks, and thus, again, the public, against such political intervention as Vice-President Agnew's. The Vice-President's statements seemed to show contempt for any kind of criticism of any government by its citizens. In an article in *Life*, he said, "Consider the idea of protest purely, removing it from any issue. . . . It does not offer constructive alternatives and it is not conducive to creating the thoughtful atmosphere where positive answers may be formulated." In his speech about television, he said that "when Winston Churchill rallied public opinion to stay the course against Hitler's Germany, he didn't have to contend with a gaggle of commentators raising doubts about whether he was reading the public right." This, of course, is not true. Churchill had many vocal opponents, both in the press and among politicians. A more nearly correct statement is that Hitler didn't have to contend with any commentators when he was rallying his people against Churchill's England.

As for the Vice-President's idea of the role of the press in a democracy, it is as strange as his concepts of rights and of censorship. In his speech on newspapers, he said that "the time for naïve belief in their neutrality is gone." But are publications obliged to be neutral? There is nothing in the Constitution that says the press has to be neutral. Nor, for that matter, is there anything that says it has to be objective, or fair, or even accurate or truthful, desirable though these qualities are. For who is to be the judge? The press is simply *free*, and its freedom, like any other freedom, has to be absolute in order to be freedom. It is free to print any information it wants to print and to write from any point of view whatever. The framers of the Constitution wisely left it up to the individual citizen, not the government, to decide which publications to read and which to believe, and to find his own way, in an atmosphere of freedom, to the truth. In a democracy, the people are free only as long as the press is free, and, in the long run, the majority is only as free as the most unpopular minority. Once this or any other Administration gets the machinery in place that can control the press or deny the rights of a dissenting minority, then the rights of all the people, even of those who support the government, are lost. Although this Administration may have intended only to produce greater support for the President's policies, in the belief that this would help him withdraw in an orderly way from Vietnam, the campaign of intimidation it has launched against the protesters and against the press has set this nation on a dangerous course that will be hard to reverse—a course that could lead us to a day when we put an end not to the war in Vietnam but to democracy in America.

DECEMBER 20, 1969

THE reports of the massacre in the South Vietnamese village of My Lai, in which American troops are said to have rounded up several hundred villagers and then gunned them down, have left the nation stunned and vexed. We sense—all of us—that our best instincts are deserting us, and we are oppressed by a dim feeling that beneath our words and phrases, almost beneath our consciousness, we are quietly choking on the blood of innocents. Often, when we open our mouths to condemn, excuses pour out uncontrollably instead. When soldiers of other nations did such things, our outrage was clear and strong, and we had no trouble finding the words of condemnation, but now we find that that outrage was poor preparation for facing what appears to be an atrocity our own people have committed. We try to turn the old phrases of condemnation against ourselves, but they seem to ring false—perhaps because they rested in the first place on a complete dissociation of ourselves from the people we condemned—and the beginnings of a new, craven logic that finds such atrocities to be the way of the world steal into our minds. When others committed them, we looked on the atrocities through the eyes of the victims. Now we find ourselves, almost against our will, looking through the eyes of the perpetrators, and the landscape seems next to unrecognizable. The victims are indistinct—almost invisible. A death close to us personally seems unfathomably large, but their deaths dwindle in our eyes to mere abstractions. We don't know what kind of lives they led or what kind of things they said to each other. We are even uncertain of the right name of the village we are said to have annihilated. Our attention turns to the men who are charged with the crime. Could *we ourselves* have committed it? (Already we have dissociated these men from "us.") Explanations of how such things can happen which never occurred to us when others did them are suddenly ready to hand, and we try to use them to comfort ourselves. From the President on down, we have responded in a muted, tired way. Some people look to the trials of Lieutenant William Calley, Jr., and Sergeant David Mitchell to resolve the issue. But the massacre—if, indeed, there was a massacre—has raised questions that go far beyond the question of the guilt of the men charged with being participants, and although some of these broader questions may be raised at the trials, the only proper purpose of the trials is to decide the fate of the accused individuals. If the men accused are convicted, the question of how much responsibility the rest of us bear will be left to us, and will be resolved by what we say to each other and what we say to ourselves, and, above all, by what course we follow thereafter in our Vietnam policy.

Although it may be that the My Lai massacre is an "isolated incident," in the sense that no other report of mass killing of civilians by troops on the ground has been brought to light, there can be no doubt that such an atrocity was possible only because a number of other methods of killing civilians and destroying their villages had come to be the rule, and not the exception, in our conduct of the war. And the scale of this killing and destruction had been great enough even at the time of the My Lai massacre to defeat completely our original purpose in going into Vietnam, which was to *save* the South Vietnamese people from coercion by the enemy. A report in these pages revealed that in August, 1967, in Quang Ngai Province—where the alleged My Lai massacre took place seven months later—a carefully devised and clearly articulated policy of reprisal bombings against villages that helped the Vietcong, or even tolerated their presence under duress, was widely in effect. This reprisal policy was announced to the South Vietnamese population in the clearest possible terms by the dropping of psychological-warfare leaflets. One such leaflet, the title of which was "Marine Ultimatum to Vietnamese People," announced, in part, "The U.S. Marines issue this warning:

THE U.S. MARINES WILL NOT HESITATE TO DESTROY, IMMEDIATELY, ANY VILLAGE OR HAMLET HARBORING THE VIETCONG. WE WILL NOT HESITATE TO DESTROY, IMMEDIATELY, ANY VILLAGE OR HAMLET USED AS A VIETCONG STRONGHOLD TO FIRE AT OUR TROOPS OR AIRCRAFT."

The same leaflet announced the names of hamlets that had already been bombed, saying, "The hamlets of Hai Mon, Hai Tan, Sa Binh, Tan Binh, and many others have been destroyed." And, in case the villagers didn't fully understand us after they had read this—or, for that matter, after their village had been bombed—another leaflet, titled "Your Village Has Been Bombed," was dropped, telling why we had bombed it. At one point, the second leaflet informed the surviving villagers, "Your village will be bombed again if you harbor the Vietcong in any way." This policy did not result in a few isolated incidents of villages' being bombed; it resulted in the razing to the ground of over seventy per cent of the villages in the province. Sometimes the villagers were warned before their villages were bombed, but more often the people were bombed in their villages without warning. With this kind of policy in effect, and with foot soldiers burning as a matter of course almost every village they entered, our men had come to regard the whole population of the province as their enemy. The orders coming from Washington assumed that the population would be friendly to us, and ordered the troops to separate the enemy from the population. But this order couldn't be applied in Quang Ngai. The military were unable to distinguish between friend and foe, so they improvised their own policy, which was to wage war against everybody. Although the reports that the military sent to Washington formally referred to civilian houses they had destroyed as "military structures," they were already fighting a war completely different from the war that our policymakers told the American people they were fighting. Therefore, the issue of the massacre at My Lai is inextricably bound up with the issue of our entire presence in Vietnam. And although any men who are accused of participation in the massacre cannot be exonerated on this account, when we ask ourselves who is responsible we cannot rest the blame on them alone, nor can we exonerate ourselves by imposing heavy penalties on them.

However, if by blaming only these men for the massacre we cast our net too narrowly, there is another way of looking at the massacre that casts the net too widely. Now that it is Americans who are accused of an atrocity, we hear on every side that "war is hell" and that "human nature has its dark side." The sudden popularity of this line of thinking has led many people to say that up to now America has had an innocent, naïve impression of the wicked-ness of the world, as if to suggest that our failure to commit such atrocities in the past was due to a lack of worldliness and sophistication. This view tempts us toward a touch of actual pride in the massacre, as if we had gone through an initiation ceremony into adulthood as a nation, or as if committing great crimes were part of being a great nation, like having a huge gross national product, or going to the moon. But if war is hell, man has made it so. Or, to be more precise, if a particular war is waged particularly hellishly, it is not man but particular men who are responsible, and in this case *we* are those men. To lay the responsibility on Man, or on War, is to make nobody accountable, and is to move in the direction of regarding the massacre as part of a natural, acceptable course of events. We also attempt to lighten our burden of responsibility by drawing dubious distinctions between this mas-sacre and the massacres committed by others, such as the Nazi reprisal killing of all the men in the Czech village of Lidice during the Second World War, on the ground that for those others the killing was part of a national policy, whereas for us it is not. This again points the finger at the impersonal force of War and away from us. But is it a virtue to have a sensible, humane policy if in our acts transgressions of it are the rule? An announcement of a policy is nothing more than a promise, and a promise not fulfilled is certainly no better than a promise not given. Was it a saving grace for a high official in our pacification program to say, as such an official did in August of 1967, that "Quang Ngai Province is going to be one of the success stories of 1967" when at that very moment our bombers and troops were completing the destruction of the entire society in Quang Ngai? This is the point at which official pronouncements stop being "policy" and become rationalization and propaganda. Nor can we excuse ourselves by saying that we have not known what we were doing. We have known what we have wanted to know. It may be that the truly staggering gap between our lofty intentions and our brutal actions is due more to self-deception than to ordinary deception. But we tend to forget that, just as surely as ordinary deception requires a conscious will to fool others, self-deception requires an unconscious will to fool ourselves. And we are as accountable for our self-deceptions as for our deceptions. With the report of the My Lai massacre, we face a new situation. It is no longer possible for us to say that we did not know. When we look at the photographs published in *Life* and see bodies of children and women in piles, and look into the faces of an old woman and a young girl who (we are told) are about to be shot, we feel that a kind of violence is being done to our feelings, and that the massacre threatens to overpower us. To block it out, we may freeze. If we face the massacre for what it is, we are torn by almost unbearable grief, but if we turn away and let the rationalizations crowd into our minds to protect us, we are degraded. We want to go on with our daily lives, and we may wonder, Why should *my* life be interrupted by this? Why should I take on this suffering on behalf of these victims? However much we may resist it, the choice has been made for us, irrevocably. Whether we manage to bear the grief or whether we freeze, the massacre enters into us and becomes a part of us. The massacre calls for self-examination and for action, but if we deny the call and try to go on as before, as though nothing had happened, our knowledge, which can never leave us once we have acquired it, will bring about an unnoticed but crucial alteration in us, numbing our most precious faculties and withering our souls. For if we learn to accept this, there is nothing we will not accept.

FEBRUARY 28, 1970

B ECAUSE it is possible to defend liberty only as long as we still enjoy liberty, it must be defended as soon as the first sign of a threat to it appears. The government's campaign against the press, which has proceeded swiftly from threats of action to action, in the form of subpoenas of reporters' notes and tapes and films, has already heavily damaged the press's access to the news—particularly its access to news of what radical groups are doing. And this campaign is only one part of a rapidly developing national crisis that has seen powerful, illegitimate pressures from many quarters—from Congress, from the courts, from the police, and from the Administration itself—brought to bear on every form of dissent, whether it occurs in the news media, in political life, or in demonstrations. Yet when we turn on our television sets or pick up our newspapers, we find that the politicians and the men in the press from whom we might expect a defense of liberty are strangely silent and seem to be in disarray. Instead of mustering and rallying their forces, they appear to sit puzzled and becalmed—almost oblivious of what is going on. The concerned citizen is apt to follow the crumbling of our democracy in the back pages of his newspaper. It is as though the people who have spoken out in the past had decided that the nineteen-sixties were our decade for protest and the nineteen-seventies are to be treated as a decade of business as usual, no matter what. A couple of weeks ago, hoping for signs of leadership in the current crisis, we were heartened when we learned that the Democrats were going to put on a television program called "State of the Union: A Democratic View," to "answer" President Nixon's State of the Union Message, and we decided to watch it. The first fifteen minutes of the program concentrated on the still relatively uncontroversial issues of environmental pollution and inflation. (Up to now, they have been controversial only in the sense that the Republicans and the Democrats are vying for the honor of taking the stronger stand against them. On pollution, the real controversies, which will probably be vast, are yet to come.) The second fifteen minutes concentrated on the same two issues, and so, to our astonishment, did the final fifteen minutes. The issues of Vietnam, of race relations, and of civil liberties were never raised. We were left with the disturbing thought that even though the Democratic Party has no formal machinery of censorship, something like a total suppression of three of the major issues of the day—indeed, of the whole last decade—had been achieved.

The Democrats' complete silence on these issues throughout the program struck us as an extreme instance of the more general avoidance of controversial issues which has been noticeable among politicians and on the networks and in the press. Although some newsmen made statements opposing Vice-President Agnew's campaign to interfere with the press, they have moved noticeably toward compliance—perhaps unconscious compliance—with his demands, as though a new and unacknowledged balance of political pressures had suddenly made itself felt after the Vice-President's speeches. Editorial criticism of the Administration has lost its edge, and criticism of Administration policies by politicians has seemed to lose its claim to newsworthiness.

The tone of the networks' response to the Agnew attack was perhaps set by their initial decision to adjust their programming to carry his speech about television live, instead of simply leaving it to be covered in the regular newscasts. One could only conclude that their idea was that by giving the speech this dramatic coverage they could exonerate themselves in advance from the charge of "unfairness" to the Administration. It was as though they thought that when their own interests were involved it was unfair to apply the same standards of coverage that they applied to the rest of the news. And so a move that was perhaps inspired by a desire to bend over backward in an attempt to be fair actually turned out to be a form of compliance with Agnew's new standard of what news coverage should be. As we have watched the news on television and read the papers since the Agnew speeches, we have had the feeling that the Administration has been allowed to assume a leading role in establishing the relative importance both of news stories and of issues. The new "fairness"—i.e., "fairness" to the Administration—has become indistinguishable from fear of the Administration. In hundreds of tiny ways, news coverage now seems to reflect an eagerness to please the people in positions of power. While Agnew's speeches attacking the press have been given heavy coverage, Senator Fulbright's hearings on Vietnam, which once got extensive live coverage on television, received only a few cursory glances in the late evening news. Agnew's long and empty trip to Asia and Secretary Rogers' trip to Africa have received heavy front-page coverage, while the story of the Chicago trial and the story of the subpoenas of press documents have only occasionally emerged from the back pages. We have an impression that the President's picture is being run more often in the papers than it used to be. In editorials, it has suddenly become popular to praise President Nixon's "effectiveness" or "adroitness" in political maneuvering, but without asking what the goals of his maneuvering are. The Administration wheels out what are at the moment issues—such as inflation and pollution—which everyone can agree on and which can be used in a diversionary fashion, and throws a spotlight on them, and the press dutifully drops what it's doing and rushes to fill up its front pages with the new stories. The eagerness for uncontroversial issues is keen. On every side, we hear newsmen and politicians saying, "Pollution is the new hot issue on campus," or "Some of our finest and most responsible young people are now becoming deeply concerned with pollution." Some of these young people are, some of them aren't, and all of them should be, for the pollution issue is a crucial one. But the Administration's message to the young people seems to be "Forget the war in Vietnam and the race question and the threat to civil liberties, and get together with the President on pollution." It can be hoped, at least, that the young people will not be diverted—that they will take on pollution without forgetting everything else.

One of the most distressing results of the new standard of news coverage has been the minimal space given to statements by the very few politicians who have been warning of growing repression. A particularly striking example of this was the coverage in the New York press of a brave and important speech that Mayor Lindsay made on February 11th, at the hundredth-anniversary ceremonies at Hunter College, in which he spoke for the first time on the current danger of repression and of the failure of nerve in those who should protest against it. The Mayor said, in part:

Once again, people who are disturbed by legitimate concerns are being tempted into a simplistic faith in repression as an answer to deep-seated, complex dilemmas. And what is disturbing is not only this new pull toward repression but the strange silence of so many in public life. . . . Look at what has happened in Washington in the last few weeks. The Senate passed a drug law which included a direct challenge to the right of privacy—authorizing federal agents to enter the home of a private citizen with no warning whatsoever. No one voted against that bill. It passed that same week a crime law which directly impairs certain basic rights of defendants in a criminal case—including the right to examine wiretaps for signs of illegal evidence, the right to remain silent, and the right to effective freedom from illegal searches. One senator voted against that bill. That same week, the House of Representatives passed a so-called defense-facilities bill. Put bluntly, what this bill does is to extend government investigation into the private political associations of people in private industry—in so-called sensitive facilities. . . . And in this same period of time, the Justice Department issued—then retracted—wide-ranging subpoenas, unparalleled in scope, for the notes, unedited tapes, and film of reporters for the news media—using as its excuse investigation into subversion. . . . If those in public life can forthrightly condemn the actions of militants and radicals who threaten our freedom, surely we can expect them to be at least as concerned about threats which emanate from the government itself. Yet we have not heard these concerns. And that is what is most disturbing of all.

The *News*, which gave the speech its most extensive coverage in the city, carried the story on page 28. The *Post* carried a story of about a hundred words on page 49. The *Times* quoted two and a half sentences from the speech in a story on page 44—an inner page of the second section—under the headline "Mrs. Wexler Installed as 9th President of 100-Year-Old Hunter College." Coverage such as this compounds our danger by muffling the voices of those who do speak out against the danger. At one point in his speech, the Mayor asked, "Where is the outcry at these threats to our freedom? Where are the defenders of the Bill of Rights? Where are the resolutions, the outraged expressions of alarm from prominent figures in public life?" But his call was lost in the very silence he was challenging.

MARCH 7, 1970

A S a number of observers have pointed out, many developments in the conspiracy trial of the Chicago Seven, including the Justice Department's decision to invoke a law against crossing state lines with intent to incite a riot, and the apparently prejudicial handling of the defense case by the judge, have had a damaging effect on the rule of law in the nation. (The defendants' decision to use the court as a theatre for political struggle has also been unfortunate, and has raised questions for judges which have yet to be satisfactorily answered, but the danger to the law at the hands of defendants who do not respect the law is almost inherently less than the danger at the hands of attorney generals, judges, and policemen who do not respect the law. It is important to remember, when the effects of bad conduct by the judge are weighed against the effects of bad conduct by the defendants, that the trial could not possibly have resulted in the defendants' putting the judge in jail.) But in the precedents set by the Chicago trial there are still graver dangers—dangers that are not strictly legal—for the trial not only resulted in a new injustice but also compounded an old one. During the Democratic Convention, almost the entire national press and all the networks were in agreement that what was happening on the streets of Chicago was what *Time* called "sanctioned mayhem" and what the Walker Commission called a "police riot." The Chicago Police Department claimed that it had been greatly provoked by violence on the part of the demonstrators, but the fact that about twenty newsmen were assaulted by policemen on the first night of the rioting suggests that this was far from being the full story. (No one has yet claimed that any member of the press assaulted any policeman.) Later, a federal grand jury handed down sixteen indictments in connection with the Convention rioting. Eight were brought against policemen and eight were brought against demonstrators, as though to suggest that there had been equal amounts of violence on both sides. Before five of the Chicago Seven (the eighth indicted demonstrator was removed from the court for contempt) were convicted and sentenced, other courts had acquitted seven of the eight policemen (the trial of one policeman has not been completed), so the final result seemed an astounding reversal of justice. The principal rioters, who were the police, went free, and the principal victims of brutality in the riot, who were the demonstrators, were punished. Among the lessons that a policeman might learn from this trial is that he can get the organizers of a demonstration thrown in jail by beating up the demonstrators. Among the lessons that an organizer of a demonstration might learn is that even if he behaves himself at a demonstration he may end up being tried and imprisoned if the police don't behave themselves. It is interesting to reflect that there almost surely would not have been a trial in Chicago if the police had not rioted.

No one in government, of course, was able either to predict or to plan or to control the long train of events that led to the trial, but, with exceptions (and Attorney General Clark was a conspicuous exception), people in positions of authority—in the Chicago Police Department, at the Chicago City Hall, in the federal courts in Chicago, and in two Administrations in Washington—behaved as though they were acting together to protect the interests of a state that had little interest in the rights of its citizens. Also, by the time of the Convention the F.B.I. and the police were employing an army of undercover men, paid informants, and detectives who could be relied on to support the government's interpretation of events and provide it with rationalizations for further action. It was these men who supplied the overwhelming preponderance of the significant testimony for the prosecution at the Chicago trial. In short, the government identified the defendants as criminals by attacking them itself. And by prosecuting the Seven and obtaining convictions against five of them, the government rationalized and justified one piece of repression by committing another.

Once the government had become mired in these acts of repression, it soon learned that its second natural enemy, after the demonstrators themselves, was a free press. It appears that on the streets in Chicago the police singled out newsmen as particularly frequent targets for assault. Later, Mayor Daley challenged the objectivity of the news coverage, and, incidentally, provided an uncannily accurate preview of the wider campaigns that are being waged against the press by the present Administration as part of *its* attempt to suppress dissent.

Perhaps one reason Americans have found it difficult to identify and combat these trends is that Americans have always tended to associate threats against democracy with fanatical leaders of dynamic, highly organized movements that act outside the established institutions and are eager to sweep them aside in a crusade for the domination of society. The rhetoric of American politicians and the American press is filled with warnings against the "extremes of both sides," and people have tended to measure the safety of democracy by the weakness of movements on the far right and left. This has perhaps made people slow to recognize the diffuse, unorganized, unplanned threat that gathered at the dead center of our nation's political life at the time of the Democratic Convention—a threat that had grown behind a screen of rationalizations from bureaucracies and rhetoric from nerveless, self-deceiving politicians, and then had suddenly burst into public view in a display of shocking brutality. For our part, we remember our feeling of incredulity at the Convention while we watched former Vice-President Humphrey deliver his acceptance speech. His boyish face was flushed with pleasure as he emerged into the spotlights, and his eyes seemed to shine with the good intentions he is famous for. Near the beginning of his speech, he quoted at length from St. Francis of Assisi. He went on to say, "Majority rule has prevailed, but minority rights are preserved." And he ended by declaring, "With the help of that vast, unfrightened, dedicated, faithful majority of Americans, I say to this great Convention tonight, and to this great nation of ours, I am ready to lead our country!" For a moment, it was almost impossible for us to believe that we had seen what we had seen during the past few days—the police savagely beating demonstrators on the streets, a Convention delegate being taken off to prison by Convention security guards, Dan Rather, of C.B.S., being punched and knocked to the floor by security guards on the Convention floor, and delegates pledged to Eugene McCarthy shouting into microphones that had just gone dead at a signal from the Convention chairman. We were forced to conclude that in America, if repression came, political leaders might still be quoting St. Francis of Assisi at you when the police began beating on your door.

APRIL 18, 1970

IN 1968, America had a kind of national debate on the Vietnam war, and it appeared that, as far as the *debate* was concerned, the dissenting forces won a victory of sorts. All of the political candidates for national office incorporated a good deal of the rhetoric of the peace movement in their public remarks, and all of them seemed persuaded that withdrawal of our troops was the only course the next President could afford to follow. The war was shorn of its justifications not only in the minds of its veteran critics but also, somewhat surprisingly, in the minds of its former supporters. The demand for military victory in Vietnam all but disappeared from national politics, and the considerably slackened debate centered almost exclusively on the question of how long it should take us to get out. Hawkish sentiment appeared to undergo an odd twist, in which anger at critics of the war intensified but support for the war actually declined. (A rally held in Washington last week in support of military victory in Vietnam drew, according to police estimates, only fifteen thousand people.) And yet now, nearly two years after the beginning of the 1968 campaign, in a peculiar atmosphere of mental exhaustion, in which both opponents and supporters of the war seem to have lost their forensic stamina, our involvement in the conflict continues on almost the same scale, and even threatens to expand into Laos and Cambodia. It is as though the public had shrugged its shoulders and decided to accept the war as something that cannot be affected by human effort. The war has outlived the *issue* of the war.

In the days when the debate was still vigorous, opponents of the war used to find it helpful to expose false claims made by the government, and to point out ironies and contradictions in government policy. They used to say things like "The body count is exaggerated, and anyway a body count is no real measure of success," or "The pacification program isn't going as well as the government says it is," or "The South Vietnamese elections are rigged, and the Saigon regime is a dictatorship and doesn't have the support of its own people." And finally they pieced together the ultimate irony—that we seemed actually to be physically destroying the country we were supposed to be saving. In the last year or so, however, opponents of the war have found that it is inadequate to repeat these arguments. Perhaps one reason is that the gap between the official explanations and the realities we are faced with daily on television and in the newspapers has become so staggeringly huge and so obvious that when one persists in making these points one feels almost ludicrously simpleminded. Also, pointing out discrepancies between the official versions and the realities seems to presume a rationality in the whole enterprise that is now revealed to be entirely lacking. It is as though we were taken on a tour of an alleged health resort that turned out in fact to be a concentration camp, and were then obliged to write a report describing in great detail the specific differences between the facilities of a health resort and those of a concentration camp. We might well feel slightly mad as we wrote things such as "Whereas in a health resort there are doctors giving people medicine, here, on the contrary, we find armed guards systematically murdering the inmates." We might have the same sense of absurdity as we wrote that "whereas the American forces are supposed to be building democratic political structures in the villages of Vietnam, we find that they are bombing the villages and shooting the villagers." The disparity between the official policy and the reality is now so great that it appears as though policy is developing in accordance with a set of rules that will be responsive to the political situation in America but that the actual conduct of the war is developing according to a completely separate set of rules, determined by the conditions of unspeakable brutality and confusion in Vietnam itself. (Our soldiers in Vietnam have started referring to the United States and other places outside Vietnam as "the world"—as though Vietnam were on another planet.) The war, which now grinds on without evoking either much support or much new criticism, or much national debate of any kind, seems to have acquired an insane life of its own, and to have developed in utterly unexpected ways that neither its critics nor its supporters ever anticipated. Several recent news stories have brought this feeling home to us with particular force. A number of them have been so strange as to almost defy rational comment, and we have been trying to imagine what this Administration would say about them if we were still in the period when the government felt obligated to justify and rationalize the consequences of its policies in Vietnam. What comment might the Administration make, for example, about recent reports that the Saigon police beat up disabled veterans of their own Army when they attempted to demonstrate for a rise in their disability allowance (which can be as low as two dollars a month)? What might government officials say about the recent United States Army report that at least thirty-five per cent of the combat soldiers in one brigade are regular users of marijuana? What justifications could be offered for sending a half-stoned army into the villages of Vietnam to wield the greatest volume of firepower that any army has ever possessed? (Around the same time, there has been the peculiar discovery, which we mentioned recently in these pages, that the general we support in Laos may be fighting in order to gain control of a multi-million-dollar opium trade in the contested regions.) And what arguments could be advanced in defense of the First Infantry's decision—at what turned out to be the cost of three American casualties—to carve a mile-and-a-half-long boulevard in the Vietnamese jungle in the shape of its divisional insignia? Situations such as these show that the Army, like the nation itself, now has no idea at all of what it is supposed to be doing in Vietnam. They reveal that the war has lost even the pretense of a purpose, and has become nothing more than a bloody playground for our idealism and our cruelty.

MAY 23, 1970

SEVERAL months ago, the *Times* ran some remarkable stories about the unusual way in which an airline pilot dealt with a desperate armed hijacker and managed to bring his passengers, his crew, and his plane to safety. The pilot, whose name is Donald Cook, was on the way from Los Angeles to San Francisco when the hijacker, an A.W.O.L. marine named Raffaele Minichiello, appeared brandishing a gun and demanding that the plane fly to Rome. Captain Cook's first move was to persuade Minichiello to agree to his landing at Denver and letting the passengers off. When this was done and the plane was aloft again, Cook decided that the safest thing to do would be simply to land in New York, refuel, and then take Minichiello to Rome. Later, Robert C. Doty, of the *Times*, quoted Cook as saying that Minichiello "seemed to want to be met here by someone shooting" and wanted to "fight someone and die." Still later, when Cook was interviewed by Joseph Lelyveld, of the *Times*, he said, "We had arranged that there would be a minimum ground crew when we landed at Kennedy. . . . When we got there, there was the car with the replacement crew, but there were also many other vehicles and many other men. Some of them were carrying weapons and wearing military-type flak jackets. . . . This boy was no dope. He was a very intelligent young man. He panicked and he started to scream, 'Get those people away from the airplane'. . . . I said, 'This boy is going to shoot us.'" Cook said that the agents ignored his plea and continued to move in on the airplane. He added, "We had seen him go from practically a raving maniac to a fairly complacent and intelligent young man with a sense of humor, and then these idiots from the F.B.I.—I don't know if 'idiots' is a word you want to use, but it's the way I feel—had irresponsibly made up their own minds about how to handle this boy on the basis of no information, and the good faith we had built up for almost six hours was completely destroyed." An Assistant United States Attorney whom Lelyveld also talked with explained that the F.B.I. agents had been trying to "crawl up through the belly of the plane either to get the drop on [Minichiello] or to get a shot at him." Eventually, the plane did take off for Rome, and on the way Minichiello at one point left his gun within Cook's reach, but Cook made no move to get it. When Minichiello asked him why he hadn't, Cook answered, "Raffaele, all of us have been in the service and all of us have had an opportunity to fight in wars and none of us want to fight in wars now or kill anyone. I couldn't consider it unless it was a mandatory thing. Besides, we've got to like you, and we really think we can bring this to a conclusion without our

being killed and without your being killed." At the end of the flight, Minichiello apologized for giving the crew so much trouble, and Cook answered,
"That's all right, we don't take it personally." And, with what we regard as a
touch of the sublime, Cook told reporters that the crew wished they had
met Minichiello "in other circumstances." Finally, Cook said of the dilemma
he had faced, "The F.B.I. just thought they were playing Wyatt Earp and
wanted to engage in a shoot-out with a supposed criminal. They would have
wound up unnecessarily killing this boy, and, probably, completely destroying
a seven-million-dollar airplane and wounding or endangering the lives of four
crew members."

We believe that Captain Cook is an authentic hero of our times. Isn't his
remark about the crew's wishing they had met Minichiello "in other circumstances" all the more to the point when one considers the police and National
Guardsmen at Jackson State and Kent State and the students they killed, and
when one considers the American soldiers now fighting in Cambodia and
the people whose villages they are destroying? As we hear the calls to unleash
American power in Indo-China and the calls to "untie the hands" of the
American military, it strikes us that, generally speaking, America could use
more of Captain Cook's instinct for protecting life and less of the F.B.I.'s
eagerness to "get a shot" at its quarry regardless of who gets caught in the
crossfire.

Traditionally, of course, mankind has had a special place in its heart for
warriors who, with pure and single-minded devotion and unlimited courage,
have plunged into battle with total abandon, withholding nothing. Some of
the most shining deeds in history have been performed by men or by whole
peoples who, for an ideal or in order to protect their countries, have cried
"Victory or death!" and hurled themselves against overwhelmingly superior
enemy forces. In the same way, we have all admired men who have seemed
to pass beyond the normal limits of human endurance in struggles against
the sea or against some other force of nature. It is also true, of course, that
when these qualities of unlimited commitment and energy have been har-
nessed to personal ambition or to campaigns of territorial conquest they have
brought about some of the darkest episodes in history. Yet, terrible as those
episodes may have been, the scope and duration of the suffering they caused
were limited by what seem to have been several natural checks. The passage
of time, the diversity of mankind, and the sheer size of the globe were enough
to defeat or transmute forces bent on unlimited conquest or destruction.
Although it sometimes took centuries, the energy of the most powerful armies
spent itself in the vastness of the populations they sought to conquer. Sometimes it was not men but nature that eroded the strength of invading forces.

It is said that the Russian winter was as much responsible as the Russian Army for Napoleon's retreat from Russia. Until recently, nature and man were inexhaustible adversaries of the single-minded will of the conqueror and destroyer, but in our times the destructive power of man has gained the upper hand. Since the development of nuclear weapons, everyone has known that an international crisis could lead to the extinction of the human species, and since the discovery of the dangers of environmental pollution everyone has known that business as usual could bring the same result. Measured against our new powers of destruction, both man and nature are frail and vulnerable. Now we must learn to *protect* our old adversary the sea, and, what is more difficult, we must learn to protect our human adversaries—as well as those we regard as innocents—against the full power of our own wrath. In the light of this peril, it becomes plain that any single-minded and open-ended campaign, whether it is for military victory or for economic achievement, will lead us into the worst kind of trouble, and will, in the long run, keep us from reaching any goal that such a campaign might be aiming for in the first place. Our competitive instincts and our passion to win battles against other men have become suicidal. The more violence we unleash in order to annihilate our enemies, the closer we come to nuclear war, and to the annihilation of everyone, ourselves included. It used to be thought that men who wished to put an end to war were idealistic dreamers and that those who were willing to go to war were "realists." Now the reverse is true. Often in the past when the question of whether or not to go to war arose, the aim of preventing one's own people from suffering was considered a "reality" and the aim of preventing another people from suffering was considered an "ideal." Now, in a country such as ours, which possesses nuclear power, even if one accepts this callous view of what a reality is, it is those who call for victory who are the dreamers and those who call for restraint who are the realists. What used to be the question was whether men would continue waging wars as they always had or whether they would make a seemingly utopian dream of a world without war come true. Now, with the survival of man at stake, what used to be a dream has become a necessity. We can no longer emulate those who cry "Victory or death!" because in our times victory *is* death.

As we try to cope with this unprecedented situation, we cannot afford to let ourselves forget that there is still a deep and ancient instinct in all of us that wants to see issues shape up in the form of battles—that wants other people to commit themselves as our comrades-in-arms or as enemies and then fight to the death. It may be that it will prove particularly difficult for the American people to learn to temper this instinct. Our present leaders like to remind us that we have until now achieved victories, or at least been on the winning side, in all the wars we have entered. We have grown accustomed to victory, and it may come hard to many of us to learn that our appetite for victory has become deadly even to ourselves. And if this appetite is stronger in some Americans—our policemen, our soldiers, and our veterans among them—than it is in others, it may be in part because in the event of a battle they will have a chance to do what they have been trained to do and know how to do and what they have always been praised for doing. When the government sends the Army to perform such subtle and complicated tasks as keeping peace on the nation's campuses and building democracy in Vietnam, it should not be surprised if, almost unknowingly, the Army turns these tasks into the straightforward business of fighting conventional wars. If you give a man a gun with a bayonet and some ammunition, he is likely to stab and shoot.

It is true that from the start our policies in Indo-China have been haunted by a tendency to slip into the anachronistic idiom and inappropriate tactics of conventional wars, but in recent weeks it has begun to look as though the present Administration were entirely baffled by the shape and texture of the perilous realities we face, and had come to believe that through unilateral action we could force the world back into a less dangerous age. It looks as though the Administration believed that fighting the Indo-China war as a conventional war would transform it into a conventional war, with only conventional risks. Of course, the citizenry that rallies behind a government to give unshakable support to its war effort is as much a part of the conventional war as the army that fights to the limits of its resources in the field. In an attempt to stir up this kind of support, the President has raised the spectre of "humiliation and defeat" for America, and has told us that our willingness to support him is a test of our "courage" and our "character." But to believe that the North Vietnamese Army challenges our courage in this way requires us to accept the enormous misconception that the strength of America is gravely threatened "both abroad and at home," in the words of the President, and that we can repel the threat only by calling on untapped reserves of energy and determination. Such demands, of course, have been the rallying cry of nations fighting for survival in the past, but how strange they sound coming in our times from the government of what the President himself calls "the richest and strongest nation in the history of the world" as it invades one of the poorest and most helpless nations in the world. The Administration speaks of the need to prove our "credibility." The truth is that the world is already well persuaded of our capacity for violence and our willingness to use it. As everyone knows, our capacity for violence is unlimited.

God save us from ever *proving* it. When a call to support a policy that is moving in this direction is made, the citizens—who know somewhere in the back of their minds that their homes and families are threatened more directly by a wider war than they could be in any way by our present enemy—are likely to discover a worm of doubt inside them that makes them wonder whether this is what patriotism really does require, and tends to take the wind out of the warlike passion they are called on to display. Indeed, hawkish sentiment on the war has never really been very outspoken or very impassioned. Often its existence has been merely deduced, as is revealed by the phrase "the silent majority." When those with hawkish views *have* shown anger, they have vented it not on the North Vietnamese but on other Americans, such as demonstrators and the press. Even in what are regarded as the most hawkish quarters, there has been a reluctance to give strong support directly to the war. And when one looks for the kind of unity and resolve that governments ordinarily expect in support of their policies in wartime, one must turn to the anti-war movement to find it. It is in this movement—especially among the young, who have never learned the taste for military victory—that one finds the solidarity and the spontaneous determination of a people that is fighting for survival. But in this case it is the survival of the human race. It is generally recognized that the current generation of young people have lived their whole lives in the shadow of nuclear destruction. Surely Indo-China, being one of the places where the shadow falls most heavily, must loom pre-eminent in youth's struggle to insure that man will have a future. In this struggle, America's ability to impose its will on other nations by force is useless. And since it is compassion for our own people and for other peoples that keeps us from proving our character to the hilt, our government's indifference to the terrible fate it has decreed for the Cambodian people is alarming. It is profane that the first thing the American government told the American people about Cambodia was that American forces had begun to destroy it. One newspaper, limping along, like everybody else, to keep up with the President and the military, ran an article entitled "Cambodia at a Glance," which informed its readers of such facts as that in Cambodia "most of the population is rural and farming is [its] major occupation," and that "mineral resources are undeveloped." The title seemed to suggest that if you wanted to learn anything about Cambodia you had better look quickly. Now, on television, Americans are getting their first look at Cambodians. Most of the Cambodians are lying dead in their shattered villages. On the evening of the invasion, when the President went to his map to show the American people where Cambodia is ("Here is South Vietnam, here is North Vietnam," etc.), we felt that we were being given a geography lesson by military invasion. We don't want to learn about our brothers on the earth in this way.

MAY 30, 1970

ALL that can be said for certain about the Administration's motives in going into Cambodia is that few people, inside the Administration or outside it, can agree on what they are. This in itself is a disturbing situation. Stewart Alsop, whose column in *Newsweek* we often turn to for information on what our leaders in Washington are thinking, declares that "what the President is really doing is to conduct a great military retreat—the greatest in American history." In his view, the President's alarming remarks about resisting the forces of "anarchy" all over the world were nothing but a bellicose disguise for a policy of withdrawal, and the invasion of Cambodia is only "a limited spoiling attack, designed to protect the rear guard of the American retreat." As for the President's critics, they "don't want to admit that the President is engaged in a great retreat . . . because if they did they would have much less left to criticize." One of these critics is former Secretary of Defense Clark Clifford, a man whom we would expect to have reliable information on what is happening in Washington. In an article in *Life*, he declares that "President Nixon, while he proclaims his dedication to a political settlement, by his actions still seeks to gain the military victory that cannot be won." In other words, Mr. Alsop says that the President is talking like a hawk and behaving like a dove, and Mr. Clifford says that the President is talking like a dove and behaving like a hawk. Several months ago, when Attorney General Mitchell told civil-rights leaders that in judging the Administration he belongs to they should "watch what we do instead of what we say," it seemed that he might be offering the public a useful guide for judging government policy in the era of the credibility gap. But how can one apply this standard when the most authoritative sources are unable to determine either what the Administration is doing *or* what it is saying?

As the press gropes through this tangle of uncertain rhetoric and uncertain intentions, many newsmen have decided that the invasion should be regarded as a Presidential "gamble," in which the President is weighing the military advantages that might be gained from it against the domestic and diplomatic costs. In this view, if the military succeeds in its stated objectives the President will "win" the gamble, whereas if it fails he will "lose." What strikes us most forcibly about the invasion, however, is that its military objectives appear to have been worthless in the first place. According to the President, the aim of the invasion is to protect America's troops as they withdraw from Vietnam by destroying the enemy's supplies in Cambodia and thus setting back the enemy's schedule for attacks on American troops. The President stated that he was particularly concerned about the safety of the two hundred and fifty thousand troops that would be left in Vietnam when his current plan of withdrawing one hundred and fifty thousand troops within a year had been carried out. Yet the military's most optimistic estimate of the setback in the enemy's schedule which can be gained by the invasion of Cambodia is eight months. Thus, the enemy will be back at full strength at least four months before the current twelve-month withdrawal is complete, and the American troops that remain in Vietnam will be as vulnerable to enemy attack as they would have been if the invasion had never taken place. It might be argued that eight months of reduced enemy activity would permit the training of the South Vietnamese Army to proceed more rapidly. However, this hope has now been destroyed by the South Vietnamese government's announcement that its troops will stay in Cambodia to fight the enemy after the American troops leave. If "Vietnamization" of the war in South Vietnam is the ultimate aim of these moves, it is hardly well served by having South Vietnamese troops in Cambodia. (We can well imagine the Vietnamese telling the United States that they will leave Cambodia just as soon as they have "Cambodianized" the war there. Perhaps they will even attack "sanctuaries" in Laos in order to protect their own withdrawal from Cambodia.)

However, according to the President and members of his Administration, the invasion was intended not simply to do something but also to prove something—something about America's "character" and "courage." The President said that the invasion would prove to the world that America would not act like "a pitiful, helpless giant" when free nations were threatened by totalitarian nations. And he said that the invasion would put America's enemies on notice that Americans were willing to take "decisive" action against them. One might say that the invasion had a propagandistic intent as well as a strictly military intent, and this may help explain why the distinction between action and rhetoric which led Mr. Clifford and Mr. Alsop to such different conclusions is not a reliable guide to policy. Of course, there is nothing new about a government's making a "show of force," but usually a government makes it in order to threaten a specific enemy with a specific action. This Administration, on the other hand, has not specified just who is being threatened, or with what. Is it the North Vietnamese, and is our action a signal that we will invade North Vietnam if they persist in opposing us? Is it the

Chinese? Or is it the Russians? Many observers believe that it is not only the Russians but the *Egyptians* as well. These observers see the invasion of Cambodia as our way of telling the Egyptians and the Russians that we are willing to come to the support of Israel. It also used to be thought that a show of force, to be useful, had to threaten the enemy with an action that would be militarily effective. But in Cambodia the military futility of our invasion undercuts any point we might be trying to make about the effectiveness of our power. We should have learned from our experience in Vietnam that you can't build confidence or "credibility" by stubbornly persisting in a futile venture. There can be no credibility unless the original cause is sound. A show of force in a futile cause amounts to a demonstration of futility, and the bitter ironies of our involvement in the war in Vietnam will follow us wherever we may extend that war. Yet the President's remarks about the risk of "defeat" for America suggest that he has almost come to believe that by widening the war, and by presenting it as part of a global conflict between the forces of freedom and the forces of totalitarianism, we could leave behind the ironies and frustrations that Alsop and Clifford are attempting to analyze. It is as though the President believed that a wider conflict would somehow become a simpler conflict. Ordinarily, governments seek to prove the consistency of their policies, but, according to one interpretation of our invasion of Cambodia—one that James Reston, in the *Times*, reported to have been advanced by the President's foreign-policy aides—the President's aim was to prove the "unpredictability" of our actions. As this theory has it, if we behave in surprising, irrational ways our enemies will not be able to guess what we are going to do next, and will deal cautiously with us, as one would with a madman. If this is why we invaded Cambodia, then the futility of the invasion begins to make a certain amount of sense, for what could be more unpredictable than a nation's taking actions against its own interests?

JUNE 6, 1970

WHEN a totalitarian government—Communist or Fascist—engages in a brutal and repressive campaign in another country, there is no clash of principle between what it is doing abroad and what it is doing at home, since totalitarian governments are founded on brutality and repression to begin with. For a democratic country, however, a repressive venture abroad contradicts and undermines the principles on which the government is founded, and in the long run it is likely to provoke a clash between democratic and anti-democratic principles in every area of its political life. Such a clash appears to have begun in America. All of us who remember one or both of the world wars know that even a war that is considered just by the overwhelming majority of a democracy's citizens imposes a temporary strain on the liberties that the citizens normally enjoy. A war that is considered anti-democratic imposes on the democracy strains of an entirely new order. The character of a war is likely to determine the effect it will have on the home government. In considering the war in Indo-China, one may find it useful, for the sake of a limited comparison, to think of South Vietnam as a kind of fifty-first state, or as an American protectorate, and to imagine what the reaction of the American people would be if that region continued to be ruled as it is now being ruled. It is no longer possible for the American people to delude themselves into thinking either that the South Vietnamese government is a democratic government or that it is an independent government. There are over four hundred thousand Americans in Vietnam, and all of them are there to influence and support the South Vietnamese government. Almost every one of the officials of that government down to the level of district chief has a full-time American adviser. Most of its financial resources are American. Its Army is trained, supplied, and advised in the field by the United States Army. Yet, as many people now recognize, the South Vietnamese government is a military autocracy. And the "independence" of the South Vietnamese government, which its leaders sometimes ostentatiously display by making anti-American speeches, is nothing more than the freedom of a dog on a leash that barks at its master. In short, it is now common knowledge that American arms, American money, and American administrators have become the sinews and the lifeblood of an anti-democratic regime in Southeast Asia. It is hardly surprising that an increasing number of the American people, who have been taught to cherish liberty, should find this situation repugnant. Indeed, it is their very love of democracy and their desire to protect our own democracy that impels their opposition. And the fact that the forces against which the American forces are fighting would not establish a democratic form of government, either, is no comfort. It is true, of course, that some dissenters have turned against democracy itself because of the war. One of the tragedies of the war is that some people have looked on our conduct of it as the measure of the government's concern for democracy in all its activities, both at home and abroad, and have said, "If this is democracy, then I don't want it." Others, who have perhaps paid less attention to the war and have not found their own lives immediately affected by it, have been unable to believe that America could be engaged in repression anywhere, and have continued to support the war. And then there are a few who support the war because they have never been devoted to democracy, and would actually be pleased if the government took its administrative procedures in Vietnam as a model for government in America.

Our politicians are caught in the same predicament as the rest of us. Some have joined those who oppose the war. Some have supported the war and have also supported repressive measures against the domestic opposition. But the most poignant, perhaps, are those who believe in democracy but want to believe in the war, too. They are forced to turn their backs on the realities of the war and on the damage that the war is doing at home. It is from these men that the most tortured and transparently contradictory interpretations have come. Hubert Humphrey, a man who has spent most of his life fighting for democratic principles, and who has now turned against our war policies, found himself in this tragic bind during his term as Vice-President. He forced himself to keep up a highly inappropriate cheerfulness during some of the darkest moments in our recent history. At the end of the 1968 Democratic Convention, which had degenerated into violence both outside the Convention and on the Convention floor, he was unable to do anything but ignore the entire disaster and speak of "the beginning of a new day" as though "the politics of joy" were a reality in America. More recently, our Secretary of Housing and Urban Development, George Romney, has found himself entangled in the same dilemma. In a speech to the general assembly of the United Presbyterian Church, he first called the Vietnam war "the most tragic event in our history," and said, "I don't think the United States should ever again commit our boys to a conflict without following the Constitutional provision for declaration of war unless we are defending ourselves from attack." But later in the speech he defended the decision to enter Cambodia, saying, "Assume we are at war with Russia and assume they had sanctuaries in Canada and we did nothing about it. Then how would you feel?" It seemed that he had forgotten that the point of the first part of his speech had been that the war in Vietnam was *not* analogous to a war in which we had to defend our country from an attack by Russians operating from Canada. But his confused rhetoric and that of the other confused men in public life are only a symptom of a deeper and more dangerous confusion, which has arisen from the government's peculiar attempt to administer the provision of enormous support for an anti-democratic regime abroad and at the same time to administer a democracy at home.

Recently, the President referred to "forces of anarchy" that must be resisted "both abroad and at home," and the Vice-President, making a similar comparison between events in America and events abroad, said, "I have sworn I will uphold the Constitution against all enemies, foreign and domestic. Those who would tear our country apart or try to bring down its government are enemies, whether here or abroad, whether destroying libraries and classrooms on a college campus or firing at American troops from a rice paddy in Southeast Asia." It need hardly be said that it is extremely dangerous to establish these equivalencies. The Administration, which has been lumping together the few violent opponents of the war with the millions of Americans who have been opposing the war by peaceful means, has now blurred these crucial distinctions even further by throwing both groups in together with the Vietcong and the North Vietnamese. But whereas in Vietnam the military can simply shoot its enemies, with no questions asked, a democratic government must cope with its critics (it is incorrect and inflammatory to call them "enemies") with nothing more forceful than argument and persuasion. Any politician who in this way confuses the government's struggles abroad with its struggles at home is truly in the advance guard of the cause—which has been favored by the most radical left-wing groups—of "bringing the war home." The intended result of America's support of the Saigon regime has been to export a democratic form of government to Vietnam, but it is beginning to look as though the actual result were to import anti-democratic principles into our own political life in the United States. The Vietnamization of the United States appears to be proceeding much more rapidly than the Vietnamization of Vietnam.

JUNE 27, 1970

SINCE the beginning of the Cold War, this country has had an extraordinarily difficult time preserving its sense of proportion in matters that concern the political left. Even when the influence of the left has been virtually negligible, men like Senator Joseph McCarthy have been able to create an atmosphere of panic and suspicion among large parts of the public by falsely claiming the existence of leftist conspiracies in high places. In recent years, the problem has been complicated by the appearance of a small, disorganized, but indubitably real and active extreme-left-wing movement, which, although it has almost no support in the nation as a whole, has been able, through the actions of some of its more militant members, to do real damage to the functioning of many universities. The current Administration's response to this new danger has been to exploit and exaggerate it by creating the impression that just about anyone who questions the Administration's war policies is an extremist, and in so doing it has created a threat to the

freedom of the nation as a whole which is vastly greater than any threat that
the extreme left could ever have posed in the first place. This campaign has
put university administrators, who must actually deal with the dangers of
disruption, in a very difficult position. At the time the campaign was launched,
many of them had already had to face the awful choice of suffering the
occupation of university buildings, the destruction of university property,
and the disruption of classes or calling in police and National Guardsmen,
who were likely to use a degree of force that might bring about serious
injuries—perhaps even death—and would almost certainly aggravate the crisis
rather than solve it. Now, in addition to the task of opposing the real dangers
that threaten their universities, the administrators, because of the inflamed
state of public opinion, have been burdened with the task of opposing the
circulation of unreal fears that have been spread publicly by political leaders.
In recent weeks, some of the most distinguished and respected voices in the
country have spoken on the question of campus disruptions. In their remarks,
they have met the problem of disruption within the universities head on, but
they have met less forcefully the problem of the spreading public misinformation outside the universities, and we fear that some of the statements they
have made about the nature of the radical left have been inaccurate in a way
that will further inflame the public, rather than reassure it. Senator Margaret
Chase Smith, who was one of the few senators who had the courage to speak
out against McCarthy's campaign of intimidation, and whose voice carries
tremendous weight in matters that concern our freedom, has likened the
disruptive activities of today's radical groups to McCarthyism. In a recent
speech to the Senate, she said, "I spoke as I did twenty years ago because of
what I considered to be the great threat from the radical right—the threat
of government repression. I speak today because of what I consider to be
the great threat from the radical left that advocates and practices violence
and defiance of the law—again the threat of the ultimate result of a reaction
of repression. . . . The Senate was silenced and politically intimidated by one
of its own members; so today many Americans are intimidated and made
mute by the emotional violence of the extreme left." President Nathan Pusey,
of Harvard, another of those who opposed McCarthy in the nineteen-fifties,
has added his voice to that of Senator Smith, saying, "Now, less than twenty
years later, our campuses are experiencing a not dissimilar period of torment,
whiplashed as they are by a resurgence of his [McCarthy's] hateful technique.
Again people are looking for scapegoats. But this time the attack comes not
from the outside but from within, from extremist splinter groups of the New
Left." President Pusey also likened both McCarthy and the New Left to Hitler
and the Nazis, on the ground that all of them relied on the tactic of telling

"the big lie" in order to gain support. The *Times*, too, has likened the American left to the Nazi movement, saying in a recent editorial that "it is not surprising that the new breed of campus revolutionaries intent on destroying all freedom except their own are now turning to what they call 'trashing'—the setting of fires, hurling of rocks, smashing of windows—ominously reminiscent of the shattered storefronts with which the Nazis sought to intimidate their political opponents of a generation ago."

On the whole, the comparison between today's radical left and McCarthyism and Nazism is a confusing one—and anything that adds to the already vast current confusion is dangerous. It is true that none of these groups have respected democratic freedoms, but in almost every other respect the differences between today's radical left and the two other movements seem to us immense. (Most of the comparisons that have lately been made—by all sides, including the radical-left side—between Germany in the nineteen-thirties and forties and America in the nineteen-sixties and seventies have been confusing. The Vietcong are not the Nazis. Americans are not the Nazis. Ho Chi Minh was not Hitler. Nixon is not Hitler. The radical students are not the Hitler Youth.) What is perhaps most striking is the disproportion between the danger posed by today's left and the dangers that were posed by McCarthyism and by Nazism. McCarthy had widespread public support, and he had access, as a United States Senator, to the enormous power of the government. Today, the extreme left has almost no support in the general public and no chance of winning access to state power, whether through revolution or through electoral politics. McCarthy, because of his power, succeeded in frightening scores of politicians as well as millions of citizens into silence, and even greatly respected public figures like Senator Smith could oppose him only at great political risk to themselves. Today, there is not even one politician who is so afraid of the extreme left that he does not dare to denounce it; in fact, the nation's politicians have denounced the left almost unanimously and have found it very advantageous politically to do so. McCarthy was able to prevent people from speaking out anywhere, at any time—to silence them completely. The left today is able to prevent people from speaking at certain times, from certain platforms, but it cannot prevent them from speaking at some other time or in some other place. In this society, although groups with anti-democratic tendencies who work outside the government can have a damaging effect on American political life and can mount dangerous attacks on certain institutions, such as the universities, it is only groups who have the backing of state power, or might be able to gain access to state power, who can pose a mortal threat to American democracy.

Senator Smith, after levelling her most strongly worded denunciation at the left, went on to recognize these crucial distinctions when she pointed out that, ultimately, it would be not the extreme left but the government that, in the name of opposing the left, would actually impose repression. In other words, the left is important because it could provide the government with a pretext for intimidating the public, not because it could do the intimidating itself. McCarthy, on the other hand, was able to intimidate the public through his own efforts. And this, of course, suggests that the analogy should be not between McCarthyism and the left but between McCarthyism and government attempts—and potential attempts—to intimidate citizens into silence.

We know from the McCarthy period that the fear of an imaginary danger from the left can inflame a large section of the population with anti-democratic passions just as surely as any real danger from the left. Comparisons like the ones that have recently been drawn, which tend to make the left seem more powerful and dangerous than it is, may build up still further the public's already exaggerated fear of the left and thus serve to create public support for repressive tendencies in the government. Moreover, these comparisons have been drawn at a time when, as a result of the invasion of Cambodia, the minority of students who are inclined to violence has been swamped in a gigantic outpouring of sentiment and energy on the part of students who are dedicated to non-violent political activity. Thus, oddly, the comparisons have come just when the influence of the extreme-left groups is the weakest it has been in several years. Indeed, one of the few hopeful signs of the moment is that on many campuses—perhaps on most—students have been able to break away from their futile and destructive but peculiarly fascinating internal grappling and, together with faculties and administrators, turn their energies outward. It would be a tragic irony if, at just the moment when the power of the extreme left is fading, an artificial intensification of the fear of the extreme left were to provoke the repression we all hope to avoid.

JULY 18, 1970

ALMOST since the beginning of the war, journalists have been saying that the government was suffering from a "credibility gap." The phrase was never intended as a compliment, but in the light of the present Administration's behavior during the Cambodian invasion it has an almost reassuring sound. It at least suggests that there is some strained connection between what the government says is happening and what is really happening. However, since the beginning of the invasion (or incursion, or intervention), the official account of our situation and our real situation have moved light-years apart—too far apart to be measured any longer in terms of gaps. It is as though, in his numerous television appearances, the President had stepped into the shoes of a playwright or scriptwriter, and had decided that he could create new characters, phase out old characters, invent thrilling new episodes, and move the plot in almost any direction his imagination might take him. For example, in his speech announcing the invasion the President told us that the reason for it was that the enemy was enlarging and linking up his bases along the South Vietnamese–Cambodian border. Later, we learned from the press that the enemy had actually been moving *deeper* into Cambodia and *away* from his bases ever since the coup that overthrew Prince Sihanouk. This became utterly clear in the following months, when our troops failed to encounter the enemy in force during their stay in Cambodia. But if the Administration's version of events in Cambodia has some of the characteristics of a play, it is a very bad play. If a film, say, were to show an army about to make an assault on the enemy's "headquarters for the entire Communist military operation in South Vietnam" and then were to suddenly drop all reference to the headquarters and simply cut to shots of the same army walking around in the woods picking up weapons and rice, the audience would probably demand its money back. This Administration has been behaving as though with each passing day the public completely forgot what had happened the day before. For example, each time one picked up one's newspaper during the period of the invasion an Administration official was saying something different about the crucial questions of what role the South Vietnamese were going to play in Cambodia after we had withdrawn into Vietnam and how much support they would get from us if they stayed. Starting with the President's statement, at his most recent open press conference, that he expected the South Vietnamese to come out at the same time we did, because the air and logistical support they relied on would be withdrawn at that time, Administration officials, at one point or another, took just about every position on this issue that it was possible to take. Now, in the aftermath of all these statements, which seemed designed more to affect public opinion at a particular moment than to enlighten anyone about what our policy really was, no one has any idea how long the Vietnamese will be in Cambodia or any idea of how much support we are going to give them.

However, among the various inventions and suppressions of fact there is one development that looms as paramount. And this development alone has been enough to make one wonder from time to time whether the President is perhaps surpassing himself in dramaturgy and describing some war other than the one we have all been reading about every day in the newspapers. This development is that while the "allies" have been busy with their frenzied and confused activity of the last few months—while they have been sending American troops and Vietnamese troops into Cambodia, and sending Vietnamese of Cambodian origin into Cambodia, and sending Cambodians of Vietnamese origin into Vietnam, and sending Thais of Vietnamese origin into Cambodia, and sending our planes to bomb South Vietnam, Cambodia, Laos, and North Vietnam—the allied Communist forces have been quietly taking control of most of Cambodia. On June 28th, the news came out—rather inconspicuously—that the Lon Nol government had yielded control of about two-thirds of the Cambodian countryside to the North Vietnamese and their Cambodian allies, and that it had decided not even to contest their control of the northern third of the country. For the last several months, everybody's attention has been riveted on Phnom Penh—as though we all thought that Phnom Penh was Cambodia—but surely the fall of at least a third of Cambodia, and probably a lot more, is a piece of news of the most extraordinary importance. For seven years, we have fought to prevent one half of one Southeast Asian country—Vietnam—from falling under the control of the government of the other half. We are still suffering the anguish, disruption, and death that this intervention has brought to the Vietnamese and to our own people. Yet now, apparently as a consequence of our own acts, the event we have sacrificed so much to prevent in Vietnam has actually taken place in Cambodia. Indeed, by the criterion of the justifications that have been offered for our intervention in Vietnam, the takeover in Cambodia is a more shocking event than a similar takeover in Vietnam would be, because in this case there can be no doubt in anyone's mind that the takeover has been accomplished largely by means of foreign invasion. Yet our government has so far failed to give any acknowledgment whatever to this takeover, which may well be the most momentous single development of the entire Indo-China war. The lack of interest displayed by the press is perhaps more understandable. The press is in a very difficult position just now. The government not only is trying to manipulate public opinion by continuously releasing a garbled and untruthful version of the facts of the war but is also expending much time and effort in direct attacks upon the press and attempts to discredit it in the eyes of its readers by accusing it of disloyalty to the country. Reporting this war is a hazardous and confusing business even without interference and pressure from the government, and newsmen might well be inclined, perhaps unconsciously, to play down events that the government has taken no cognizance of.

The President's failure to acknowledge this consequence of the invasion is all the more striking because it was supposedly to prevent the enlargement of the enemy base areas that the President sent our troops into Cambodia in the first place. As has been noted above, the President's contention at the outset of the invasion that the enemy was moving to link up his bases in Cambodia was not true at that time. Now, however, it *is* true, at least along the northern third of the border, for the North Vietnamese control not only that part of the border but the whole northern third of the country. In short, at a time when the North Vietnamese were not expanding their bases the President found it expedient to say that they were, and now, at a time when they *are* expanding their bases, and expanding them on a totally unprecedented scale, he finds it expedient to pretend that they are not. The logic of these positions reminds us of Secretary Laird's warning at the beginning of the invasion that the United States might be forced to resume the bombing of North Vietnam, although at that very moment the United States *had* resumed the bombing, temporarily. Just as Secretary Laird threatened then that the United States might be forced to do something it had already done, the President warns the American people now that the North Vietnamese may try to do something *they* have already done.

It might be argued that one reason the President has said nothing about the fall of a large part of Cambodia to the North Vietnamese is that he fears that if he does, he will be subjected to pressure from hawkish circles to invade Cambodia again—this time in direct support of the Lon Nol government. However, we believe that there is another reason for the President's silence. It is this: If the United States lets Cambodia fall, why should it save South Vietnam? Yet even the most unswerving hawks—the people who have argued that a non-Communist South Vietnam is all that stands between world peace and a third world war—have behaved as though it were the most natural thing imaginable for the North Vietnamese to take over Cambodia. Even such stalwart supporters of the war as Senator Barry Goldwater and Senator John Stennis have publicly stated that they would oppose a move to support the Lon Nol government. And in doing so they—together with the Administration, and everyone else who has kept silent—have, whether they know it or not, tacitly recognized that the justifications for America's entire venture in Indo-China, from its beginning to the present day, have been nothing but one long tangle of illusions and contradictions.

AUGUST 22, 1970

I N the last several months, the public's confidence in the government has
been further threatened by the introduction of a form of official deception
that may be altogether new in American political life. Two incidents,
which represent high points in the new trend, tell a good part of the story.
After President Nixon made his famous remark, at a press conference in
Denver, that Charles Manson, who is on trial in California, was "guilty,
directly or indirectly, of eight murders without reason," officials of his Administration issued a series of statements about the incident that ran as follows:
(a) Minutes after the press conference was over, the President's press secretary,
Ronald Ziegler, issued a "clarification" asserting that the President had meant
to say Manson was "allegedly" guilty of the murders. When Ziegler was asked
whether he was retracting the President's statement, he replied that he thought
he had done so. (b) Shortly after Ziegler's statement was issued, Attorney
General Mitchell, who had been at the President's side when the remark was
made, told newsmen, in effect, that the remark had never been made at all.
He said that he did not think the President had "made a charge or implied
one." (c) That evening, the President issued a statement asserting that Ziegler's
remarks earlier in the day had been "unequivocal," and adding, "The last thing
I would do is prejudice the legal rights of any person in any circumstances."
(d) Several days later, Mitchell said a few more words to the press on the
subject, and this time he declared that as soon as the President had uttered
the remark about Manson, he himself had been aware that the President had
made a slip of the tongue, and the reason he had not said anything about it
at the time was that "it is not the proper posture of anybody to correct the
President of the United States when the President is speaking." The second
incident involves a statement made by Communications Director Herbert
Klein about another of the President's remarks: namely, his remark, back in
April, that one objective of the American troops' mission in Cambodia was
going to be the capture of COSVN, which he described as "the headquarters
of the entire Communist military operation in South Vietnam." In mid-June,
as the American ground operations in Cambodia were coming to a close,
Klein said, "There has been a great deal of misunderstanding regarding COSVN,
and I think the briefings indicated we would capture some of the headquarters
areas. Some of these were found in the so-called 'The City'—this great
underground complex which included their schools and signals and everything. Basically, the key part, the general staff and the radio, was never part

of the plan. It would have been a longshot chance had we been able to capture them."

Ordinarily, when democratic governments try to deceive the public, they limit their deceptions to matters of which the public can have only a hazy and indirect knowledge, such as foreign wars or the activities of vast, amorphous bureaucracies. But when a government expands the field of deception to include deceptions about what its highest public officials have recently stated before the public, as Klein and Mitchell did in the incidents we have mentioned, it is invading one of the few areas in political life of which the public can have direct, first-hand knowledge. The citizen who has to rely on the reports of journalists and politicians for most of what he knows about public events can see and hear with his own eyes and ears, in his own living room, the President and other officials making public statements on television. He may doubt the truth of what the official says, but he cannot doubt that the official has said it. For this reason, a lie about a recent public statement—and particularly a televised public statement—is one of the most extreme, brazen kinds of affront that an official can offer to the public's intelligence. Such lies, far from concealing inconsistencies of policy, actually flaunt them before the public. They are based on the insulting assumption that the public can believe two contradictory things at the same time, or else that each time a policy statement is made, all previous statements on the same subject, however recent, are erased from the public's mind.

This new kind of lying, similar to the Big Lie practiced in totalitarian countries—in which the government tries to convince the public of a grossly false but self-consistent version of the facts—is nonetheless different, because it destroys all consistency, even the internal consistency of the government's position. In short, the government defies and obliterates its own word, and policy statements become unintelligible as well as untruthful. When this happens, the points of certainty that might serve as a common basis for constructive discussion are lost, and the kind of rational public debate that is essential to the functioning of a democracy becomes impossible.

SEPTEMBER 12, 1970

ALTHOUGH men's religions and political philosophies have sanctioned the maintenance of infinite distinctions of rank, privilege, and class among the living, almost all of them have left the determination of things in the afterlife—or in the lack of it—to Nature and to God. There are few philosophies more unnatural, in our view, than those which, not being satisfied with manipulating and ordering the living, wish to extend their influence over the dead as well. We were prompted to these reflections by the recent news accounts of a black woman's attempts to have her son, who had been killed in Vietnam, buried in a Florida cemetery that had previously been reserved for whites. At first, the cemetery refused permission, and one man, who was white, and whose brother and sister were buried there, said that he would consider disinterring his relatives and burying them somewhere else rather than let them remain in the cemetery with the black soldier. Race hatred aside, we were struck by the gross materialism implicit in these responses. Whether or not men's spirits are immortal, we know that their bodies are not. Yet it is precisely a sort of monstrous notion of immortality that was suggested by the Florida cemetery's extreme regard for the company that its corpses kept. The incident reminded us of an experience we once had in another country. A few years ago, we visited Red Square, where for the last forty years the body of Lenin has been preserved and kept on public display in a mausoleum. We were taken to see it as part of a guided tour. After being led down a short marble staircase, we found ourself in a small, refrigerated underground vault. Lenin's corpse was lying under glass, and his face, which had turned a yellowish green, was illumined by pink spotlights overhead. Four soldiers stood at rigid attention at the four corners of the vault. When we were back in the daylight and were being guided past several ordinary graves where lesser figures in Soviet history were interred, we had a feeling of extreme revulsion. One of the graves was that of Joseph Stalin. Until several years before, when Stalin's reputation suffered its sharp decline in official circles, his corpse, as everybody knows, had been on view alongside that of Lenin in the vault we had just visited. We wondered, briefly, whether his corpse was being kept preserved in its new resting place, so that it could be lugged down into the vault again in case his reputation improved, or whether this time the Soviet government had relinquished him once and for all to the earth. We hoped it had taken the latter course, and we left Red Square wishing that men would occupy themselves with the living and let the dead rest in peace.

OCTOBER 10, 1970

TO the various credibility gaps and failures in communication that have been commented on so much recently, one must now add the widening gap between the President and the Vice-President. The lines of communication between them began to break down when the Vice-President called for "positive polarization" and a general heating up of national debate just a few months after the President asked us all to lower our voices and a few months before the President recommended that when the going gets hot the rhetoric should get cool. The break widened when the Vice-President called for the resignation of Joseph Rhodes, Jr., whom the President had just appointed to his Commission on Campus Unrest. And then the other day the Vice-President challenged the wisdom of all nine of the President's appointments to the Commission and condemned the Commission's findings and recommendations as "imprecise, contradictory, and equivocal." He pointed out that nine was "not a very large number of people," and suggested that nine other appointees might have come up with quite different conclusions. He asserted, however, that his statements represented his "personal views," and not the views of the Administration. In any case, it seems to us that, taken together, the differences between the President and the Vice-President have assumed the proportions of a debate. In view of the fact that statements by the President and the Vice-President pretty much dominate the news these days (you have to look deep in the back pages of the papers to find the replies of other men—such as Senator Fulbright, Senator McGovern, and Dr. Spock—whose views have been questioned by the Vice-President), we would like to suggest that the time has come for a televised debate between Mr. Nixon and Mr. Agnew. And if this cannot be arranged, we would like to suggest a debate of a wholly new kind. Now that the Vice-President is speaking with two voices on matters of official policy—his official voice and his "personal" voice—it occurs to us that recent advances in television technology might make it possible to arrange a debate between the Vice-President and himself. On one side of the screen you would have the personal Mr. Agnew, expressing his own views, and on the other side you would have the official Mr. Agnew, representing the Administration. The press has already begun to show some acceptance of the idea that Mr. Agnew has two legitimate voices with which to speak out on political matters. The *Times*, for example, concludes an editorial in which it opposes Mr. Agnew's views on the threat of polarization in America with the sentence "It would be an inestimable tragedy if the Administration shared Mr. Agnew's insensitivity to this threat." In view of the fact that Mr. Agnew is himself the second-highest-ranking official of the Administration, this amounts to saying that it would be an inestimable tragedy if Mr. Agnew shared his own insensitivity. The debate we are proposing would perhaps help to clear such matters up. Admittedly, it might not be a very high-toned affair. There could be no assurance that it would not descend on both sides to character assassination and some rather crude charges about lack of patriotism, and the like. However, there would be the advantage that we would be permitted to hear every shade of the Vice-President's opinion, and that should satisfy everybody, including the Vice-President.

Last week, when we turned to the *Times'* new page for guest columnists, we expected to find the usual parade of Presidential official advisers and ex-advisers, but instead we found, to our considerable dismay, two modern-day witch doctors performing a dance of death on the printed page. Actually, both of these men, if they are not official advisers to the President, at least advise him informally, and each was described by the *Times* as a "friend" of the President. One, Dr. Arnold Hutschnecker, is the President's former physician and the author of some plans for controlling crime, and the other, Dr. Billy Graham, is often mentioned as the President's spiritual mentor. That is to say, these are men who have looked after the body and the soul of our President. The first, Dr. Hutschnecker, is a theorist whose field is the kind of thought control and behavior control that in modern times has had its fullest expression in the totalitarian states of Hitler's Germany and Stalin's Russia. The second, Dr. Graham, who in his article ponders the timing of Judgment Day and the Second Coming of Christ, is an exponent of a medieval kind of apocalyptic thinking. Thus, at the bottom of the page you have an exponent of the most virulent forms of modern barbarism and superstition, and at the top of the page you have an exponent of the barbarism and superstition of the Middle Ages.

In the more modern article, which is titled "A Plea for Experiment," Dr. Hutschnecker uses the *Times* column to solicit governmental and private funds with which to institute a "pilot project" for his idea of subjecting all six-to-eight-year-olds—and perhaps all fifteen-year-olds, too—to "tests" that would uncover those with "delinquent tendencies," so that potential future delinquents could be given "therapy." Dr. Hutschnecker proposed his plan to the Administration several months ago, and it was said to have met with some expressions of interest. However, the plan was leaked to the press, and an extremely unfavorable, if somewhat lighthearted, reaction seemed enough to consign it to the dustbin, where it clearly belonged. In the original report,

Dr. Hutschnecker suggested that therapy could be carried out at "special camps," run by, among others, "parapsychologists." His article in the *Times* assures us at one point that "a delinquent sticks out like a sore thumb" in a certain test he recommends, but at another point it states that actual delinquents cannot be discovered by means of testing; rather, delinquent "tendencies" can be readily spotted. There seems to be a contradiction here, but we are confident that if Dr. Hutschnecker's "special camps" for "therapy" were to be put into operation, the troublesome distinction between children who actually commit delinquent acts and those who the state predicts *will* commit delinquent acts could be eliminated. Other "special camps" in recent history have succeeded very well in eliminating this distinction, and also in eliminating the delinquents and "potential" delinquents themselves. In case anyone has any doubt about the reliability of the main test he proposes, Dr. Hutschnecker assures us that a memorandum he received describing it included not only eleven pages of text but sixty-six more pages of "bibliography and related data." *That* ought to keep any doubting intellectuals quiet. The title "A Plea for Experiment" raises some interesting questions. Apparently, the laboratory for this "experiment" is to be the lives of a number of six-year-old children, and, if Dr. Hutschnecker gets the Presidential approval he is still hoping for, perhaps the lives of all the six-year-olds in the country. But if you make man himself your "laboratory," where are you going to apply all the marvellous results you achieve with your "experiments"? Where but to the mangled survivors of the original experiment?

Turning to the top of the page, we get Dr. Graham's opinion on the question "When Is Christ Coming?" (That is the title of his article.) He gets one answer from the nineteenth-century French chemist Marcellin Berthelot, who apparently said, "Within a hundred years of physical and chemical science, man will know what the atom is. It is my belief when science reaches this stage, God will come down to earth with His big ring of keys and will say to humanity, 'Gentlemen, it is closing time.'" (A while back, Daniel P. Moynihan, another adviser to the President, used the phrase "the sheer intellectual vulgarity of the parlor apocalypse style." Perhaps this is an early example of what he had in mind, though the word "vulgarity" seems a bit mild.) It is to the Bible, however, and not to any secular authority, that Dr. Graham principally turns for his prediction. "Millions of Americans are caught up in a desperate attempt to know the future," he points out. "The phenomenal rise in the sale of crystal balls, Ouija boards, and Viennese fortune-telling tarot cards is only a part of the new 'groping' into the future." Everyone can put away his Viennese cards and his Ouija board now, because Dr. Graham, although he modestly confesses that he does not know "the hour, the day, the month of the year" of the apocalypse (a manner of speaking that suggests he does at least know the year of the apocalypse), has ascertained that the hour of doom and of the Second Coming of Christ is imminent. But the Christ who will come again will not be like the one who visited the earth 1,970 years ago. Forgiveness and mercy will not be His message. Christians must now fear a new kind of Christ, Dr. Graham warns. "The prophecies of the Bible do not predict a world of gradual progress toward a materialistic paradise," he tells us. "They see a world torn by lawlessness, war, famines, and pestilences on a scale that only God himself can terminate if the human race is to survive. . . . These events will culminate in God's intervention and the literal return of Jesus Christ to this planet. The Bible does not teach that the earth or the human race will come to an end. The Bible teaches that the world will be renovated by fire." Dr. Graham's Christ has apparently forgotten about salvation and is now interested, like an interior decorator, in "renovation." "This fire," Dr. Graham goes on, "will destroy all that is evil and prepare the earth for the Kingdom of God." We are not sure just what kind of fire Dr. Graham is talking about, but we can make a guess. It is the fire that waits in the underground silos of the Soviet Union and of the United States. But it is man who is in control of this fire. And man cannot save his soul by incinerating his body. To regard a decision that is in man's hands as the will of God is not to worship God. To wait for the bomb to go off is to lay the groundwork for the ultimate heresy, which is the worship of death. Dr. Graham concludes with the pronouncement "Thus the future does not belong to Communism! The future does not belong to capitalism! The future belongs to God!" For "God," read "death." We trust that, God willing, the future belongs to man.

DECEMBER 5, 1970

WE'VE been following the reports on the recent commando raid on the prisoner-of-war camp in North Vietnam, and we were particularly interested in this exchange between Senator Fulbright and Secretary Laird, which we read in the *Times'* account of the recent Senate Foreign Relations Committee hearing:

MR. FULBRIGHT: I don't like to say it was all a bad idea simply because it failed, but it did fail. There was something wrong with the intelligence.
MR. LAIRD: This was not a failure, Mr. Chairman, and I would—

MR. FULBRIGHT: Well, it was a failure.

MR. LAIRD: These men knew full well the chance that there might not be P.O.W.s present.

MR. FULBRIGHT: I'm not complaining about the men but those men responsible for it.

MR. LAIRD: I would like to tell you, Mr. Chairman, that we have made tremendous progress as far as intelligence is concerned—

MR. FULBRIGHT: You mean since Friday?

MR. LAIRD: —but we have not been able to develop a camera that sees through the roofs of buildings. We had— The intelligence in this mission was excellent. But let me give you the intelligence rundown, as far as the location of troops were concerned, the location of buildings, the makeup of the camp, where the SAM missiles were located, where the anti-aircraft was located, where the radar blanks were in the radar screen, so that we could make penetration without detection.

MR. FULBRIGHT: But, Mr. Secretary, I don't think this is relevant. There weren't any prisoners there, so what difference does it make?

MR. LAIRD: There were prisoners there, Mr. Chairman, and we knew full well . . .

In Secretary Laird's remarks there is to be found a remarkable definition of "success" and "failure"—a definition that implies a radically altered notion of what the government's responsibility for its actions is. Success is measured wholly in terms of the vigor and health of the war machine, without any reference to what's happening to the war itself. The world outside the confines of the government's own organizational machinery disappears from view, and success and failure are judged by standards that are completely internal. One might compare the government to a doctor who tries to judge the health of his patient by taking his own temperature; or one might compare it to those "permissive" educators who grade their pupils on the basis of effort rather than on the basis of results. Under this system, even a moron can get an A in nuclear physics, and though in certain schools—particularly schools for the handicapped or the mentally retarded—this system may be wise and merciful, it is foolish and dangerous when the government uses it as a way of not facing its mistakes and of giving itself straight A's for everything it undertakes.

We have long believed that certain fundamental errors lie at the root of our country's travail in Vietnam. For one thing, the forces sent to Vietnam were entirely inappropriate to the task they were asked to perform; in fact, it is hard to imagine that any forces from any country could have performed the tasks that our government assigned to its Army. It has now become apparent that sending the Army to build democracy in Vietnam was like sending a carpenter to sew up a dress, or sending a fireman to settle a marital dispute, or sending a psychiatrist to put out a fire. And the results in Vietnam have been as ludicrous as the means. But if you apply the Laird Principle, and forget what it was that you wanted to accomplish in the first place, and forget what the results were, too, then the whole war can be seen as a "success." Laird's answers to Fulbright provide a good metaphor for the entire war effort. If a hearing were to be held on the success or failure of the war up to this point, it might, we imagine, proceed as follows:

Q: We went into Vietnam to help the South Vietnamese fight Communism and build themselves up so that they could stand on their own. Why have we failed?

A: I'd like to say that as far as the actual operation of the war is concerned, this has been a tremendous success. As to the efficiency and morale of our armed forces, this is the most sophisticated, finest Army we've ever had. Let me give you a rundown on some of the things we have accomplished. We've got the best Air Force we've ever had. As to pilot performance, these are the finest pilots who have ever flown planes, and they've got the most sophisticated ordnance that has ever been put together. This has been a tremendous plus for our side. We've got B-52s that can tear up a strip of jungle a mile long; we've got a pinpoint, surgical precision in our air strikes that we never had before; we've got some ordnance for any job you want done. When you put all this together, it means that our men have been able to apply more ordnance in this war than in all our other wars put together.

Q: But the enemy continues to infiltrate its men into South Vietnam, and continues to fight in South Vietnam, and now in Laos and Cambodia as well.

A: Well, we're going at this thing from every side. I don't want to just emphasize the negative side and forget the great work that our Rural Development boys have been doing, because we've had a whole string of successes on the positive side. We've built some of the most modern housing the rural people have ever seen. Some of them had never seen a television set until we brought one along, and our agricultural team has been doing a lot of work with new advances in farming. We've got a machine called the Transphibian Tactical Destroyer that weighs ninety tons and can cut a highway through any jungle. In the entertainment field, we've shown thousands of films throughout Vietnam, and we've kept our military bands busy, too. We've developed a tremendous store of techniques there. We replaced their tradition-oriented village system with a progress-oriented democratic system, and we've got a team of some of the highest-paid professors in the country to tell us how to put their country together again in line with modern processes, with the disruptive elements shut completely out of the picture.

They were two thousand years behind us when we got there, and we've brought them into the modern age. In terms of the development process, we introduced a lot of potential workers into the urban areas, and now, with our resettlement programs, we're getting some of them back into the countryside again. We've made amazing advances in this field, too.

Q: Then why do the villagers hate us?

A: Modernization can't happen overnight. It took us two hundred years to do it. As to the hostility that sometimes is generated, we've got planes dropping billions of leaflets explaining our system in the kind of language they understand. This is the biggest, best-organized, most sophisticated psychological war effort we've ever launched, and I want to take this opportunity to pay a tribute to our Psy War team. They're just tops. And that goes for Intelligence, too. We've got an infrared device that can just about read a fellow's mind from ten thousand feet. We've got the whole country rigged to the most sophisticated computers. They've given us more reports per square inch of enemy-controlled territory than we've ever had before.

Q: Well, then why do the enemy always know when we are going to attack, whereas we never know when they are going to attack? Everything you say is very impressive, but what has it got to do with building a strong democratic government in Vietnam? Why aren't we achieving our objectives?

A: Well, in answer to your question I'd say that we've made fantastic progress. Our machine has outproduced, outgunned, and outtalked their machine in every hamlet of Vietnam. As to whether we're achieving our objectives, I'd say that this is the best-co-ordinated, best-financed, most highly motivated operation we've ever mounted. In other words, we've succeeded.

Q: Then why have we failed?

A: You can't have everything.

DECEMBER 19, 1970

W HEN the President announced his "second inflation alert," in a speech to the National Association of Manufacturers, he concluded with a lengthy encomium on "the power and genius" of "the American economic system." Among other things, he said, "Here is a system that makes possible massive aid to education, vital new programs to improve the health of our people, and a wide range of efforts to protect and restore our environment. A strong economy makes us strong enough to better our lives." Passing over the fact that many nations with economies feebler than this

country's have much better records in health and education, we were particularly curious about just how the American system had proved better able
to protect the natural environment than other systems. It seemed to us that,
however great the benefits of a strong economy might be, environmental
pollution was clearly one of its disadvantages, and that, as things were set
up, the relation of the strength of the economy to the health of the environment was precisely the opposite of what the President suggested. Likewise,
the freedom from strong government regulations that industry now enjoys
in the matter of pollution had seemed to us to be a primary cause of the
continuing pollution. A few days later, a story on pollution appeared in the
Times. Headed "Polluters Sit on Antipollution Boards," it revealed that "the
membership of air and water pollution boards in thirty-five states is dotted
with industrial, agricultural, municipal, and county representatives whose own
organizations or spheres of activity are in many cases in the forefront of
pollution," and that "the roster of big corporations with employes on such
boards reads like an abbreviated blue book of American industry." The story
went on to say that the conflicts of interest inherent in this state of affairs
naturally impeded the control of pollution. That being so, we began to wonder
again how America's economic system helped contribute to pollution control.
It appeared that this powerful economy "makes possible" a "wide range of
efforts" to control pollution only in the sense that if it weren't for this economy
we wouldn't have the problem of pollution to cope with in the first place,
and it looked as though the President were offering his congratulations to
the very people who were at the root of the problem, much as if he were to
congratulate a criminal for having given a policeman an opportunity to make
a heroic arrest.

   A couple of weeks ago, we suggested that Secretary Laird's testimony
before the Senate Foreign Relations Committee on the recent raid upon a
prisoner-of-war camp in North Vietnam contained some new definitions of
"success" and "failure," and we gave our version of what a defense of the entire
Indo-China war based on these definitions might sound like. It now seems
to us that the President's remarks on pollution and the American economic
system contain new definitions of "problem" and "solution." A number of
slogans about problems and solutions have been going around recently. Many
radicals have been saying that "either you're part of the solution or you're
part of the problem." Environmentalists have answered that often, when it
comes to pollution, "the solution *is* part of the problem." The President's
answer to these slogans might be "The problem is the solution." This slogan
has the advantage of obliterating the distinction between problems and solutions once and for all, and would save everyone the trouble of discussing

the subject any further. If a speech were to be given in which the problems of the nation were set forth in accordance with the new definitions, it might, we imagine, sound something like this:

"The American people want peace in Vietnam, an end to the arms race, and a just and open society here at home. No one wants these things more than I do. But we have to consider our problems with balance and perspective, and we must reject the arguments of the self-styled nay-sayers and the professional pessimists who have eyes only for what's wrong with America. Now, I know that many sincere and dedicated young people are disturbed by our continuing presence in Vietnam, and that they would like us to withdraw. That's what I want, too, but this doesn't mean that our presence in Vietnam has been all bad. Indeed, it is the presence of a huge American military force in Vietnam that makes possible our wide range of efforts to effect a withdrawal. We can say with confidence that if we didn't have our troops there, the goal we are all hoping and striving to reach—withdrawal—could never be attained. Our forces are fighting for peace, and it is only through their efforts that we will eventually be able to leave. But we have a duty to protect our troops. We *are* going to withdraw, I assure you, but if we withdraw immediately, then who is going to protect our troops as the withdrawal continues? Once again, it is only the continued presence of our troops that will make withdrawal possible.

"I also share the fears of the many loyal Americans who are worried about the spiralling arms race. No responsible person can seriously oppose disarmament in this nuclear age. But I'd like to point out that if we hadn't developed the powerful, highly effective weapons system that we've now got deployed around the world, 'disarmament' would be nothing but an empty slogan. Our missiles and our conventional forces are what put the teeth in our program of disarmament. And when the time comes, we're going to have the know-how and the resources we need to put through our disarmament program. But we've got to protect our disarmament program with great care, and this is why we're going ahead with the M.I.R.V., the A.B.M., and the new hardened missile silos. These are bargaining chips, and this means that when we get to the bargaining table, we're going to have a lot to bargain with.

"And now I'd like to say a word about race. Our nation has a tremendous challenge to face here. The movement to bring about a just and open society has called forth some of the most idealistic impulses of our finest young people, and it has brought forth a new awareness and a desire for equality among some of our most capable and responsible black citizens as well as white citizens. And America deserves to be proud of this. But I'd like to say that if it hadn't been for our one-hundred-and-ninety-year history of racism, none of this would have been possible. It is fashionable now to look at only the negative side of our system of slavery before the Civil War. To be In now, you have to join the noisy minority that can see only the bad side, but I want to point out that without slavery we would never have had a Martin Luther King or an Abraham Lincoln—two of the finest men we've ever had in our public life. I'm the first to admit that America faces many problems that challenge our ingenuity and our will power, but we can't just look at what's wrong. Every great nation has great problems. As the greatest nation, we naturally have the greatest problems any nation on earth has ever had. We've got some really tremendous problems—race hatred, the threat of nuclear war, a declining economy, civil unrest, the threat of repression from extremists of the left and of the right—but without problems what would we do for solutions?"

JANUARY 23, 1971

IT has come to light that the United States government and its South Vietnamese allies are planning a mass deportation within South Vietnam that appears virtually certain to open an entirely new and bloody chapter in the Indo-China war. A recent story in the *Times* reveals that a project to deport hundreds of thousands of people—and, in the end, perhaps millions—from the five northernmost provinces of South Vietnam to southern provinces is "now in its final planning stages." So far, the American and South Vietnamese government officials concerned have been covering up the enormity of this measure with the customary euphemisms. In the *Times* article, a Vietnamese official says that several "village representatives" from northern provinces will be brought down to the south to look at the land where their villages are to be relocated, as though to suggest that this forced mass deportation would be nothing more than a kind of real-estate deal. In reality, if this brutal project is carried out, it will be nothing less than the first openly totalitarian act in the history of this nation's relations with other nations, and one of the few such acts in any nation's history. The closest precedent may be the Soviet Union's infamous deportation in the nineteen-thirties of Ukrainians, White Russians, Armenians, Jews, and Georgians to Siberia. It is true, of course, that through bombing and through thousands of small-scale projects of forced deportation the American military have already uprooted something like six million Vietnamese from their homes. The obliteration of their villages was also covered up with euphemisms—words and phrases such as "pacification," "resettlement," "rural development," and "Operation County Fair." At the "county fairs," along with free buffet lunches from portable Army kitchens, piped-in music, showings of cartoons and propaganda movies, and handouts of candy to the children, there were offered such novel attractions as the torture of the customers and the machine-gunning from helicopters of anyone who didn't want to attend. In cases where there was resistance from a village slated for "resettlement" (and who can doubt that the current project of mass "resettlement" will be met with heavy resistance?), the military very often simply bombed the village out of existence. These are the true precedents for the new plan, and they afford the best indications of what its execution will bring. Yet, terrible as the effect of these policies has been, the policies have been different in several crucial aspects from what is now being proposed. The forced emigrations and the killings of civilians that have so far taken place have occurred in a twilight zone of public confusion and half-knowledge and with official approval that has been only tacit. The new project, on the other hand, cannot take place without the full and energetic support of the entire military command and civilian administration, and without being fully and frankly announced to the American public and to the world as a major new policy of the United States government.

Ordinarily, this is the kind of plan that it is better not even to mention, since by merely discussing it one runs the risk of making it seem acceptable, of helping to raise it from the level of a wild, unthinkable scheme to the level of one of those myriad "options" that the government is "keeping open." And one wants at all costs to avoid adding one's voice to the voices of the official analysts who, for a price, will discuss, in their own weird, ambiguous, pseudo-scientific language, the "pluses" and "minuses" of any option, scenario, or game plan that is put before them, whether for building an orphanage or for carrying out mass murder. However, since the current project of mass deportation has moved beyond the option stage and got into the planning stage, one is compelled to discuss it. In fact, it is a striking demonstration of how deeply the nation is sunk in anesthesia when it comes to events in Vietnam that the press and television have failed to comment on this project since it was reported in the *Times*—a project that, if we imagined its being undertaken in the United States, by, say, the Chinese, would consist of deporting the entire population of New England to the Southwest, destroying all the cities and towns, defoliating the landscape, and shooting all the people who refused to leave or who hid in the woods.

One must remind oneself that five and a half years ago, when the Marines landed in the provinces of South Vietnam now scheduled for depopulation, the officials of the American government imagined that the job of the American military forces was to help a friendly population repel a foreign enemy. But in actuality, as the Marines soon came to realize, most of the population supported the supposed foreign invaders and regarded the Marines themselves as the real invaders. The people of these provinces had supported every insurgent force in South Vietnam since the late nineteenth century, and if in 1965 they had any doubts about the justice of the National Liberation Front's cause, these doubts were dispelled when the Marines landed. The Marines, and the Army units that joined them in the spring of 1967, adjusted quickly to this unexpected situation and altered their strategy accordingly. And if they did not announce to the world that they were fighting a war against nearly the entire population of the provinces they were in, they did announce it to the South Vietnamese people. In leaflets titled, among other things, "Marine Ultimatum to Vietnamese People," they announced a policy of reprisal bombings against villages in South Vietnam that supported the National Liberation Front in any way. After this policy had been in effect for about two years, most of the villages in these provinces had been bombed, and about half of the population of these provinces was living in camps. Every soldier, whatever he had been told before he arrived in South Vietnam, learned from bitter personal experience that he was engaged in a war against the South Vietnamese people. The bomber pilots who bombed villages day after day knew it; the Psychological Warfare officers who dropped leaflets knew it; the G.I.s—who were indeed often attacked by small children and old women, as they have claimed—knew it. The highest levels of the military acknowledged this situation in many of their statements, although in other statements they denied it. Some officers began to read the works of Mao Tse-tung, in which it is said that guerrillas live among the people the way fish live in the sea, so a new strategy was developed in the hope of catching the fish by drying up the sea—which is to say, by tearing the entire Vietnamese society to pieces and then putting it together again according to some plan that was being worked out in the think tanks in Washington. At that time, officials proudly announced that millions of Vietnamese had been pulled out of their homes in order to "deprive" the enemy of their support, and the official analysts spoke of "war-induced urbanization." But in adopting this strategy based on the insights of Mao Tse-tung the Americans obliterated the very purpose for which they had been sent to Vietnam. The aim had been to save the society, and counter-insurgency had been the means to that end. Now this policy was reversed; destroying the guerrillas became the aim, and destroying the society became the means. However, if the men in the field had some knowledge of what was really happening, Washington did not know, or pretended not to know, or refused to know. What all this meant was not that the military were doing things the wrong way, or that the "mix" of bombing and camp construction was unbalanced, or even that a sound policy had been corrupted by bungling or by berserk execution. What it meant was something much harder for the officials and experts in Washington to accept: namely, that the South Vietnam they had sent the troops to protect had been a hallucination, which had little resemblance to the actual country in which the men were fighting. In the last analysis, what the men were fighting to protect, and are still fighting to protect, was not a country but this hallucination. The truth is that the job that the politicians had assigned the military, the job of protecting the people of South Vietnam from a foreign enemy, was simply not there to be done. There was no such job. If you send someone to protect a friend from a common enemy, how does that someone proceed when he discovers that the friend isn't a friend after all and doesn't want his help? The answer is that he leaves. But this alternative was not open to our military. Having been sent to do a job that turned out not to exist, our military men, who were forced, after all, to live and work in the real Vietnam, and not in the imaginary one in the politicians' heads, began to do something else. They began to make war against the people whom they were supposed to be saving but who didn't want to be saved. To be sure, this was not a job that anyone had explicitly ordered them to do, nor was it a job that served to advance any objective ever stated by our government, but it did have the reassuring advantage of being, in a sense, real.

Now this war against the South Vietnamese people, based on willful official ignorance, and working at cross purposes with official policy, has got completely out of control. None of the scenarios are turning out as they were supposed to, particularly in the northern provinces, and all the game plans have gone haywire. Instead of producing a peaceful, prosperous, democratic society, they have produced massacres, a desolated landscape, and squalid detention camps. For six years, the "social engineers," both in and out of uniform, have been at work with their hot dogs and their napalm, their fertilizers and their crop poisons, trying to build public-relations utopias on the burned villages and the corpses of villagers, and the result has been a swamp of red tape and blood. And now, perhaps themselves dismayed and revolted by the monstrous results of their experiments, the social engineers have come up with their "final solution" to the problem of the northern provinces—the deportation project. Like scientists whose experiment has failed, they have decided to get rid of the whole mess, so that they won't have to think about it anymore. However, the new "solution" is not really new at all. It is only the old solution writ large. The social engineers are trying to escape from the present debacle by recommitting the very errors that led to it, but on an even huger scale, by doing to whole provinces what they used to do to one village at a time—as though they thought that through the sheer grandiosity of their new plan they could escape responsibility for the chaos and suffering they had already caused. If the plan goes into effect, it will signal the full official acceptance of a way of looking at the people of South Vietnam that has dominated our policy unofficially since the beginning of the war. In this view, the problem in South Vietnam is not the traditional village system, or flaws in the pacification program, or even the Vietcong or the North Vietnamese. The problem is the South Vietnamese themselves. Ordinarily, we regard people as *having* problems, but in Vietnam we regard them as *being* problems. Get rid of them—send them somewhere else—and you solve your problems. There will be no more starving, begging refugees, no more children throwing hand grenades, no more massacres of villagers. Get rid of the whole civilian mess, with its crying children and their crying mothers, its old people and its babies, its pigs and its chickens, and its sly but intractable spirit of resistance and defiance, and at last the Army and the Air Force will have a clear field of fire for hundreds of miles, and will be able to start fighting the war the way a war should be fought.

But fighting for what?

FEBRUARY 13, 1971

OVER the last few years, a false, simplified picture of American politics has been superimposed on the political realities. The rigid formulas and clichés that make up this false picture are familiar—all too familiar—to everybody. We are speaking of that view which divides all Americans into two groups—the wild men who oppose government policies and the responsible people who support government policies. On the one hand, the young, long-haired, loud-mouthed, pot-smoking extremists; on the other hand, the old, short-haired, reserved, cigar-smoking Establishmentarians. Abbie Hoffman versus Mayor Daley. Insofar as you oppose government policies, particularly in regard to Indo-China, you're supposed to look and act like Abbie Hoffman. Insofar as you support government policies, you're supposed to look and act like Mayor Daley. And so on and so on. One of the people who fit the clichés least well is Senator McGovern. Senator McGovern takes a strong position against the war, yet his manner and temperament—or "style," as these things are called—are notable for their steadiness and calm. This combination of content and "style" throws many political observers into confusion, because, according to the accepted beliefs of the day, anyone who opposes the war as forcefully as Senator McGovern does is bound to be an inflammatory, somewhat hysterical figure. Many commentators have run headlong onto the horns of this apparent dilemma. One of the most recent casualties was David S. Broder, of the Washington *Post*, who wrote an article called "The Aspirants' Style," in which he compared the "styles" of Senator Muskie and Senator McGovern. Mr. Broder wrote that "McGovern's instinct is to pounce on an issue; Muskie's is to ponder it. Muskie's judgments seem more impressive, in part because they come rumbling up in that throbbing bass of his, while McGovern delivers his opinions in the voice of a tenor choirboy. But McGovern's are a darn sight plainer. There are many who suspect that in the end clarity may be McGovern's undoing. . . . The prevailing wisdom in the Democratic Party is that Muskie's big-daddy moderation is more in keeping with the mood of the country than McGovern's brash-sounding prairie radicalism." But just a few sentences after referring to Senator McGovern as "brash-sounding," Mr. Broder assures us that McGovern isn't "the soft, sweet, simple clergyman's son he appears." In fact, Mr. Broder goes on, "he has an instinct for the political jugular and a talent for finding an issue." In conclusion, Mr. Broder says, "Given Muskie's lumbering caution, maybe it's well he has a terrier-like McGovern at his heels." What we seem to have here is a head-on collision of two clichés. On the one hand, because of his views, McGovern's "style" is seen as "brash-sounding" and "terrier-like." On the other hand, because of his quiet behavior, it is seen as appearing "soft, sweet, simple." Put it all together and you've got the soft, terrier-like, sweet, brash-sounding, simple tenor choirboy who represents the radical prairie state of South Dakota.

FEBRUARY 20, 1971

AFTER a period of uncertainty, the American–South Vietnamese campaign in Laos once again makes it clear that the United States is trying to win the war in Indo-China. When one uses the word "win" in connection with this war, it is necessary to specify exactly what one means. Our objective in going into Vietnam was to help a government fight its enemies until it could stand on its own. Attaining this objective, and nothing more than this objective, is what it would mean for the United States to "win" in Indo-China. It is this objective that has eluded us for a decade, and it is this objective that President Nixon seems to be still pursuing by extending the war into Laos. This, apparently, is what he is talking about when he uses the code words "peace with honor." "Honor" here means winning. The real difference between a dove and a hawk is not that a dove wants the war to stop and a hawk wants it to continue; it is that a dove wants us to get out of Indo-China whether the Saigon government collapses or not, and a hawk doesn't want us to leave until the Saigon government is strong enough to stand on its own. In saying that the President remains a hawk, no one is suggesting that he loves war and hates peace, or that he wants our troops to stay in Indo-China just because he likes having them there. One is saying that, whatever he may want, he will end up keeping our armed forces in Indo-China, because he is unwilling to give up trying to achieve the objectives this country has failed for ten years to achieve. This is not something that the Administration always readily admits to. It claims that the campaigns in Cambodia and Laos are designed to protect our forces as we evacuate them, but this is almost self-evidently not the case. Our troops could leave speedily and safely without first attacking all the neighboring countries. The real purpose of these new military campaigns is to insure the survival of the Saigon government, not *because* we are leaving but *in order that* we may leave, and this is precisely the policy that the United States pursued under two Presidents before President Nixon.

Does this mean, then, that after several years in which it seemed plausible that the United States had changed its policy we have returned to the situation in 1967, when President Johnson was still convinced that the war could be won by military measures? Unfortunately, it appears that we are actually in a more discouraging position than we were then. What we see around us is a breakdown—or, rather, the evidence of a cumulative breakdown. It is a breakdown of Constitutional restrictions, public debate, and political action, and also a breakdown of will, judgment, and moral scruple. In short, it represents an extreme—although not, one trusts, final—collapse of the delicate constraints that a free people exercises over its war machine and its leaders. In Congress, in the press, and all over the country, there is a numbness, and even a paralysis, among the people from whom one might expect leadership in the current crisis. In 1967, with each escalation of the war one could expect a stiffening of the opposition. Each new move called forth a fresh response. In 1967, also, one could expect that as politicians and the public learned more about the dangers of the war, and as the stories of crimes committed by Americans in Indo-China multiplied, the public's revulsion against the war would deepen, and would perhaps serve, in the end, to get us out. It seemed then that there were certain obstacles to new escalations— certain principles in the Constitution, certain limits to the abuse that the

Congress was willing to take, and certain simple standards of decency that most Americans shared. But now it seems that all these obstacles have been faced and crushed. Two new borders have been crossed, the bombing of North Vietnam has been intermittently resumed, and the entire nation knows that, except for nuclear war and genocide, there is almost no crime that Americans have not committed in Indo-China. Our B-52s are ranging freely across the newly violated borders. When the B-52 strikes, it leaves a path of craters a mile long. In the month before the Laos campaign, there were roughly six thousand B-52 strikes throughout Indo-China. Yet, knowing all this, and having been moved to widespread protest on several occasions, the nation has now grown silent. Having looked at what we have done to Vietnam, we are doing it again in Cambodia and in Laos. Now that we have accepted all this, and have continued with the war, what is left that can stir us into finally leaving Indo-China? Is there any limit to what we will accept? Certainly it has been one of the particular triumphs of this Administration that, along with continuing to expand the destruction of Indo-China, it has destroyed the debate over Indo-China in the United States. The Administration's degree of success in this can be judged from the fact that few men in Congress or elsewhere challenged the Administration's statement that the incursion into Laos was not a "widening of the war." But if it was not a widening of the war, then what *would* be a widening of the war? As for the press, it seemed so preoccupied with the "news embargo" that it presented the actual move into Laos almost as a footnote. Everywhere, except in Vietnam itself, where energetic preparations for the new move were under way, Americans seemed dispirited and tired. It is as though expansion of the war had been accepted as a natural law, like gravity, which no one can control and only madmen would even consider opposing.

But in reality to what extent has this war ever been under anyone's control? To what extent has it been obedient to any American's will or judgment? Have our Presidents been in control of the war? What has this war been if not the story of the breakdown of the government's control over its own actions? Does the record show that it ever enjoyed the power to do anything but bring senseless destruction or leave? Doesn't the record show that our Presidents and their advisers and our generals and all our other "leaders" who have "run" this war have been trapped in isolation and in ignorance of the war, their judgment destroyed by the flood of spurious "information" given them by overfinanced armed bureaucracies that had gone wild in a part of the world no bureaucracy understood? Now it appears that, in our weariness, the rest of us are in danger of succumbing to the hypnotic effect of the self-propagandizing machine that has put our leaders to sleep, one by one. Perhaps

there are a few people in the White House or in the Pentagon who regard
the opening of this new campaign, and the silence that has greeted it throughout the country, as a triumph for their point of view. What has happened,
however, is not that the Administration has won something and its opponents
have lost something. What has happened is that a war that no one—not
even the most belligerent hawks—ever wanted, or even imagined, has won
a victory over America. This is not really a victory of one point of view over
another; it is a victory of momentum over all points of view, a victory of
violence over restraint, a victory of fatigue over vigilance and control. The
events of the last two weeks represent the subjugation of men by impersonal
forces and the transformation of human organizations into blind machines,
which have got out of control. It is something like a death of the spirit. This
is no person's hour of triumph. This is the hour of the B-52. The B-52 casts
its shadow over Indo-China, and over America, too. It has thrown off its
harness, its victims have no place to hide, and its keepers are asleep.

FEBRUARY 27, 1971

I N the weeks since the invasion of Laos, the political world we have lived
   in for a decade has noiselessly disintegrated, and a new political world
   has emerged in its place. We can as yet only dimly perceive the shape
of this new world, but we do know that certain reassuring limits, restraints,
and protective barriers have faded away, leaving us, to our surprise and dismay,
face to face with great dangers that were never, perhaps, very far from our
minds but that only a month or so ago seemed comfortably distant. And we
know that among these dangers is the fundamental, final danger that only
our own age has had the misfortune to face. The extent of this abrupt but
profound change, which one began to sense only during the early days of
the move into Laos, was made clear when the President, in what is unquestionably the most alarming set of remarks made by any President since the
beginning of the Indo-China war, told newsmen that he refused to "speculate
on what South Vietnam may decide to do with regard to a possible incursion
into North Vietnam in order to defend their national security," and also said
that he was "not going to place any limitation upon the use of air power
except, of course, to rule out a rather ridiculous suggestion that is made from
time to time . . . that our air power might include the use of tactical nuclear
weapons," and continued, "As you know . . . this has been speculated on for
a period of five years and I have said for a period of five years that it is not

an area where the use of nuclear weapons, in any form, is either needed or would be wise." The unrestricted use of air power over North Vietnam would, in effect, reverse the decision to end the bombing which President Johnson announced along with his decision (closely linked) not to seek a second term of office. An invasion of North Vietnam would enlarge the war beyond anything ever undertaken in Indo-China by any President, and would stand a strong chance of bringing China into the war. If this were to happen, the President's assertion that the use of nuclear weapons is "not needed" and is "unwise" would not be very consoling, for what is "not needed" and "unwise" in one set of circumstances can come to be considered needed and wise in a different set of circumstances. The President's remarks force us to look at the war in an entirely new light.

For two years, we have been told that what we were witnessing in Indo-China was the last days of a war, and most Americans have seemed to believe it. At the very worst, a few observers have feared a prolonged American presence in South Vietnam. But now a strong possibility has suddenly emerged that the ten years of war in Indo-China, for all their horror, have been only the prologue to a war throughout Southeast Asia—a sort of practice session, in which the military and the other bureaucracies and public-relations outfits have tested their "conventional" weapons exhaustively, have learned how to deceive themselves and the rest of us, and have learned the techniques for brushing aside or overriding the Constitutional restraints that the people, and other branches of the government in our democracy, might try to impose.

Some words written by Simone Weil in France in 1933 seem pertinent to this moment. She said that society was dominated by "a vast machine in which men are continually being caught up and which nobody knows how to control; those who sacrifice themselves for the sake of social progress are like people who try to grasp the wheels and clutch at the transmission belts in a vain effort to stop the machine. They are crushed in their turn." As we look to the future, it now seems possible that the war may prove to have been the assembly area for a vast machine whose first, and perhaps final, act might be to provoke a war with China. The nature of this machine has become clear during its ten years of development in Indo-China. The machine's normal state is one of ceaseless, dynamic agitation and expansion. Unlike many institutions, it has a natural tendency not to be passive and inert but to move and gather momentum. The difficulty is not in setting it in motion—as with, say, the judicial system—but in getting it to stop. The machine has no restraints within itself and can be restrained only by outside forces, such as the elected officials of government. It is the machine's nature to make war. If the outside restraining forces collapse, it will make war the

way a dog barks. It is a strain for the machine *not* to make war. This characteristic can be detected in the remark of an official to the effect that a
recent decision to expand the bombing of North Vietnam constituted a more
"permissive" policy. The machine rejects all defined purposes. When it uses
language, it uses language exclusively as a weapon. Ultimately, it could operate
much more smoothly if it didn't have to issue any explanations or justifications
at all. For example, at the beginning of the war one purpose of expanding
the war was said to be the "containment" of China, but now it is precisely
our expansion of the war that threatens to draw the Chinese beyond their
borders. This explanation of purpose now works against the machine's own
expansion, and has become an irritating impediment, which the machine casts
aside. The machine requires simplicity. The democratic system of government, with its checks and balances, with its public opinion (which costs so
much to manipulate), with its demonstrations and its annoyingly skeptical,
questioning press and Congress, is too complicated for it. And the machine's
greatest enemy is the most complicated thing of all—human society itself.
Faithful always to its internal laws of growth and attentive always to its own
propaganda, the machine is constructed to disregard the outside world altogether. But human society—seemingly such a soft, disorganized, defenseless
thing—tenaciously sets up endless obstacles to the machine. It is human
society that fouls up the machine—that crawls up out of the ground again
after the around-the-clock shelling and bombing, that disrupts the game plans,
and that refuses to bend to the violence. Sometimes the only way to simplify
things enough is to destroy the society altogether. In Indo-China, the machine
has made war on Indo-Chinese society from the start. It has efficiently torn
the society apart as part of its game plan for the war. Now it appears that
those who "control" the machine are undertaking further simplifications.
There is the reported plan to move millions of people from the northern
provinces of South Vietnam to the southern provinces; one reason for the
invasions of Cambodia and Laos is surely that the military thinks the war
will be simpler to fight there, away from the hostile civilian population of
South Vietnam; and one temptation to invade North Vietnam is that the
machine might then be able to fight a highly recognizable enemy—namely,
the Chinese Army. And, finally, the machine's tendency to create simplicity
through violence, and its tendency to reject anything as disorderly as human
lives, makes one fear that it is moving unswervingly toward the ultimate
simplification.

     The question before us now is whether there is any force in the country
that is able or—what is more to the point—willing to oppose such a machine
as this. Unfortunately, as was recently noted in these pages, the people in

Congress and in the country as a whole who have protested past escalations of the war have remained comparatively silent and inactive during this most recent and most grave escalation. In fact, the active, vigorous people in Indo-China and the silent, discouraged people at home are all, in different ways, under the sway of violence, the one group being intoxicated by it and the other stunned. Why, at this most dangerous hour since the beginning of the Indo-China war, is the country so quiet? When events seem to move unexpectedly and decisively against one, there is always a temptation to detach oneself and become a spectator, or simply to sleep. There is a temptation to endow the machine with godlike invincibility. Then the spirit of defiance and of action itself is numbed, and even victims of the machine are capable of nothing more than a feeling of admiration for its great power as it rolls over them. There is actually a paradoxical tinge of smugness in this piece of self-deception, inasmuch as one feels that it has taken a literally omnipotent force to crush such a fighter as oneself.

Yet there is something more to be said about the machine and men. Simone Weil went on to write:

> The helplessness which one feels at a given moment—a helplessness which one should never consider total—neither excuses one from remaining true to oneself nor justifies surrender to the enemy, whatever disguise the enemy assumes. And whether it calls itself Fascism, democracy, or the dictatorship of the proletariat, the supreme enemy remains the administrative apparatus, be it civil or military. The true enemy is not the one in front of us, who is our enemy only insofar as he is the enemy of our brothers; the true enemy is the one who calls himself our defender and makes us his slaves. In no matter what circumstances, the worst betrayal is to consent to subordinate oneself to this administrative apparatus, and, in its service, to destroy, in oneself and in others, all true human values.

MARCH 13, 1971

IN 1971, it is nearly unbelievable that American or South Vietnamese officials could be considering an invasion of North Vietnam. Yet in South Vietnam both President Thieu and Vice-President Ky have openly advocated such an invasion, and here President Nixon has said he "would not speculate" on whether an invasion might take place, Secretary Laird has refused to "be involved in speculation" on the subject, Henry Kissinger has said that an invasion is not "the dominant probability at this moment," and

Secretary of State Rogers has registered opposition to a proposed congressional resolution against the use of American ground troops in support of an invasion. It has been suggested that these statements by the South Vietnamese and these equivocations by the Americans are only threats designed to frighten the North Vietnamese into submission, and do not indicate that an invasion is actually planned. If this is the case, the four American officials have certainly succeeded in creating a climate of complete ambiguity. It is impossible for us, as citizens, to know, from the outside, what the intentions of our government are in Indo-China. From the gravest matters, such as the fate of the South Vietnamese forces in Laos, to the most trivial, such as the piece of pipeline that was shown at a news conference as if it were a trophy of the current operation but was later revealed to have been found in an earlier operation, the Administration and the military have been displaying a virtual compulsion to confuse us. What we do know, however, without reference to any statements by any officials, is that an invasion of North Vietnam, whether by the Americans or by the South Vietnamese, is a move that might well send this nation over the brink.

Even if this move is not made, we can see, as we look around us at the altered political landscape, that this war—the very war that was supposedly "not an issue" in the 1970 election—has propelled itself into a position of dominance in our national life. Under the cloak of public relations that has hidden the true nature of the war—from its earliest days, when we were told that the expanding war was not a war at all (it was a "conflict"), to the present, when we are being told that the still expanding war is practically over—the war and the war machine that runs it have gradually been moving into the dead center of our national life. We used to see the war as just one of many issues in our political life. Now things have been reversed and we find that our political life is one of many issues of the war. The question is no longer whether our political system will allow the war to drag on after a decade of failure; it is whether the war and the war machine will allow our political system to survive after nearly two hundred years of success. The war machine now sits astride our lives like a fourth branch of the government—a branch that may well outlast some of the other branches. Wherever we go, the war is with us. Wherever we turn, the war is there. In whatever we undertake, the war intervenes. It is all around us, and it is within us. In part, this fearful recognition of the war's place in our lives takes the form of absorbing a heavy dose of bad news from the past that is only now penetrating that shield of secrecy and propaganda which is part of the war machine. From Senator Ervin's hearings on official surveillance, we are learning that in 1968, when citizens' demonstrations against the war were reaching their peak, the nation became riddled with thousands of military and civilian domestic spies, who began collecting information on individuals deemed "detrimental to the United States." This in itself, though it is only a subplot of the broader story of the growth of the war machine, could threaten our entire system of government. At the same time, through the court-martial of William Calley, we have been brought face to face with some of the worst things a nation can learn about itself as we hear the dispute over whether Lieutenant Calley shot and killed a monk or merely struck him in the mouth with the butt of his rifle. To judge by the testimony, Calley's only regret after shooting people in the ditch was that he couldn't then force them to walk ahead of him through enemy minefields—a common procedure, according to Calley. These pieces of bad news from the past help us reconstruct the interior, hidden history of the war in America and in Indo-China. In the meantime, fresh bad news—including the first openly and broadly censored news since the start of the war—is reaching us by television and in the press. In America, Senator Fulbright, who keeps closer track of the balance of power between the executive and the legislative branches of the government than any other legislator, tells us that a breakdown in that part of our system is not merely imminent, as a reporter on "Face the Nation" suggested to him, but actually under way. He points out that when the President violates the laws passed by Congress, as he has done by claiming the right to send troops into Laos for purposes of "protective encirclement," a senator can do nothing more than "complain" and "make speeches." Senator Fulbright, along with a number of other legislators, has been trying to reassert a measure of congressional control by introducing legislation that would limit the President's freedom to use our military forces as he pleases. But this legislation either has been defeated or has been rendered nearly impotent through compromises. The way things are going now, unless Congress resolves to withstand the erosion of its powers it may very soon be nothing more than two large rooms full of men in business suits who make speeches written by other people—men who may possess convincing rhetorical gestures, charming smiles, and excellent television "images" but who will have no power. This has happened in our time to more than one country's congress or parliament that has not been vigilant against military and executive power.

In Indo-China, we see—or, rather, we half see—the spectacle of an Asian army that is financed by America and equipped with American weapons being sent in American helicopters to fight in a foreign country in order to "save American lives," as the President has unabashedly stated. The small amount of news we have had out of Laos indicates that this has been an unwilling army. In some instances, the American helicopter crews are reported to have forced the South Vietnamese soldiers out of the arriving helicopters. At other times, it is reported, South Vietnamese soldiers have clung to the runners of helicopters leaving the battle zone to carry out the wounded. In front of the South Vietnamese troops are the North Vietnamese; behind them are the Americans, cracking the whip over their heads.

The crimes in Indo-China and the breakdowns in our political system at home help to teach us how much the war has already altered us. We are only beginning to realize how extensive the damage is. And yet, hard as it has been to recognize its true scope, the damage that has already been done is of little or no significance compared to the damage that would threaten the entire planet if the invasion of North Vietnam now being discussed were to take place. For the first time in the course of the Indo-China war, moves that appear to have a strong chance of leading to a third, and perhaps final, world war are under open consideration. While the South Vietnamese are advocating an invasion and our officials are making ambiguous remarks about the prospect, the North Vietnamese have been hinting that if an invasion took place the Chinese might enter the war. If this were to happen, some official of our government would no doubt announce that we were in a "whole new ballgame," which would mean that none of the policies or promises made in the past were binding any longer, including the prohibition against the use of nuclear weapons. And this is all that would be needed to bring on general war. It seems remarkable that in the present circumstances there is almost no discussion of these dangers in the press or in Congress. Could it be that the press and Congress have some inside information that enables them to dismiss these apprehensions as ridiculous? Have they found out for certain that no invasion will take place, and decided not to tell the public, or have they found out that the Chinese won't come into the war if an invasion does take place? The truth is that there is no member of Congress, no member of the press, no China scholar—there is simply no one—who knows what the Chinese might or might not do, and that there are very few people who know what our own government and the South Vietnamese government are going to do.

Since the spread of nuclear weapons, the shadow of universal death has passed over us from time to time. This danger is always with us somewhere in the background, but certain combinations of events, such as those leading up to the Cuban missile crisis, draw it into the foreground. Once again, this danger is near. But this time it has come upon us in a peculiar way, in conjunction with a war that has been spreading disorder and confusion in the nation for a decade—a war that has destroyed our sense of proportion and numbed us spiritually. Now our perception of the nuclear danger has been clouded by the confusion that surrounds the war. Five years or so ago, when everyone knew that the war was getting larger, the slightest suggestion of an invasion of the north caused an uproar. But now, when the war is supposed to be "winding down," these suggestions pass almost unnoticed, although there is no reason to believe that the consequences of an invasion now would be any different from what the consequences would have been then. This war has gone to our brain. It has drugged us. Our reflexes have slowed down. Our alertness has been blunted. Now, as this small war—this "brushfire war"—threatens to bring us to the edge of the ultimate war, we drowse on. We act as though the big bang were only a footnote to little Vietnam.

MARCH 20, 1971

IN the winter of 1968, when an American officer explained the bombardment of the city of Ben Tre, in South Vietnam, by saying, "It became necessary to destroy the town to save it," it was almost immediately obvious that, with unwitting, insane brilliance, he had penetrated to the very heart of what was then the Vietnam war. And since then we have seen two more countries being saved in this same strange way. Recently, a second saying, with an equally broad and equally unintended meaning, emerged from the war as a companion saying to the first. This was Lieutenant Calley's remark, at his court-martial, that the alleged shooting by American soldiers of people they had just pushed into a ditch at My Lai "wasn't any big deal." Calley was talking about the extinction of one group of villagers—itself hardly a small matter—but his remark, like the earlier remark, sums up a prevailing attitude toward the entire war. For ten years, the military, and government officials from the top to the bottom of three Administrations, have been trying to tell the American people that the war wasn't any big deal. This message has come in a hundred forms. It is behind that whole new lexicon of anesthetic language which has emerged from the war. At different times, we've been variously told that it wasn't a war but just a rather heavily armed aid program; that it was a war but that it was over, or virtually over; and that it was perfectly normal to fight a war for ten years, and if you thought that was too long, you were a "neo-isolationist." Denying the reality of the war has become a bureaucratized and institutionalized occupation. It is the full-time job of thousands of public-relations men. When we think of propaganda, we usually think of a maniac with a bullhorn shouting hysterical slogans to an excited mob; it's time we recognized that the American kind of propaganda isn't like this. Ours is soothing. It puts people to sleep instead of stirring them up. It is quiet, persistent, and pervasive. Whereas the impassioned voices get tired, this voice goes on like interminable Muzak. In this soporific climate, the war intermittently vanishes and reappears. We read that South Vietnamese troops were accidentally bombed with napalm, and we suddenly realize that we had forgotten all about napalm, which is used no less than it was six years ago, when it seemed that all anyone talked about was how awful napalm was. The planes, too, disappear and reappear. On television, you hear Douglas Pike, a respected academic expert on contemporary Vietnamese society, say that the "military aspect" of the war ended in 1968, and that in the last five or six months there has been "very little American military offensive activity." Then you remember that the heaviest bombing campaign in history is at present under way in Indo-China. This scholar is able to give highly detailed descriptions of the power struggles within the North Vietnamese government, and is even willing to speculate on what the precise vote was in the secret meetings of the North Vietnamese Politburo, but the American planes over Indo-China—and there are more than a thousand of them—have become invisible to him. A few days later, we read that the President has described himself as "a pacifist." He predicts that this may be the last war we'll ever fight in. But just the previous day this pacifist sent up a thousand planes to bomb Indo-China. Had they been dropping stones instead of high explosives, the damage to the four countries they flew over would still have been great. The President says that the war is almost over—is getting smaller every day. Some generals go even further, and say that the war actually is over. In short, no big deal. But then what are the thousand planes doing? Furthermore, to judge from the tepid response in our country to the growing danger of war with China, we can no longer see the threat of even the biggest deal of all— what would truly be the last war, for everybody. Like the war in Indo-China, that war would be fought for nothing. And if we reach that dread pass, and if any Americans survive, there may well be one among them who will say, "We had to destroy the world in order to save it. But don't worry. It wasn't any big deal."

APRIL 10, 1971

T HE nation has reached a decisive moment. Regardless of what strategists may say about options and game plans in Indo-China, and regardless, even, of whatever ends are being pursued in this war, the nation's response to the massacre of hundreds of villagers at My Lai may determine whether the nation lives or dies. With the conviction of Lieutenant Calley, the moral anguish that some Americans have been experiencing for years has touched nearly all of us: to judge by the latest Gallup Poll and an invaluable New York *Times* survey, the questions that have long occupied the minds of a few people have become for multitudes the stuff of daily conversation and concern. These powerful new currents of feeling have divided old allies and made unlikely new ones. The reactions range across the full gamut of opinion, from Representative John R. Rarick (who sees Lieutenant Calley as "a great American") and Governor George Wallace (who visited Calley in order to pay his respects) to those who have for the first time turned against the war in revulsion, and it is not yet possible to judge what shape this new mood will finally take or how it will affect our government's policy. It appears that the conviction of Lieutenant Calley has forced every American, whatever his position on the war, to face what war itself is, what the nature of the war in Indo-China in particular is, and what his own responsibility is. Everyone has had to ask himself, in effect, whether the crimes committed at My Lai were isolated atrocities in a just war or whether they represented the essential nature of what we were and are doing in and to Indo-China. Each of us has had to ask himself just how deeply implicated he himself is, by his actions or his inaction, in murder. If Calley is guilty, who is *not* guilty?

Yet a democratic nation, even if it finds itself mired in crime, can redeem itself. Even if its crimes are unforgivable, it has—because it *is* a democracy—a chance to retrieve its honor. It can acknowledge what it has done, admit responsibility, and set itself on a different course. Democracy exists so that people may make choices such as this. This is what it means to be free. However, if a nation denies the truth and refuses responsibility, then brutality enters its bloodstream and threatens the survival of democracy. We in America are still a free people, and we can choose what this nation will become. But first we must choose to remain free.

The issue of freedom is not like other issues. In a sense, it is larger than any other issue, because without it there are no issues, there are only orders. Freedom must be defended as soon as the earliest signs of a threat to it appear, because while other losses can be recovered, the loss of freedom is usually irrevocable. And recently we have found around us much, much more than early signs of a threat. On every hand, the late signs have been out. It is not only in Indo-China that boundaries have been overrun and familiar restraints ignored. Throughout our political life at home we have been finding disintegration and acts of usurpation. And, for the first time, elements that could one day form the basis of an American form of totalitarianism have come into clear view.

The first unmistakable indications that our trouble was deeply rooted at the dead center of our political life came in the summer of 1968, at the Democratic Convention, in Chicago. For a few days, we were given an intimate glimpse of a new, frightening America. On the streets of Mayor Daley's city, police were wantonly attacking demonstrators, newsmen, and bystanders. At the Convention itself, delegates were being subjected to open manipulation by a majority that had control of the public-address system, and delegates and newsmen were roughed up by "security" agents, who were suddenly ubiquitous. One newsman was knocked to the floor, and one delegate was thrown in jail. At a downtown hotel, the police raided the headquarters of one of the candidates and clubbed several of his workers. In effect, this was how, in 1968, we as a people were responding to the war. Some of us were dissenting, and some of us were seizing control of the microphones and clubbing the dissenters. A temporary, local police state had emerged.

The aftermath of the Convention was as important and as revealing as the Convention itself. When power is abused in a body politic, two courses of action are open. The body politic can admit the abuse and take measures to correct it, or it can deny the abuse and institutionalize it. America institutionalized the abuses of the Chicago Convention. The victims of the brutality were convicted, the police perpetrators went free, and the press was condemned by prominent members of both parties for having covered the Convention "unfairly." A new way of dealing with official abuses of power had been found: Suppress the truth and punish the victims. All this was in plain view on television. But a number of things were happening in 1968 that were not visible to the public at all. The public didn't yet know that Lieutenant Calley and other men in his company had extinguished the hamlet of My Lai, and there were a lot of other things about the war in Indo-China that it didn't know. Nor did it know that in the F.B.I., in all branches of the military, in the C.I.A., and in many other arms of the government, thousands of secret agents were being sent out to spy on people who were not suspected of any crimes but were simply deemed politically suspect by the government, or just by J. Edgar Hoover or some other ideologue who happened to be in a position of control in the spying apparatus.

A dangerous pattern had been established in our national life. Vast bureaucratic machines in the government, in the military, and in industry— sometimes under orders and sometimes on their own initiative—were becoming involved in many brutal or senseless, or sometimes merely foolish, activities, which they disguised with propaganda that tended eventually to fool the propagandizers as much as it fooled the public. In the case of the government, the elected officials who nominally control and oversee these bureaucracies on behalf of the public—men who might never have dreamed of advocating massacres, massive reprisal bombings, invasions, the killing of demonstrators, or secret surveillance of civilians—had shown themselves willing to defend these things *once they had happened* and had been renamed "pacification," "protective reaction," "protecting American lives," "overreacting," or "guarding national security." And not only were the officials ready to defend these things but they were ready to vote their support for them again and again, and to continue they were ready to vote their support for them again and again, and to continue them and expand them. Outrages committed in the public's name began to be presented as *faits accomplis*. We have consistently underestimated the importance—the nearly decisive weight—of the accomplished fact in recent events. The accomplished fact deadens the spirit of public action, which is at the heart of political freedom, and it teaches people not to think or feel. Of Vietnam, people began to say glumly, "We're there," as though this were the beginning and the end of the argument. The choice presented to the people was not whether or not their sons would fight in Indo-China but whether or not they were willing to give their assent to what their sons had already been made to do in Indo-China. Once the question was put this way, the people, on the whole, seemed to accept the war; at any rate, the men who were elected to public office accepted it. With regard to the war, the country faced—and still faces—the same choice it faced after the Chicago Convention: whether to correct the abuse or to institutionalize it. The year 1968 is remembered as a year of opposition, but it should be remembered as a year of collapse. It wasn't enough for the anti-war movement simply to stir things up and attract notice; it had to prevail—to end the war. But it failed. Public belief in the war was shaken, but calm—an acceptance of the war—was restored. And the war continued to expand. Now, with Lieutenant Calley's conviction, the public's acceptance has once again been shaken, and the outcome is again in the balance.

Nobody can be sure whether the war in Indo-China is a cause or a symptom of the spiritual crisis in our nation; it is doubtless both. But it seems clear that already a nearly intolerable strain has been placed on our system of government. The delicate relationships defined by the Constitution between the three branches of government, between the government and the press, and between the government and the people are out of kilter. The threat to the rights of the people has been building up for several years. Freedom of speech has been imperilled by a bullying campaign against the press on the part of the Administration—a campaign that has had a severely damaging effect on the news. A heavy fog has moved in over the news. What investigative reporting we have been getting out of Vietnam—such as the story of corruption in the PX system, the story on "refugees" from the Cambodian invasion, and the story of the My Lai massacre itself—has reached us through the investigations of a few congressmen or through the efforts of self-employed reporters. As soon as any men of the press have taken a look at things themselves and given their own accounts of what was going on—as they tried to do during the Laos invasion, despite stringent Administration-imposed handicaps—the Administration has stepped up its pressure. Now the discrepancy between events and the Administration's version of them is too great to continue. According to the polls, the public no longer trusts the Administration's statements on the war. This means that we have reached a point beyond which the Administration will no longer be able to win support for its war policies unless it changes its policies or actively manages the news. Recently, the Vice-President demanded the right to edit a taped interview he had given which was about to appear on television. He was refused, but if he ever gets his way in a matter like this, the free press will be in the most serious peril. The right of assembly has also been endangered. The constitutionality of a provision of the 1968 Civil Rights Act which makes it a crime to cross state lines with "intent" to participate in or incite a riot has been challenged but has not yet been ruled on, and meanwhile that provision has been encroaching on the right of assembly. This right was further endangered by the shootings at Kent State and by the county grand jury's decision not to indict the National Guardsmen but—once again—to indict the victims, or at least those who were still alive. The "no-knock" and "preventive-detention" provisions of the District of Columbia Crime Control Act have violated, respectively, the public's right to be secure against unreasonable searches and seizures and the traditional presumption of innocence.

The very shape of the government has been badly warped by assaults on the principle of the separation of powers. The lines defining that separation have grown indistinct. The President has taken over Congress's prerogative of declaring war and, in general, its powers in the field of foreign policy. He

has stated that he "alone" has responsibility for the recent invasions of countries in Indo-China. Having invaded two more countries, he has refused to
"rule out" an invasion of a third—North Vietnam. If he did order this invasion,
we could find ourselves at war with China, though Congress would not have
given a word of assent. Congress, for its part, while abdicating its foreign-
policy duties, has meddled in affairs that are properly within the jurisdiction
of the courts, by passing laws, such as the crime bills, that override rulings
made by the Supreme Court. On paper, the three branches of government
have powers that can be described as roughly equal. In times when the
branches respect the limits of their authority set forth in the Constitution,
their powers are roughly equal in reality, too. But when this respect dissolves,
as it has done lately, a hierarchy of powers never mentioned in the Constitution begins to take shape, and the executive branch is found to be the most
powerful, the Congress to be the second most powerful, and the Supreme
Court to be the least powerful. Thus, it is not surprising that at the moment,
as the system shows signs of breaking down, the executive branch has flouted
Congress, and Congress has flouted the Court. This is merely one of the
signs that the rule of law, unless we are watchful, may be replaced by the
rule of force. Nor is it surprising that organizations for which there is no
provision at all in the Constitution have begun to crop up—institutions like
the domestic-surveillance branches of the military. The shadow of Big Brother
looms higher behind our backs. The other day, at a Senate hearing on secret
surveillance by the government, an Assistant Attorney General told Senator
Sam Ervin that the federal government had the right to put Senator Ervin
himself under surveillance, although it might be "a waste of the taxpayers'
money." This was not the remark of a man who understands our system of
government. In the context of a hearing on the propriety of secret surveillance,
it was a threat.

However, it would be a mistake to believe that our trouble has been due
primarily to usurpers who were trampling over indignant, loudly protesting,
but helpless defenders of liberty. Our trouble has been due equally to the
acquiescence, and even the co-operation, of those from whom one might
have expected resistance. Each move of usurpation has been accompanied
by a submissive giving way somewhere else, as in a ballroom dance. Congress
had handed over its warmaking powers to the President with hardly a murmur
of protest long before Mr. Nixon began to formulate his doctrine of executive
supremacy in decisions of war and peace. The passage of repressive crime
legislation was not forced on Congress; it was Congress's own idea. The press
had failed in Vietnam long before this Administration launched its open
attacks on the press: the wholesale killing of civilians has been going on in

Vietnam at least since 1965, but although American reporters there were for the most part free to report what they wanted to, it took years for the fact even to begin to be widely known. (Now, with the Calley court-martial, this news has invaded everyone's life, and the accumulated horror is shaking the nation.)

New exigencies began to take precedence over freedom. In each case, the principle of freedom—the very cornerstone of our system of government—was reduced to a question of simple efficiency. Consideration for the rights of criminal suspects was said to be slowing down the rate of convictions. Congress's duty of passing judgment on questions of war and peace was said to be encumbering the speed and flexibility of executive and military decision-making. The freedom of assembly was said to be weakening the war effort. The freedom of the press was leading to revelations that were getting in the way of the government's propaganda about the war. And this logic was accepted not only by Presidents and generals but by congressmen, newsmen, and ordinary citizens as well. People began to act as though they were in tacit agreement that freedom had had its day in America, that it was an anachronism left over from "simpler times." Even some members of the antiwar movement began to lose their grasp of the distinction between freedom and tyranny, but in a different way. They began shouting, "Totalitarianism is here!" But to call what we had—or what we have today—in America totalitarianism is to have a dreamer's notion of what the evils of real totalitarianism are, as anyone who is at all acquainted with the history of Nazi Germany or Stalinist Russia well knows. Now, having used up their strongest words, these people have no words left to name the darkness looming ahead of us that we must struggle to escape. In this atmosphere, the final loss of freedom might be experienced as some kind of minor adjustment. There is a lot of talk about the abstract notion of "the free world," but real freedom cannot exist apart from specific rights and specific structures of government. When they are lost, freedom is lost.

Our system of government is an instrument of great intricacy and ingenuity—even of some beauty—but in itself it does not promise the good life; it promises only that the people will get what they deserve. We have always cherished our system because we have believed that it offers the best chance to preserve and to develop human qualities. But there is evidence that the ten years of war have brutalized us, and have soured our vision of the things we want to preserve and develop. When the news of the massacre at My Lai reached the headlines, many people said that, in the light of what we had just learned, the war would surely have to end. Instead, we appeared to grow accustomed to the massacre—and to the war. (And last week, inconceivable as it may seem, voices in some of the highest places in the land were still being raised in defense of what happened at My Lai.) Over the years, as the war dragged on, we lost all sense of proportion. Finally, a bloody war took second billing in our press to an issue like revenue-sharing, or to a prizefight. Three years ago, a call to end the bombing of North Vietnam had the country in an uproar for months. A few weeks ago, the resumption of this bombing hardly made the front page.

As long as the war continues, each one of us faces the choice that the nation faces: whether to repudiate the war and call for its ending or to accept it and make it—and its massacres—part of us. Something worse than the beginnings of a collapse of our system emerged in the last three or four years. The standards with which to measure the collapse themselves collapsed. The vision we needed in order to spot the infection was itself infected. The minds we needed in order to perceive the derangement were themselves becoming deranged. It appeared that we had lost the sounding boards of mind and conscience against which a free nation tests its policies and actions. It is one thing to be at war, but it is another thing to be at war without knowing that you are at war. The men who were leading us were losing track of the difference between war and peace. The men who were voting for crime bills were losing track of what justice is. The men who were threatening our freedom were losing track of what freedom is. Now the conviction of Lieutenant Calley seems to have shocked the country in some new way and awakened it out of a long sleep. We seem to have been given another chance—possibly our last chance—to regain our soul.

APRIL 17, 1971

AS we listened to the President's speech last week, we felt as though he were speaking from another country. He seemed not to have lived through what this country had lived through since Lieutenant Calley's conviction. The conviction and sentencing of Lieutenant Calley had made tangible the enormous burden of responsibility that America bears for the holocaust in Indo-China. For many of us, the Calley verdict did what the horrifying day-by-day reports of the war had failed to do, and even the reports of My Lai itself, and even the Calley trial: it drove us into a corner. It was as if the moment we passed judgment on this one man for what he had done in Indo-China, we were forced to judge ourselves. The anguish of Indo-China became wholly ours, and our country began to endure a torment that cannot abate until the war ends. This torment took a thousand forms. Some people who had once supported the war now joined those who opposed it. Others who had supported the war turned, in confusion, not only against the war but against everything that reminded them of the war, denouncing the war *and* the anti-war movement, the Army *and* its critics, the massacre *and* the conviction. People who had already opposed the war for years now began to feel their own complicity as taxpayers (followers of orders, albeit of civil orders). Some people were moved to heightened compassion for those who are suffering in the war. Others seemed to ruthlessly stamp out all feeling within themselves for innocent victims of the war, including the ones murdered at My Lai. Many—perhaps most—reactions ran deeper than rational explanation can follow. One young veteran of the war who had lost an arm said that the conviction showed he had lost his arm for nothing. (One cannot imagine that he would suddenly regain his faith in the cause for which he made his sacrifice if the conviction were to be reversed or dismissed.) Many veterans volunteered public confessions of crimes they themselves had committed. All over the country, the most profound questions a people can ask about itself were reopened, and we were arguing over who we are and what we stand for. Yet beneath the seemingly endless divergence of views one sentiment did appear nearly unanimous: America had to get out of Vietnam as soon as possible in order to save itself.

In his speech, the President also spoke of "anguish," of "despair," and of redeeming the nation—seemingly the right words. "I believe, as Thomas Jefferson did, that Americans will always choose hope over despair. . . . We have it in our power to prove to our friends in the world that America's sense of responsibility remains the world's greatest single hope of peace," he said, and he went on to speak of his hope—shared by so many of his countrymen— that America might "come out of this searing experience with a measure of pride in our nation, confidence in our own character, and hope for the future of the spirit of America." But the anguish that the President was speaking of was not the country's anguish. He was speaking of something else—of our resolve not to "give victory to the Communists" by leaving "precipitately." This is not what has been bothering America in the last few weeks—or in the last few years, for that matter.

The speech was certainly meant to draw our attention away from the questions that have been torturing us, but the devices it employed were so transparently calculated to divert our attention that our attention was drawn back, in an unexpected, roundabout way, to those very questions. The President wanted us to think only about American casualties—which are lower now than they were a few years ago—and to forget the Vietnamese casualties.

But when he said that "one American dying in combat is one too many," pictures of Vietnamese, Cambodians, and Laotians dying had to flash across our minds. Against the background of the Laotian invasion, in which South Vietnamese had so recently died in great numbers "to save American lives" and to speed our withdrawal (as though the South Vietnamese Army were in Indo-China to protect us, rather than the other way around), the President's omissions were more vivid than his statement. With an almost eerie consistency, each of the President's phrases had an unintended echo in the realm of our real concerns. He mentioned "the barbaric . . . use of prisoners," but though the Presidential compassion for prisoners went only as far as our own men in North Vietnam, it was impossible when he used this phrase not to think of the victims at My Lai—prisoners who had been murdered by the score in cold blood. And when the President spoke of his fear that "we would lose respect for this nation, respect for one another, respect for ourselves," he was speaking of what he believed might happen at some future date if he "should move to end this war without regard to what happens to South Vietnam," but it was impossible not to think of the agony we were going through *right then* in the aftermath of the Calley conviction. As we can see all around us, what endangers America is not what might happen to South Vietnam after an American withdrawal. What endangers America is what we're doing to ourselves and to South Vietnam while we remain there. It isn't "how" we end the war that will determine "the kind of people we are," as the President believes, but whether and when we end the war. The President once said he was afraid that America would become a "pitiful, helpless giant" if it failed in South Vietnam, but the real danger—a danger that becomes more urgent than ever in the light of the President's failure to acknowledge the spiritual crisis in the nation—is that we will become a heartless, headless giant.

MAY 8, 1971

STRANGELY, after so many decades of trying to assess the weight of a public event by counting the number of people who attend it, nobody has figured a way of accurately gauging the size of a crowd. During the afternoon of the demonstration against the war which took place on April 24th in Washington, commentators were giving wildly fluctuating estimates of the number of demonstrators, ranging from a hundred and fifty thousand to three-quarters of a million. But the truth is that no one knows how many people were demonstrating in Washington on April 24th. This country can photograph a piece of paper from an orbiting satellite, listen to conversations through walls, see enemy soldiers in the dark with infrared devices, and monitor the phone conversations of thousands of suspicious characters all over the country, but it can't figure out how many people attended a planned demonstration on a sunny spring day in the national capital. Presumably, it was an ascertainable fact, but this time the fact was not ascertained.

We went to Washington, too, and tried to put together a picture of the crowd's size in our own way. We also failed completely. First, we tried walking from the back of the crowd to the front. We walked for about an hour in the middle of a steady flood of people heading down Pennsylvania Avenue toward the speakers' stand, but the crowd jammed up before we could get within earshot; in fact, most of the people who went to Washington that day never got within earshot of the speakers. Then we escaped sidewise; took a long cab ride around its vague edges, which extended into the side streets of Washington; got off somewhere near the front of the crowd; and tried to walk to the back. After an hour or so, we gave up in exhaustion. And it was just as well we did, because we learned later that the crowd was backed up in buses and cars almost all the way to Baltimore. If most of the people who went to Washington didn't get near the speakers' stand, there were, for all anybody knows, as many again who never got as far as Washington. One friend of ours set off at four in the morning in a chartered bus from New York City, and the bus got stuck forty miles outside Washington at eleven o'clock and had to head back to New York at four in the afternoon, after the would-be demonstrators had had a picnic on the highway. The words "crowd" and "demonstration" only begin to suggest the mass of people that moved in on Washington on April 24th. It was more as though a new city had been superimposed on the city that was already there. The new city was made up of entire separate neighborhoods, each with a different mood. It underwent no common experience—not the experience of hearing the speakers, and not even the experience of being in Washington, since so many people never made it in. There was no point from which the whole gathering could be seen at one time. There was no single moment when its elements were all gathered together. To a participant, it was inapprehensibly huge. There was no way to grasp its size. Humanly speaking, it was measureless.

As for the composition of the crowd, most of the press said that it was the usual crowd of "kids" augmented by a small proportion of "older" people. What struck us was that the people who make up a crowd of "kids" today are a lot older than the people who used to make up a crowd of kids. It looked to us as though there were at least as many people in their late twenties and early thirties as people of college age. Our guess is that many of the people we saw were literally the same people who have been marching since 1965, and who are now six years older. Meanwhile, a whole new generation of demonstrators has grown up underneath them. We got the feeling that if the war were to go on for another ten years, and if these people were to continue coming to Washington to demonstrate, the press might still be referring to them as "the kids" when they were in their forties. Watching these veteran demonstrators—many of them accompanied by children who were born in the sixth or seventh or eighth year of the war—we felt once again that the war was sitting like a roadblock in the life of the country. The years roll by, but we Americans are not permitted to change. The repetition of horror deadens our spirit. Our hearts ache to move on to new things, but the war holds us in the roles it has cast us in. We grow old holding placards in demonstrations, denouncing over and over a grotesque war that we must now recognize as the most enduring institution to have emerged from the rapid flux of American life at mid-century.

MAY 15, 1971

THERE have certainly been many wars as brutal as the Indo-China war, but there have probably been only a few wars as senseless. This senselessness manifests itself at every level—from the decisions made by each unit in the field on up to the decisions made by the politicians in Washington. It is impossible to examine any aspect of this war closely without very shortly finding oneself staring into a frightening emptiness in which all human purposes—even debased human purposes—have dissolved. It is as though, in the Indo-China war, we have discovered the secret of taking stupendous, devastating action without any thought or feeling whatever. Perhaps crimes in other ages were inspired by debased thoughts and debased feelings, but the worst crimes of our period seem to occur in the wake of the death of all thought and all feeling. We have learned to fear the fanatic who will commit any crime in the name of his cause. We have yet to learn how to fear his first cousin, the man who is utterly indifferent and who has no cause at all but will nevertheless commit any crime. The massacre at My Lai teaches us what this kind of crime looks like. The Nazis' massacre of the people of Oradour was in many ways similar. But one difference is that whereas the Nazis thought they had a purpose and were killing people defined by their government's policies as enemies, our troops had little or no sense of purpose and were killing people defined by our government's policies as allies. Many armies have dealt harshly with enemy populations, but ours is certainly one of the first to deal so harshly with its allies. Indeed, the Vietnamese civilians are something more than our allies; their well-being is supposed to be the whole raison d'être for our presence in Vietnam. Of course, many people have argued that neither the villagers of My Lai nor any other villagers can really be regarded as our allies, since any one of them is likely to suddenly turn around and throw a hand grenade at our men. But if they are not our allies, then we have no allies in South Vietnam, and therefore no cause, either. The My Lai massacre was not committed in a moment of ideological frenzy. The men who went into My Lai did not particularly picture themselves as crusaders for the American way of life, or for freedom, or for the free-enterprise system, or for anything else. They were confused, frustrated, frightened men who were sent into the countryside to kill but had no cause to kill for. This kind of killing is different from the killing done by crusaders and fanatics. The soldiers did not rush into the village shouting the name of their leader or the motto of a messianic cause. Instead, it appears that they acted in a spirit of either total indifference or licentious brutality. On the one hand, you have a My Lai veteran's word that everyone was "having a good time," and on the other hand you have evidence that men gave in to an unrestrained blood lust and proceeded, after raping and shooting, to horribly mutilate corpses. Some men acted like robots; others acted like animals.

In a recent article in *Life*, General Telford Taylor made an important point that bears strongly on the question of the relation between the degree of purpose and the degree of brutality in an army. In his discussion of the rules of war, he wrote:

> Quite apart from the human benefits of limiting, so far as possible, the carnage of war, military efficiency requires a disciplined awareness that soldiers are not licensed to kill indiscriminately, but only as a part of a military operation. A reign of terror against civilians will turn the population against the occupation troops and make their task the more difficult. Soldiers allowed to plunder and murder will become the less useful for military purposes, and if they lose respect for human life, will be the more ready to assault each other or their officers—as is currently reported to be happening in Vietnam. An army that shows no consideration for the prisoners of war must expect that its own men will be mistreated if taken by the enemy.

In other words, the way an army treats civilians and prisoners can lower or raise the level of brutality in the entire war. If an army forgets what it is supposed to be doing and lets its men begin to kill indiscriminately, then eventually even the distinctions between "gooks" and Americans, between friend and foe, will disappear and the whole mission will sink into a savage chaos. But something more happens as well. The collapse of standards doesn't stop with the army and is not confined to the war zone. The nation that maintains such an army in the field and forces that army to continue fighting in such a war also suffers brain damage and brutalization. A sense of purpose is just as important for a people at war as it is for an army. A sense of purpose allows a people to maintain certain standards. A leader who is fighting a war that his people understand acknowledges that the country faces an emergency and calls for support. In America today, something different is happening. The people do not understand the war, and the leaders are asking not so much for support of the war as for *tolerance* of the war. They speak of an "indefinite" American presence in Indo-China and seem to want the people to accept the war as part of business as usual, to regard it as just another "issue," like inflation or the reorganization of the Cabinet. They seem to want to wage war in a low key—almost casually. In 1940, Simone Weil wrote a passage on how a war can come to dominate the men who are waging it. In a few succinct words, she seemed to sum up the entire matter, and what she said then seems premonitory of our entire trouble today:

Once the experience of war makes visible the possibility of death that lies locked up in each moment, our thoughts cannot travel from one day to the next without meeting death's face. The mind is then strung up to a pitch it can stand for only a short time; but each new dawn reintroduces the same necessity; and days piled on days make years. On each one of these days the soul suffers violence. Regularly, every morning, the soul castrates itself of aspiration, for thought cannot journey through time without meeting death on the way. Thus war effaces all conceptions of purpose or goal, including even its own "war aims." It effaces the very notion of war's being brought to an end. To be outside a situation so violent as this is to find it inconceivable; to be inside it is to be unable to conceive its end. Consequently, nobody does anything to bring this end about. In the presence of an armed enemy, what hand can relinquish its weapon? The mind ought to find a way out, but the mind has lost all capacity to so much as look outward. The mind is completely absorbed in doing itself violence. Always in human life, whether war or slavery is in question, intolerable sufferings continue, as it were, by the force of their own specific gravity, and so look to the outsider as though they were easy to bear;

actually, they continue because they have deprived the sufferer of the resources which might serve to extricate him.

MAY 29, 1971

W E'VE been thinking about certain lists we've seen recently, and about a whole new kind of list that seems to be cropping up wherever we look. One of these was a list, quoted in this magazine a few years ago, in which the Army summed up its progress in "pacifying" a certain village in South Vietnam. The list included the following achievements: 5,269 Medcap patients, 2,200 litres of chemicals used for defoliation, 250 acres cleared by bulldozers, 20,860 sheets of roofing issued to 1,156 families, 524 hours of psychological warfare by loudspeaker, and 4 music concerts conducted. As a means of arriving at a quick judgment on a complicated matter, such a list has advantages that are obvious. It is simple, precise, and objective. Vague, intangible questions that never can be answered satisfactorily are avoided— questions such as: Did the villagers enjoy the 524 hours of psychological warfare by loudspeaker? Did that help to win them over to our side? What is the proper balance between "music concerts conducted" and "litres of chemicals used for defoliation"? Is 2,200 litres of chemicals to 4 concerts right, or should it be 4 litres of chemicals to 2,200 concerts? Should any litres of chemicals be sprayed or any concerts be conducted at all by us in Vietnam?

Another list having to do with pacification added a refinement. It listed the tasks necessary for the pacification of a village and also listed "maximum number of points" that could be won for full accomplishment of each task. Some of the tasks, together with their maximum-point score, were as follows: "V.C. local/main force units destroyed or driven out, 15 points; Census completed, 2 points; V.C. infrastructure discovered, destroyed, or neutralized, 8 points; Census Grievance Teams completed interviewing each family, 2 points; Principal grievance completely processed, 3 points." The list closed with some catch-all points, such as "Agricultural, 4 points" and "Social and administrative organization of villages completed to meet immediate needs of villagers, 1 point." (This last, one-point task, of course, is one that all governments everywhere since the beginning of history have been trying to accomplish.) When the people in charge have given themselves a score for each task, they add up the figures to get the score for the whole village. This score, together with the scores of the other villages in the country, is fed into a computer to produce one big score, which is given out as the progress in pacification to date.

The list technique for judging difficult matters has become widespread in the United States, too. We don't know why it should be on the increase just now, but we have observed that it tends to flourish in the vicinity of bureaucracies and computers. One of these lists came out of the White House not long ago. Americans naturally are concerned over whether their President understands the mood and temper of the nation, and the White House apparently felt it would be reassuring for the public if it knew just how much the President had rubbed shoulders with other human beings in his first two years in office. A report stated that the President has "met or talked by phone with leaders—both individually and in groups—from every area of American life: from labor, more than 30 such contacts; racial minorities, almost 30 such contacts; campus representatives, more than 50 such contacts; businessmen, more than 150 such contacts . . . worship services in the East Room of the White House, more than 8,000 guests attended. . . . More than 13,000 guests enjoyed the Nixons' hospitality at 132 dinners . . . and more than 40,000 additional guests enjoyed an ongoing series of breakfasts, luncheons, teas, coffees, and receptions." This list has the simplicity and precision of the first list we mentioned. One almost expects to find "4 music concerts conducted" or "524 hours of psychological warfare by loudspeaker" somewhere in it. And one appreciates the trouble the President must have gone to, cutting a notch in his telephone receiver every time he had a phone conversation with a Negro or a student.

But the most ambitious list of all was put together by a magazine. In an advertisement several months ago, *Seventeen* stated that "the February issue of *Seventeen* . . . contains an exclusive study of American youth of both sexes, aged 14 through 22, covering these areas in depth: America's Future, Campus Revolution, Consumerism, Drugs, Education, Environment, Generation Gap, Government, Health and Welfare, International Affairs, Life Style, Politics, Pollution, Poverty, Race Relations, Religion, Sex and Morality, Silent Majority, Values, War and Peace, Women's Rights." *Seventeen*'s list is like the second one from Vietnam, except that instead of giving the key for evaluating a village it gives the key for evaluating an entire generation. Also, it has the virtue of getting things of wildly disparate magnitude and character (such as Consumerism and Values) cut down to the same size for measurement. Lists have become an invaluable new tool for coping with the world. The baffling interconnectedness of things is dissolved at a stroke, and phenomena are made to line up in a neat row followed by a number. The intellectually stymieing disproportion between one thing and another (between America's

Future and Drugs, for example) is eliminated. The tiresome obligation of deciding whether something is "right" or "wrong" is likewise lifted. So when it comes to making judgments, we can throw away "traditional" thinking, with its sentences, its paragraphs, its "reason," and its "feeling." Lists are a whole new way of looking at the world. And if you don't believe it, think about what this country has done to Vietnam.

We've already got busy on a list ourself. Our list is designed to pretty much sum up the situation on the entire planet. After all, if a list can give the key to evaluating a village or a generation, what's to stop us from making up a kind of planetary point sheet? Our list draws on the lists we have mentioned so far and follows the new logic of list-making closely. We think it's nearly definitive: Values, music concerts conducted, litres of chemicals used for defoliation, guests enjoying dinner with the Nixons, campus revolutions, principal grievances completely processed, sex and morality, V.C. local/main force units destroyed, America's future, hours of psychological warfare, women's rights, agriculture, silent majority, war and peace. It still needs a scoring system, but someone might like to throw it into the computer and see what comes out.

JUNE 5, 1971

QUITE a while ago, at a time when most people were showing little interest in the war, we made the observation that the war seemed to have outlasted the issue of the war. Now things have taken a new twist, and there are people who, not being content with merely ignoring the war, are talking and behaving as though the war were actually over. They are patting each other on the back for a job well done, and are already talking confidently about the state of the world "beyond Vietnam," as though the war itself were only an unpleasant memory. In a recent interview, for instance, Secretary of Defense Melvin Laird said, "I have tried to shift the public debate and dialogue in America from 'Why Vietnam?' to 'Why Vietnamization?' . . . Now I believe the time has come once again to shift the dialogue from 'Why Vietnamization?' to 'Beyond Vietnam'—to focus instead on the question: 'What's in store for us from the national-security standpoint beyond Vietnam?' " And President Nixon has announced that "Vietnamization has succeeded." In the atmosphere created by official statements like these, it becomes harder than ever to talk about the war, because before one can get to such questions as "What is happening in the war?" or "Should these things be happening?" one has to ask the elementary question *"Is there a war going on?"* No doubt people have a natural tendency to try to forget about wars the minute they are over, but we may be the first country to try to forget about a war while it is still going on.

The notion that removing our forces from Indo-China is only a lingering detail in a job that has been substantially completed depends in part on the maintaining of a secret that many politicians know but few are willing to tell: namely, that if and when all American forces are withdrawn—whether this happens in six months or in ten years—there is the likelihood that some combination of the Vietcong and the North Vietnamese will take over South Vietnam. The President has spoken of his fear that we might "turn over" South Vietnam to the Communists, but this was probably a bad choice of words, because in fact South Vietnam was never ours to turn over. We cannot "lose" it because we have never had it in our grasp, and because we have already done something much worse and much more decisive than losing it—we have destroyed it. We destroyed the countryside in order to "deprive the enemy" of the milieu in which he thrived, but in the process we destroyed the milieu in which any independent government might thrive, including the one we support. And after reducing the society with our money and our bombs to one of the most thoroughly pulverized and chaotic societies there have ever been, we now expect the tragic imitation of a government in Saigon to assume responsibility for one of the largest, most technologically advanced war machines ever put together. This government has been called a "puppet government," but it might be more appropriate to call it a "balloon government." A puppet government administers the state apparatus in obedience to the orders of a foreign master. A balloon government, on the other hand, owes the very existence of its state apparatus to the foreign master. It may disobey the foreign master in small matters, but even its power to disobey is lent to it by the foreign master. When a balloon government is puffed up by its master, it may look fairly impressive. But when the air is let out it doesn't so much collapse as reveal that it hardly existed in the first place. There is strong evidence that the government in Saigon is a balloon government. In fact, not only the state apparatus but the entire society has been decisively altered by the American rampage in Vietnam. Thus the withdrawal of troops by no means spells an automatic end to the war. It leaves the fundamental question of the war—the question of whether we would tolerate a North Vietnamese takeover of South Vietnam—unresolved. Eventually, in the course of the withdrawal, this question *will* have to be faced, and then, unless there are negotiations, it seems probable that either the withdrawal will have to be stopped or we will have to accept the collapse of the Saigon government. If this moment of decision were to come suddenly—if the Saigon government were to begin to fall apart while our troops were still there, or if the other side were to launch a heavy attack against a greatly reduced, vulnerable American force—then this Administration, which has promised only victories in Indo-China, might undertake a reckless escalation that would endanger this country as well as Vietnam, North and South.

But in the meantime we go on dreaming. We push questions like these aside and stretch our limbs to enjoy the new, relaxed, postwar atmosphere that happens to have arrived before the war has ended. Some people in the Administration go on looking beyond Vietnam. They turn away from the sordid, ludicrous war that is taking lives now and turn to "larger" global questions of the future that seem more likely to confer some dignity on the men who tackle them. They overleap the present altogether and begin to live in a dream future. Meanwhile, there are Americans and Vietnamese in Vietnam who can't even see beyond the next tree-line, much less beyond Vietnam, and who in fact may not live to see the world beyond Vietnam at all, no matter how marvellous it may be. Of course, nobody believes that all of our country's problems would solve themselves if we managed to end the war, but still, after a decade in Indo-China, a postwar America seems to shine in the uncertain future like a New Jerusalem. Just getting back to the old problems seems almost unimaginably wonderful. But some people don't want to see the real war in the real world in this the tenth year of the war. We all yearn for the promised land of an America finished with the war. But members of the Now generation in the Administration don't want to wait until it actually happens. The real world be damned. They want to enjoy the fruits of the promised land *right now*. And never mind that we have yet to cross the River Jordan.

JUNE 12, 1971

A T the President's press conference last week, newsmen asked a number of questions about the mass arrests that took place in Washington in May. As we listened to the President giving his answers, we made a few notes. Here are some of his remarks, together with some of the notes:

"Individuals did attempt . . . to stop the government; they said in advance that's what they were going to do, they tried it, and they had to be stopped." The current Administration has often been taken in by the overblown rhetoric of the militant left. In this case, the President seems to have fallen victim to the disruptors' fantasy that it was in their power actually to "stop the government." Their slogan was "If the government doesn't stop the war, we're going to stop the government." But it would have been more truthful to say, "If the government doesn't stop the war, we're going to annoy the government," or "If the government doesn't stop the war, we're going to make some government employees late for work on May 3rd." These are lousy slogans, to be sure, but then the truth rarely makes a good slogan.

"I have pledged to keep this government going." In point of fact, although a pledge is required of the President, this isn't it. What the Constitution does require him to pledge is that he will "preserve, protect, and defend the Constitution of the United States." Important as it is to keep the government going, the framers of the Constitution apparently judged it more important to mention keeping the Constitution going.

"They [the demonstrators] were stopped, I think, with a minimum amount of force and with a great deal of patience." Seven thousand people were arrested and detained on May 3rd without any arrest forms and without any evidence, and even before the President's press conference the courts had dismissed some of the cases on the ground of improper arrest and had ordered prosecution suspended on others. Washington prosecutors have dropped most of the remaining cases. The police, however, did make these arrests with less physical violence than some police departments have used in situations that were nowhere near as chaotic. In other words, the individual policemen, on the whole, carried out illegal orders with commendable restraint. (One must add that those arrested submitted to the illegal arrests with admirable restraint, too.) One question is whether the people who gave the orders to make mass, indiscriminate arrests acted with restraint. Another question is whether they could have found a lawful way of dealing with the disruption.

"Let us separate the question into what we're really dealing with. First, there are demonstrators. The right to demonstrate is recognized and protected. . . . But when people come in and slice tires, when they block traffic, when they make a trash bin out of Georgetown and other areas of the city, and when they terrorize innocent bystanders, they are not demonstrators, they are vandals and hoodlums and lawbreakers." This sounds right. When people do these things, they *are* lawbreakers, and they must be dealt with according to the law. The trouble is that some of the people arrested were lawbreakers and some were not. And many of them were dealt with lawlessly. The results show why the police should obey the law, like everyone else. Many bystanders who had not committed any crime were swept up in the mass arrests and detained. Later, when the cases came before the courts, many people who may actually have engaged in illegal acts could not be tried,

because no evidence had been gathered. The innocent suffered and the guilty
went undiscovered. The President tried to justify the arrests by drawing a
distinction between law-abiding demonstrators and lawbreaking "hoodlums."
He seemed to be suggesting that the law should apply only to people who
obey the law. In effect, he was saying that when the government was faced
with legal demonstrations it would act within the law, but when it was faced
with illegal acts it would throw the law out the window.

"I think the police showed a great deal more concern for their rights [the
rights of those arrested] than they [those arrested] showed for the rights of
the people of Washington." A statement like this degrades the law. The logic
behind it seems to be "If *they* break the law, why shouldn't *we*? Why should
the police have their hands tied by the law when criminals ignore the law?"
If the President believes that those arrested during the Mayday protests really
were "vandals and hoodlums and lawbreakers," then he was paying the police
a poor compliment. Things can't be going so very well when a President
congratulates a police department for behaving better than vandals and
hoodlums.

A disturbing interpretation of the law itself emerges from the President's
remarks. The ordinary way of dealing with people who break the law is to
invoke the law against them. The President seems to want to replace law
enforcement with retaliation in kind—to deal with lawbreakers by suspending
the law. The police are, after all, an arm of the law. In earlier times, they
were called "the law." But if the law breaks the law, then there is no law.

JUNE 19, 1971

I T was reported recently that when six hundred and sixty disabled North
Vietnamese prisoners of war being held in South Vietnam were offered
a chance to go to North Vietnam, all but thirteen refused. The North
Vietnamese reacted by indicating that they regarded the original offer to
return the prisoners as nothing but a South Vietnamese trick. In Saigon, the
South Vietnamese declared that the North Vietnamese (for what obscure
reasons, they didn't say) had issued a message to the prisoners via the underground instructing them to refuse. According to Saigon, it was the North
Vietnamese who had been playing a trick, by offering to receive the prisoners
in the first place. In our press, other theories were advanced. It was suggested
that the prisoners were afraid of being punished in North Vietnam for having
surrendered to the enemy. It was suggested that the Red Cross, which told

the prisoners about the repatriation offer, might have failed to convince them that the offer really had come from the North Vietnamese, and was not just a trick being played by the South Vietnamese. No one on the outside can know which of these theories, if any, is correct. But on one point all the theories agree: the disabled prisoners' refusals were the result of manipulations by larger forces, and had nothing to do with their own wishes. It was taken for granted that their own wishes had been overwhelmed or annihilated by coercion and propaganda. The Red Cross representatives sought to find out what the men themselves wanted to do. By all accounts, they failed, but this was through no fault of theirs. In all probability, it would have been impossible for anyone to find out what the prisoners themselves wanted to do. Their own will in this matter had been irretrievably lost beneath the layers of coercion. They had joined the millions in this war whose will is invoked to justify the war but whose will has been rendered undiscoverable by the war. Anyone who might ask the prisoners about their own will would himself be seen as an instrument of coercion. And if a prisoner were somehow to speak his mind, his answer would nonetheless be interpreted as propaganda. In effect, the prisoners became invisible. These imprisoned men were wholly under our control, but we were wholly cut off from them. Even when the attention of the world was riveted on them, they remained invisible. Instead of seeing men, the world saw a clash of propaganda. The prisoners had moved to the center of the world stage and disappeared.

JUNE 26, 1971

THE *Times'* courageous and astounding story on the Pentagon's secret study indicates that for years the democratic system in this country has been largely short-circuited at the highest levels. In the current atmosphere of governmental lawlessness, no one can say when, or even whether, it will be possible for democracy to be restored. The country can now see that it was as much deceived about the highest levels of policymaking on the war as it was, before the massacre at My Lai was disclosed, about the day-to-day conduct of the war. Almost none of us, it turns out, were cynical enough or ungenerous enough in judging the policymakers, and almost all of us were living in a dream world furbished by official lies and by our own innocent, or complacent, desire to trust our government. Unlearning the misinformation we lived by for years is going to be as difficult and painful as reversing the effects of a brainwashing. Each of the study's revelations so far is shocking in itself—that we had secretly waged war in Laos and North Vietnam from the beginning of 1964, that the Tonkin Gulf incident was used as a pretext to whip the Congress into a crisis fever so that it would pass a resolution that the Pentagon had drawn up months before, that President Johnson's war-policy councils were planning the very military moves that Johnson, in the election campaign, was condemning his opponent for even suggesting, that President Johnson covertly sent ground troops into combat in South Vietnam. But what is most shocking of all is the growing independence of a bureaucratic machine—its feeling free enough from constraint to make decisions like these. What had emerged at the highest levels of government was a conspiracy. The weaknesses of "the conspiracy theory of history" have often been pointed out, but what other word than "conspiracy" can you use when a small group of men seize virtual control of the nation's foreign policy, and take the country into war by devising and executing elaborate plans that are carefully concealed from the public, the press, and the Congress? This is not to say that these men realized what they were doing. The popular impression is that the government got us into the war through fumbling and mistakes, and this impression need not be discarded—only added to. These men did fumble, but they fumbled secretly, and in knowing disregard of the public will. Of course, the conspirators believed that they were conspiring in the public interest, but then radical groups who throw bombs believe that they are acting in the public interest, too. The question is, Who has a right to define the public interest? In a democracy, it is supposed to be the public. A democracy has no place for men who think it is up to them to betray the public in the name of interests that the public is supposedly too foolish to recognize.

Back in the mid-nineteen-sixties, as we members of the public listened to statements by government officials and other politicians and read the reports and opinions available in the press, most of us believed we were hearing the voices that really counted. But the voices that counted in that period, and the voices that still count today, are speaking out of earshot, in secret, to each other. Part of the shock one gets in reading the documents in the *Times* comes from the effort to cross the seemingly unbridgeable distance between those documents and the world of public statements we lived in. We were not living in the real world. The "facts" on which we based opinions that inspired us to vote and to take political action were largely fake or beside the point. We didn't know what we were talking about or what we were voting for. No wonder government officials soon began to tell us we were unable to pass judgment on such complex matters without access to material that was classified and was available only to the officials. They had classified that whole period of history. In the *Times* story, we can overhear the voices that counted, and they are cold, cold voices. The secrecy that prevented the world from discovering what was going on within the councils of policy seems to have also prevented the men within them from seeing out. The men writing these memos seem to have suppressed all human faculties except certain overdeveloped accounting abilities, which are too narrow even to be called intellect. Seen through such lenses, the world grew remote and dim. One is left with the impression of diminished men straining to manipulate a vague, denatured world by means of deception and coercion.

In one memo, written late in March of 1965, an official in the Defense Department summed things up this way:

EVALUATION: It is essential—however badly SEA may go over the next 1– 3 years—that US emerge as a "good doctor." We must have kept promises, been tough, taken risks, gotten bloodied, and hurt the enemy very badly. We must avoid harmful appearances which will affect judgments by, and provide pretexts to, other nations regarding how the US will behave in future cases of particular interest to those nations—regarding US policy, power, resolve and competence to deal with their problems. In this connection, the relevant audiences are the Communists (who must feel strong pressures), the South Vietnamese (whose morale must be buoyed), our allies (who must trust us as "underwriters"), and the US public (which must support our risk-taking with US lives and prestige).

But who is this "we" whose risk-taking the "audience" of the American public will have to support with its lives? The opinions and actions of mankind are reduced to a series of "problems" to be solved, and the peoples of the earth are reduced to the single level of "audiences." At the center, at a point that seems to be equidistant from all the audiences and more remote from any of them than the highest-flying B-52, the detached problem-solver begins his ghastly, invisible performance. One audience he deceives. To another audience he whispers fragments of the truth. Another audience he kills. Among the problems he faces is that of how to go on smiling at one audience while he kills people in another audience. All his methods—lying, telling the truth, killing people, giving economic aid—are alike in his eyes, and have equal moral weight, which is to say no moral weight. All are "messages" to "audiences." The basic problem is to find the most efficient "mix." The subjects of the messages are life and death, but the atmosphere is that of a large corporation. One Presidential adviser could write of a bombing campaign that it might not succeed, but still, "measured against the costs of defeat in

Vietnam, this program seems cheap," adding, "And even if it fails to turn the tide—as it may—the value of the effort seems to us to exceed its cost."

All this is now a matter of public record, and nothing that has happened in the last three years encourages one to believe that the present Administration's record has been any better. On the contrary, the invasions of Cambodia and Laos have expanded the spheres of arbitrary action. And, as the formal suppression of news during the Laos invasion showed, this Administration has not reduced the element of secrecy, it has tried to make it respectable. We look to Congress for redress, but we find that in its latest vote Congress has turned down a bill that would help re-establish congressional control—which in this case means public control—over the warmaking power. It is as though Congress had said, "We, like all the other audiences, have been lied to, and our trust has been abused and our power usurped—but we like it. Give us more of the same." Perhaps in a later vote Congress will reverse itself. But for the time being the American system of government remains suspended.

JULY 3, 1971

T HE will of a free people to go to war combines some of a people's best instincts with some of its worst instincts to form a powerful force that, for better or worse, invades every aspect of the national life and alters every private life. It can inspire tremendous courage in citizens and soldiers, and fire a country's leaders to great eloquence; it can also be used to override freedom and to sanction crimes. It is not easily aroused, but once it is aroused it is not easily dampened. It can be manipulated but not manufactured, and it cannot be faked. During the Indo-China war, this will has been nearly absent in the United States. The public began by ignoring the war, then grew, for a while, to tolerate it, and now has come to oppose it. There are countless reasons for this coolness, and among them, no doubt, is the fact that this war was conceived as a "limited war." (In our times, a "limited war" is a war that stops short of planetary destruction.) Our war aims included such goals as "demonstrating the credibility of our deterrent," and the public found it difficult to get very fired up over these. (It also had little taste for "victory" in this particular war, as the fate of Barry Goldwater in 1964 clearly indicated.) One thing we can learn from this war is what it is like for a democracy to wage a major war without a popular mandate. In theory, of course, it is always the popular mandate that gives the war strategists permission to go ahead with their plans. But in this war public support, instead of being the foundation of all strategy, became just another strategic problem. As the Pentagon study shows, the strategists' method of dealing with this new problem was to create momentum by taking clandestine action. They acted on the hypothesis that if people wouldn't support the idea of sending our troops to Vietnam, they would support our troops once they discovered that the troops were already there. In this way, the question of whether to go to war and the question of how to prosecute the war were rolled together into a single issue, and the war strategists were able to take charge of both questions. But Presidents and Vice-Presidents still live with one foot in the public realm, and they have had to try, from time to time, to stir up the old kind of popular support that is supposed to be the basis of any war effort. One of their favorite ways of doing this has been to compare America in Indo-China to England in the Second World War. For example, when Johnson was Vice-President, he once referred to Ngo Dinh Diem as the Churchill of Asia, and President Nixon has also invoked Churchill, by referring to our years in Indo-China as one of America's "finest hours." (Things got confused when reporters recalled that Nguyen Cao Ky had told them it was Hitler whom he admired.)

Recently, we read a work written during the original finest hours—the diaries of Harold Nicolson from 1939 to 1945. There's a difference. Nicolson was a Member of Parliament and, for a time, a minor figure in Churchill's Government. His instincts were élitist, and he could write, "I know that such a life [the cultured life] as lived by Vita [his wife] and myself is 'good' in the philosophical sense. We are humane, charitable, just, and not vulgar. By God we are not vulgar!" For all that, the will of a whole people in wartime is alive on every page of his diary. To an American in 1971, what is most striking to encounter there—and, in a way, most painful, because of its absence in America today—is the paradoxical ebullience (what Nicolson calls the "gaiety") of England preparing to meet Hitler. Nicolson describes Churchill giving a speech to the House of Commons in September, 1939, before he became Prime Minister: "The effect of Winston's speech was infinitely greater than could be derived from any reading of the text. His delivery was really amazing and he sounded every note from deep preoccupation to flippancy, from resolution to sheer boyishness. One could feel the spirits of the House rising with every word. . . . In those twenty minutes Churchill brought himself nearer the post of Prime Minister than he has ever been before. In the Lobbies afterwards even Chamberlainites were saying, 'We have now found our leader.' Old Parliamentary hands confessed that never in their experience had they seen a single speech so change the temper of the House." In July, 1940, by which time Chamberlain had stepped down, Nicolson testifies again to Churchill's power to rally the House of Commons: "The House is at first saddened by this odious attack but is fortified by Winston's speech. The grand finale ends in an ovation, with Winston sitting there with the tears pouring down his cheeks." (An American in 1971 has a hard time imagining any of his recent Presidents sitting before an audience with tears rolling down their cheeks.) Here is how, at a later date, Churchill deals with news of military reverses: "He is rather grim. He brings home to the House as never before the gravity of our shipping losses and the danger of our position in the Eastern Mediterranean. It has a good effect. By putting the grim side foremost he impresses us with his ability to face the worst. He rubs the palms of his hands with five fingers extended up and down the front of his coat, searching for the right phrase, indicating cautious selection, conveying almost medicinal poise. If Chamberlain had spoken glum words such as these the impression would have been one of despair and lack of confidence. Churchill can say them and we all feel, 'Thank God that we have a man like that!' . . . Thereafter he slouches into the smokingroom and reads the *Evening News* intently, as if it were the only source of information available to him." (An American, at this point, must think of the abortive invasion of Laos.) Late in 1940, Nicolson had a glass of sherry with Churchill: "He is more solid about the face and thinner. But there is something odd about his eyes. The lids are not in the least weary, nor are there any pouches or black lines. But the eyes themselves are glaucous, vigilant, angry, combative, visionary, and tragic. In a way they are the eyes of a man who is much preoccupied and is unable to rivet his attention on minor things (such as me). But in another sense they are the eyes of a man faced by an ordeal or tragedy, and combining vision, truculence, resolution, and great unhappiness." Of his own feelings, Nicolson wrote to his wife, "I really feel that I can do some good, and I am *embattled*. I did not know that I possessed such combative instincts. Darling, why is it that I should feel so *gay*? Is it, as you said, that I am pleased at discovering in myself forces of manliness which I did not suspect? I feel such contempt for the cowards. And such joy that you and I should so naturally and without effort find ourselves on the side of the brave." Later, he wrote to his wife, "We may fail. But supposing we do not fail? That was their finest hour. I have always loved England. But now I am in love with England. What a people! What a chance! The whole of Europe humiliated except us. And the chance that we shall by our stubbornness give victory to the world." And of the resolve of the English people he wrote, "I believe that what will win us this war is the immense central dynamo of British pride.

The Germans have only assertiveness to pit against it. That is transitory. Our pride is permanent, obscure, and dark. It has the nature of infinity."

JULY 24, 1971

I F we finally lose our freedom in America, we may well lose it without knowing we're losing it. Sheer forgetfulness—not to say amnesia—may well have a crucial role to play. We call our young people the Now Generation and exhort them to study the lessons of history, but it is the older generation, the generation in control in Washington, that looks to be most tightly glued to the urgencies of the present and most willing as well as most able to take drastic steps that would cancel a two-hundred-year tradition of political liberty. In all three branches of the government, but particularly in the executive branch, actions are being taken and statements are being made which elevate presumed needs of the moment—needs of "national defense," needs for "more efficient" law enforcement—above the fundamental principles of our legal system. In Congress, we have had the House Commerce Committee attempting to hold C.B.S. and Dr. Frank Stanton, the president of C.B.S., in contempt of Congress for refusing to submit some of the editorial files (including unused film) of the organization to the committee for inspection. In the executive branch, the lawless arrests of demonstrators in Washington in early May have been followed by the attempt to suppress the Pentagon Papers. And in the Supreme Court there were the three dissenting opinions in the case concerning those papers—opinions that themselves shook the First Amendment, and one of which suggested that the *Times* might be held responsible for future deaths in the Indo-China war.

At the highest levels of government, a new, unheralded anti-democratic philosophy of government is emerging. On every hand, one finds slack, demoralized citizens and legislators, increasingly willing to turn over their destinies to eager executive-branch management teams, who are bursting with energy and organizational skill but have only the most sadly diminished and debased ideas about what to do with their burgeoning power and their mushrooming organizations, and who, if they are not held in check, will almost certainly forget about our traditional concern with life, liberty, and the pursuit of happiness, and will turn the country in the direction of their own natural bent, which appears more and more to be something like death, security, and the pursuit of efficiency. Certain of its elements can be seen in several statements by members of the present Administration. There was Attorney General Mitchell's remark, last month, that "a preoccupation with fairness for the accused has done violence to fairness for the accuser," which was followed by the question "Is justice served now by shackling the pros- ecutor and giving more weapons to the defense?" There was Vice-President Agnew's remark, more than a year ago, that an attack he was making on the press could be seen as an exercise of his "right to dissent." There was President Nixon's remark at one of his news conferences that during the May distur- bances "the police showed a great deal more concern" for the rights of the people who were arrested than those arrested "showed for the rights of the people of Washington." These remarks have a disquieting common theme. Each of them leaves one with a picture of two equal sides squared off against each other for a fight—the Vice-President squared off against the press, the accuser in court squared off against the accused, the police squared off against the demonstrator. The aim of each side, these remarks seem to indicate, is to beat the other side. Although the Administration can hardly be described as a disinterested party as far as any of the three encounters are concerned, these remarks suggest that its interest is that of an umpire, who wants to make sure that neither side has an advantage. If the newspapers have a "right to dissent," then Vice-President Agnew must have it, too. If the accused in court has certain legal rights—"weapons," the Attorney General calls them— then the accuser must have them, too. And if demonstrators violate the rights of the people, then the police should be allowed to violate the rights of the demonstrators. In the Administration's view, the Vice-President, the prose- cutor in court, and the policeman are like teams on a playing field who have been hobbled by arbitrary restrictions while the opposing teams—the press, the accused in court, and the demonstrators against the war—have been unfairly armed with advantages (rights). What the Administration wants to do is redress the balance, blow the whistle, and start the game over. The trouble with this is that the rights of the press, of criminal suspects, and of demonstrators were devised in the first place as a means of redressing what the men who wrote the Constitution saw as the enormous imbalance between the government, which is entrusted with most of the power in society (in- cluding most of the means of coercion), and the people, who are nearly defenseless. The accused, when he enters a court, cannot be armed, but the officers of the court are armed. A newspaper doesn't have the means to restrain the government from enacting a piece of legislation, but the government does have the means to restrain a newspaper from publishing an article. The laws that concern civil liberties are meant to transmute the power of the state into justice. As a result, democracy has inefficiency built right into it. It deliberately throws up obstacles in front of impetuous Vice-Presidents, prosecutors, policemen, and troops. It restrains the people who exercise power by forcing them to follow elaborate procedures. It lets citizens loose to do nearly any foolish, ill-advised thing they want to do, but it does indeed, to use an increasingly familiar phrase, "tie the hands" of the President and of every other representative of authority. Compared to a Soviet Premier, for example, our President is bound hand and foot. At least, he used to be.

One more new idea about government that has emerged recently seems to go to the heart of the matter of rights; in fact, it seems to cut out the heart of this matter. It is the idea that the government has a "right" or a "duty" to "function." Two of the highest officers in the government—the President and the Chief Justice of the United States, who is the President's appointee—have now cited it. President Nixon brought it up in his last press conference, when he said he had pledged to "keep this government going," and Chief Justice Burger brought it up in his dissenting opinion in the case of the Pentagon Papers, when he said that in that case "the imperative of a free and unfettered press comes into collision with another imperative, the effective functioning of a complex modern government." Chief Justice Burger was joined in dissenting by Justice Blackmun, who wrote that "Article II of the great document vests in the executive branch primary power over the conduct of foreign affairs and places in that branch the responsibility for the nation's safety." The assertion that the government's "functioning" may be threatened is one of those slogans (like "supporting our prisoners of war") that throw you immediately on the defensive. Who can oppose the "functioning" of government? It is a sweeping, vague assertion that stands like a brick wall in the way of any intelligent discussion. If it should win wide acceptance, it could deal a roundhouse blow to our political system. The first thing that needs saying is that the Constitution doesn't mention any duty, right, or "imperative"—to use Chief Justice Burger's word—of the government to "function," or to "keep going." Nor, for that matter, does the Constitution "place responsibility" for "the nation's safety" in the executive branch. These are dubious generalizations of a kind that the framers of the Constitution wisely avoided. What the executive branch is sworn to protect is the Constitution, which is something much more specific than "the nation's safety." The Chief Justice's phrase "the effective functioning of a complex, modern government" is a phrase that should be paused over. "Effective," "functioning," "complex," "modern" are words that stand a good chance of replacing the old words that are suited to the inherently inefficient services rendered by the simple, old-fashioned government described in the Constitution—words like "freedom" and "justice." In fact, if you stop to think about it, an effectively functioning complex modern government may be just the thing we have to watch out for. Its imperatives could well turn out to be exactly what we should fight hardest to fend off. In the old system, there is no special provision for the government's functioning, because this is the subject of the entire Constitution. To have included a clause setting forth the government's imperative of functioning would have been to devise a wholly vague principle that could be invoked against any specific right that was actually named in the Constitution, as Chief Justice Burger has invoked his imperative against the right of a free press. In effect, it would have been to create a Counter-Constitution, which could be used by men in power to bypass the Constitution itself.

OCTOBER 16, 1971

SHORTLY after the recent "election" in South Vietnam, we received a letter from a friend who happened to have been in Vietnam during an earlier election—an election held in the autumn of 1967 for President and Vice-President and for delegates to the National Assembly.

"One day, as I was walking through the center of Saigon, I came upon an odd scene," he wrote. "A dozen or so men in elegant dark suits and white shirts were standing on the steps of a government building taking turns speaking into a microphone. The usual wartime crowd of street urchins, street venders, soldiers, prostitutes, and students on motor scooters was flowing past. But no one was stopping, or even pausing, to listen. I asked a uniformed guard stationed nearby who these men were, and he answered, 'They are candidates for the National Assembly.' In the 1971 election, there weren't enough candidates (just one candidate, in fact), but in the 1967 elections there were too many (about seventeen hundred). Eleven candidates were running for President, and a television 'debate' between them was set up to help the voters sort things out. The election itself was an American idea, and I suppose this television debate was also an American idea. The trouble with it was that almost no Vietnamese had television sets.

"Having seen a bit of the campaign in Saigon, I then had a chance to see—or almost to see, as it turned out—part of the campaign in the northern provinces. The South Vietnamese government offered the use of two planes—one for ten or twelve candidates, and the other for about twenty-five journalists, who were all American. I found myself on the one for the journalists, flying up the coast to a village in one of the northernmost provinces. The heavily cratered coastal landscape was passing beneath us, and every once in a while we could see puffs of smoke rising from air strikes or artillery strikes on the ground. After landing, we were conducted to the headquarters of a province chief. An election rally was planned for the afternoon, but right then it was hot and it was way past lunchtime. The journalists, hungry and thirsty, were getting peevish. None of them spoke Vietnamese, and only one, a man from the *Times*, had an interpreter along, so there was really nothing to do but sit around in a large office and complain. The *Times* man did interview the province chief, and for a minute all the other journalists took notes. The province chief said the election would be fair. Eventually, the province chief arranged for lunch to be served at a Chinese restaurant in a nearby town. In the neighborhood of the restaurant, most of the houses were the kind made of old pieces of cardboard and bits of trash thrown away by the American forces, and the streets were dirt. Outside the restaurant, chickens pecked in the dust. Inside, the floor was mud, there was hardly room to stand, and there were thin, mangy dogs under the few tables. All the other customers were cleared out for the Americans. This was probably the best restaurant in town, but the journalists were not enthusiastic about their lunch. Halfway through, a small voice was heard outside, making an announcement. All twenty-five journalists rushed out to see what was going on. The voice was that of an extremely old man, no bigger than a child, who had a huge megaphone—it was almost as large as he was—strapped to his mouth by means of a sort of harness that went over his shoulders. He was the town crier, and he was announcing the election rally. This was the first thing of interest that had happened all day. The press went into action. Twenty-five pencils came out of twenty-five pockets and moved across twenty-five tiny pads. The *Times* man got his interpreter on the job, and the others crowded around, straining to hear. Still cameras clicked and television cameras whirred. Cameramen ran around the old man taking shots from different angles, and almost knocking him over. One went down on his back in the dust to get a shot from that angle. But, apart from the journalists, the street was empty. Millions of Americans might see and hear on television the old man's announcement of an election rally, but the Vietnamese were indifferent. Later, the newsmen moved on to the site of the rally. Martial music was being played across a dusty lot where several hundred people had gathered, most of them white-shirted civil servants let out of work for the day by the government. But when the time came for the rally to begin, the candidates failed to appear. It turned out that while the province chief had been arranging to get the American newsmen to their restaurant for lunch, he had been omitting—perhaps deliberately—to send transportation to the airport to pick up the candidates, who had arrived by then. Someone had decided that it was more important to get the American journalists to lunch than to get the candidates to the rally. After a few hours, transportation was finally sent to the airport, but the candidates had taken off for Saigon in a huff. And it was just as well, because by that time there was almost no one left in the dusty lot—no one, that is, but the twenty-five American newsmen. They had been sent to Vietnam to cover an election, but there were no candidates and no voters here. There were only the American newsmen. They were the election campaign."

Now we have all been through another election in Vietnam. Our leaders still tell us we are in South Vietnam to defend freedom. But there is no freedom in South Vietnam. The American people know this. Henry Kissinger knows it. The South Vietnamese people certainly know it. The North Vietnamese, the Chinese, the Russians, the French—everybody knows it and has known it for years. And everybody knows that everybody else knows. What's more, since the publication of the Pentagon Papers everybody has known that freedom for the South Vietnamese isn't our aim anyway. Knowing all this, one finds it hard to get very angry about President Thieu's recent failure to hold a fair election. There is something about the whole charade that might stir anger, but it isn't that the election wasn't fair. If one tries to get angry about this, a false note creeps into one's voice. For instance, in an angry editorial some weeks before the election the *Times* asserted that if the election had only one candidate the United States would be disgraced and her sons would have died in vain. The trouble here was the implication that if there were three candidates the disgrace would be lifted and the sons' deaths would become meaningful. In a later editorial, the *Times* suggested that President Nixon might use American leverage to force the South Vietnamese Supreme Court and the National Assembly into "reopening" the election. Our allies in Vietnam weren't interested in having freedom in their country, so the *Times* wanted the President to ram freedom down their throats. But although you can force people to do many things, you can't force them to be free. The *Times'* position on the election said a great deal about the pure strangeness of our current policy in Indo-China. Here was a mighty American newspaper urging the President of the United States to meddle in a rigged election in another country by coercing its dictatorial leaders into putting pressure on its own Supreme Court and National Assembly, and the newspaper was urging the President to do this not in order that the regime's people might live in freedom but in order that Americans would not have to feel the full futility and horror of a military venture that the same newspaper regarded as misguided.

In one sense, the elections in South Vietnam are red herrings. They were created for the sake of appearances, and appearances are all they can produce. Nothing real, for us or for the Vietnamese, can ever come out of them. Our anger when the fraud stands exposed is as fatuous as our satisfaction when the fraud maintains some plausibility. But it's probably better for us as well as for the South Vietnamese when the elections openly fail, since what is failing is not democracy but a lie. The important thing, in the end, is for Americans not to take sides, not to want more candidates to run, not to want reform of any kind, but to see these elections for what they are: phantoms of our own minds—the sentimental side of a violent ritual enacted by the armed and powerful on the bodies of the unarmed and helpless.

NOVEMBER 13, 1971

IN his recent article in the *Times*, "America Is Not a Repressive Society," Lewis Powell writes, "There may have been a time when a valid distinction existed between external and internal threats. But such a distinction is now largely meaningless. The radical left, strongly led and with a growing base of support, is plotting violence and revolution. Its leaders visit and collaborate with foreign Communist enemies. Freedom can be lost as irrevocably from revolution as from foreign attack." And he adds, "Foreign powers, notably the Communist ones, conduct massive espionage and subversive operations against America." He warns against "the day when the heel of repression is a reality—not from the sources now recklessly defamed [current law-enforcement authorities] but from whatever tyranny follows the overthrow of representative government," and ends by noting, "This is the greatest danger to human liberty in America." In recent years, a number of the highest authorities have slyly predicted that radical activism on the left might provoke a repressive "reaction" from the right. Since such a reaction could take place only with the co-operation of these same authorities, their predictions have, of course, the character of threats. Mr. Powell speaks differently and plainly. He sees the repression coming from the left itself. When he surveys the current scene in America, he finds a powerful revolutionary force in existence that may in the foreseeable future overthrow the government of the United States by violence and, with the help of foreign enemies, establish a repressive

left-wing regime in its stead. Powell's manner is mild and his tone is that of
a moderate man, but his America is an alarming place. Any government
official who found himself living in this America—or who *thought* he found
himself living in this America—would naturally discover that the conduct of
his office was dramatically altered. Heavy new obligations would fall on his
shoulders. The work of the Supreme Court Justices, for example, would be
greatly complicated. In ordinary times, their work of interpreting the law is
difficult enough, but in times of extreme disorder or of imminent revolution
they would have to assume the added burden of deciding when to apply the
law at all and when to suspend it. When the state's survival is in real jeopardy,
so-called reasons of state gradually eclipse legal considerations. What were
once legal questions become political or military questions. Ordinarily, some
new form of law, such as martial law or rule by decree, is imposed. The
question that judges and other men then face is not so much "Is this act legal
or not?" as it is "Which side am I on?" Powell, who sees a revolution on the
horizon, has already begun to struggle with these thorny issues. Since in his
eyes the demonstrators who blocked traffic in Washington last Mayday are
"insurrectionaries"—members of the alliance between young revolutionaries
and foreign states which threatens us—he doesn't bother to look for a legal
justification for the mass arrests that were made, in most of which no evidence
was taken and no sustainable charges were filed. Instead, he points to what
he sees as the unthinkable *political* consequences of acting otherwise: namely,
what he envisages as the "surrender" of the government to "insurrectionaries."
This makes sense if you believe, as Powell does, that the survival of our
government is seriously threatened. When he comes to the subject of wiretapping, reasons of state again apply. In explaining why he believes that the
government should be allowed to use wiretaps at its own discretion, rather
than the courts', in "national-security" cases, he offers no Constitutional justification. Instead, he points to the advantages such a procedure would have
for military strategy. (He notes, "Public disclosure of this sensitive information
would seriously handicap our counter-espionage and counter-subversive
operations.")

A great deal has been said recently about the "judicial philosophy" and
the "political philosophy" of men and women being considered for the high
court. But the differences between the various candidates have proved elusive
when they were measured by differences in philosophy: all the candidates
wish to remain as faithful as possible to the Constitution, but they recognize
that some divergence in interpretation is inevitable; all of them believe in
the Bill of Rights; none of them favor the overthrow of our government.
Powell's article gives us something that may be more important than his

philosophy—his picture of the United States in 1971. He sees no threat of repression from the authorities, but he does see a threat of repression from revolutionaries. The critical questions to ask candidates for the high court may be not about their "philosophies" or opinions but about their judgment on questions of fact. In Powell's case, one would like to ask: How many revolutionaries are there? Who are they? Which foreign powers are they collaborating with? If they assaulted the government, would the government collapse? The answers he would give to such questions are important. We want our leaders to have impeccable philosophies, but we also want them to live in the real world, because even the stoutest defenders of liberty can inaugurate repression once they start taking real emergency measures to deal with imagined insurrections.

NOVEMBER 27, 1971

THE nineteen-sixties, a period that lasted from about 1962 to about 1969, was a time of demonstrations. Above all, there was the Vietnam war itself. It was a "demonstration," in the policymakers' words, of this country's "resolve" to fight "Communism," a "test case" of its "toughness" in facing world revolution. And then, of course, there were the other demonstrations—the ones in Central Park and at the Washington Monument, which gave the lie to what the government was saying with its war. Those crowds were saying that, as a people, Americans didn't in fact have the "resolve"— or the stomach—to tear up small countries that posed no threat to them. The protest movement has been criticized for its theatricality, but what could be more appropriate than answering one "demonstration" with another? A couple of weeks ago, on November 6th, we went to the Sheep Meadow in Central Park to see the most recent demonstration of this kind, which called for "An Immediate Withdrawal of All Troops from Southeast Asia." In the nineteen-sixties, the crowds were asking for negotiations to end the war. This crowd was asking for a lot more. Its speakers were calling for an end not only to the war but to American imperialism generally, to racism, to Fascism, and to sexism, too. It was asking for more, but its numbers were fewer— perhaps ten or fifteen thousand, instead of the hundreds of thousands who used to show up. Part of the audience, moreover, was made up of small groups who were using the demonstration to advance a number of more specific causes, among them independence for Puerto Rico, self-determination for Northern Ireland, independence for East Bengal, and a trial of Governor

Rockefeller for "murder" at Attica. And every second person in the crowd seemed to be selling subscriptions to one radical newspaper or another, so the whole occasion had the air of a convention of underground-newspaper dealers. The organizers tried to put a brave face on things, but the inescapable conclusion was that—for the moment, anyway—*this* kind of demonstration was dead. It has been outlasted by the other kind—the kind we make with our B-52s in Indo-China.

We are in the strangest period of this strangest of our wars. The speakers at the demonstration in the Park could point to many successes—most notably, the fact that today, according to the polls, a majority of Americans want to get out of Vietnam even if that means that the Communists will take over. Even the President seems to be against the war. To hear him talk lately, you would think he was so opposed to the war that he had already ended it. (For example, he has been referring regularly to our "peacetime economy.") It is as though the Administration had struck a bargain with the opposition. "As far as the United States is concerned, we give up in the debate on our war policy," the Administration has seemed to be saying. "We surrender the domestic front to you. We concede all the arguments. We won't talk about preserving freedom in Vietnam anymore, or about combatting revolution based in Peking. We'll stop trying to rally support for the cause. From now on, everyone in America is a dove, with us leading the flock. All this we concede. And we ask just one thing in return: a free hand to do as we please in Vietnam."

DECEMBER 11, 1971

AUTHOR'S NOTE: In March of 1971, President Yahya Khan of Pakistan ordered his Army to attack secessionist forces that had gathered strength in East Pakistan. In the month that followed, the Army carried out massacres whose victims, according to some accounts, numbered in the millions. Additional millions fled to India. In December, war broke out between India and Pakistan, and within two weeks the Pakistani forces in East Pakistan were defeated, and East Pakistan proceeded to set itself up as the independent state of Bangladesh. As these events unfolded, President Nixon and Henry Kissinger developed the belief that India, which in August had signed a "friendship agreement" with the Soviet Union, was acting as a proxy of Soviet power in the subcontinent, and that West Pakistan, which had declarations of support from China, was in effect a Chinese proxy. They further came to believe that India intended to attack and defeat

*West Pakistan, thereby extending Soviet power in the region, and therefore they resolved
to make a display of support for Pakistan.*

L AST week, when we learned that war had broken out in South Asia,
our thoughts began to race over the entire globe, as they do now
whenever a war breaks out, or expands, anywhere. We found ourself
trying, in our uneasiness, to take an inventory of the enmities and the alliances
that are supposed to keep local wars from growing into general wars. It was
clear immediately that the standard Cold War thinking would provide a poor
guide. Here was China, once widely considered the headquarters for revolution in Asia, backing a murderous, reactionary regime in its efforts to
suppress a promising revolutionary force on China's own border, and here
was the United States joining the Chinese in ingratiating itself with that
same regime while thoroughly antagonizing its old ally India, whom it used
to refer to regularly as "the world's largest democracy." A vague American-
Chinese-Pakistani axis and a somewhat less vague Russian-Indian axis seemed
to have emerged in South Asia. But only in South Asia. Next door, in Southeast
Asia, the Russians and the Chinese were still allied against the United States
while remaining the bitterest enemies in almost every other matter. And, to
confuse the picture still further, our President was planning a friendly visit
to China even as Americans and Vietnamese continued to die in a war whose
aim was to "contain" China. As our thoughts raced on, trying to follow the
chains of possible consequences to their conclusions, it seemed to us at first
that the greatest danger lay in the possibility that, just as the Indians had
attacked Pakistan when it was in trouble militarily, the Chinese might attack
India while it was preoccupied militarily, and the Russians might then take
the opportunity to attack China, perhaps with the aim of destroying China's
nuclear installations. In the end, though, none of this looked probable to us.
One set of rules applied to South Asia, and a completely different set to
Southeast Asia, and perhaps there were grounds for reassurance in this very
confusion. None of the Great Powers had staked their prestige unreservedly
on the victory of one warring side or the other, and the ladders of escalation
that have for so long seemed to stretch directly up from the Indo-China war
and the Arab-Israel war toward general nuclear war seemed to be missing
here. Still, the entire world had been given a severe jolt. We were reminded
of something we had heard a scientist say on the radio just before the
underground nuclear blast at Amchitka. He said that the blast would send
out a shock wave across the surface of the earth that could be measured on
a seismograph in New York several minutes later. Then the wave would circle
the earth a second time and could be measured a second time. "The earth's

thin crust is just like a bell. When you strike it, the entire earth reverberates,"
he explained. Now the bell has been struck again, and again we have felt
the entire earth reverberate.

DECEMBER 25, 1971

*AUTHOR'S NOTE: In mid-December, Nixon, fearful that an attack by India on West
Pakistan was imminent, sought to forestall it by ordering a naval task force to proceed
toward the Bay of Bengal.*

DURING the last eight months or so, the world has watched the United
States create, from scratch, a new enemy. A year ago, our relations
with India were cordial; last week we were sending a naval task force,
headed by the aircraft carrier U.S.S. *Enterprise*, into the Indian Ocean. This
was no small gesture. The *Enterprise*, which carries almost a hundred planes
and is equipped with nuclear weapons, is a compact, floating holocaust. Its
presence in the Indian Ocean, together with the presence of a Soviet fleet
said to have been moved there recently, threatened not only South Asians
but the rest of us as well. Our alienation of India seemed to unfold with
systematic efficiency, as though according to a plan. First, as so many observers have now pointed out, Henry Kissinger's famous trip from Pakistan
(India's greatest enemy) to China (India's second-greatest enemy), followed
by our failure, once the revolt in East Pakistan had broken out, either to
condemn the murderous policies of West Pakistan or to cut off our shipments
of arms to Pakistan, seemed calculated to drive India into the alliance she
soon made with the Soviet Union. We seemed to have forgotten that there
were great powers in the world apart from us. Then, having drawn the Soviet
Union into the situation by our own policies, we seemed dumbfounded to
find it there. The Indians and their problems were invisible to us, and we
seemed to believe that everything that happened on the subcontinent had
originated with the Soviet Union. And last week official spokesmen were
going as far as to equate every military advance made by India, our friend
of twenty years' standing, with an advantage to the Soviet Union: by an
amazing twist, an extension of Indian influence on the subcontinent began
to seem to us the same thing as an extension of Soviet influence.

The manufacture of enemies is, in fact, an old habit of ours. In many ways,
our India policy has been following the pattern of Vietnam and the Dominican
Republic—countries in which we were also too quick to see local people as

proxies for great powers we already considered our enemies. There are few questions as important for Americans as how and why we create new enemies for ourselves. At first, perhaps, the Cold War was to blame. When we selected the North Vietnamese as foes, the blurred vision of the Cold War helped us along. In those days, we couldn't discern the difference between a member of the National Liberation Front and a North Vietnamese and a Chinese, or between a Chinese and a Russian. They all looked to us like soldiers in one threatening army—the army of World Communism. But now the Cold War is supposedly over: The Chinese and the Russians are at each other's throats; soon the President will be in Peking. (It is one of the disturbing anomalies of the present moment that the Hot War continues after the Cold War has apparently ended.) One might have hoped that as the Cold War glaciers broke up, our own aims would become less grandiose and our vision more precise. Our behavior in South Asia suggests that something different is happening. New grandiose aims, even larger and vaguer than the old ones, and a new blur, even fuzzier than before, threaten to dominate policy. We are finding new reasons for making enemies.

The aims are best suggested, perhaps, by the President's claim that we are "the Number One nation" in the world. This claim, so comical at first hearing, is turning out to have grim implications. The collapse of Cold War thinking has left the clash between the great powers drained of ideology, let alone ideas or principles. (The confused debates over the South Asian war in the Security Council of the United Nations offer spectacular proof of this.) But it has left intact the monstrously overgrown military machines that thrived and expanded in the Cold War. The collapse robbed the armies of their missions, but it left the armies in position all over the globe. It is as though the human beings had become reconciled but the missiles still had a score to settle. The aim of being "the Number One nation," or of not letting ourselves become "a second-rate power," or "a pitiful helpless giant"—if you can call it an aim—can restore our machine to full life. Walt W. Rostow's phrase "We are the greatest power in the world if we behave like it" fore-shadowed a new, circular policy, and could serve as a motto for it. Our new aim in wielding our power, in other words, can be to serve not our people but simply our power. The machine's new cause can be to advance not a cause, such as freedom or the "free world," but itself. Naturally, the Number One nation, the queen of the nations, cannot allow any form of lèse-majesté—whether it is in the form of a military challenge, as in Indo-China, or in the form of a vote, like the U.N. General Assembly vote on China—to go unpunished. And even if there are no offenses or slights, perpetual demonstrations of our "willingness" to deploy, and use, our forces are required, to head off future offenses and to make sure the world won't think that, because of Vietnam, we are becoming "isolationist." With this new aim, the questions of just where to make our demonstrations and against whom and to what end tend to fade in significance. Indeed, high officials have argued that even arbitrary demonstrations of violence can be useful. They serve to keep the entire world, including our allies, on its toes where the United States is concerned. In the new rhetoric, we are no longer "the leader of the free world" but "the leading nation"; we are in danger not of being "soft on Communism" but just as being "soft" (the Roman Empire is often mentioned in this connection); and we are in danger not of "appeasing the Communists" but of general "isolationism." Since the aim is to prove our resolve to all comers, and not just to Communists, India became as good a place as any for us to show our toughness. So in the new scheme our list of potential enemies has actually broadened.

It is a commonplace that political leaders are hungry for power and do-minion. But when one looks at our government's record in Asia over the last decade or so, it seems that if our leaders have shown any persistent failing, it has been an excessive hunger for action. They have consistently arranged their picture of the world—and, to a considerable extent, arranged the world itself (with the assistance of the Soviet Union)—in such a way that every crisis in the world becomes *our* crisis. We've claimed the globe as a stage where our passions and our obsessions are to be played out, and we haven't left room for anyone but ourselves and our enemies. Other nations are reduced to mere shadows of our obsessions. If they begin to pursue their own local crusades and vendettas, we quickly cast them, first in our imagination and then with the tremendous weight of our power, as minor characters in our grand struggle. They are visible only insofar as we can make them reflections of ourselves. And soon (who could have guessed it a year ago?) Pakistan is our loyal ally (as well as China's loyal ally), and India is our perfidious antagonist. We shape things so that when trouble starts, the adrenaline can start pounding through our veins—so that there is something for *us* to win or lose. Then the phones begin to ring in the back of the officials' limousines, lights burn late at the Pentagon, Presidential aides are interrupted at dinner parties by the beeping of their wrist radios. We have identified the enemy.

With seemingly little help from the great national governments of the world, peace has come to South Asia. In a season of miracles, let us just call it a miracle.

JANUARY 15, 1972

SCHOOLCHILDREN are often told the story of how President Lincoln scribbled the Gettysburg Address on the back of an envelope as he rode to Gettysburg on a train. The other day, the *Times* ran an account of a politician of our day preparing a speech—Senator Muskie, preparing the announcement of his candidacy:

> Mr. Muskie was closeted with advisers as he tried to figure out what to tell the American electorate about his quest for the Presidency. He had three drafts, one written by his chief speechwriter, Robert Shrum, a second submitted by Milton Gwertzman, a Washington lawyer and sometime supporter of Senator Edward M. Kennedy, and a third by John Bartlow Martin, who was a friend of President Kennedy. Senator Muskie was trying to piece together a declaration from all three drafts, adding his own thoughts. . . .

It used to be that speechmaking was subject to a mysterious chemistry all its own. At best, if the right man spoke to the right audience at the right time and in the right place, he could do what Lincoln did at Gettysburg. At worst, the wrong man at the wrong time and in the wrong place could turn an audience, or a whole nation, into a mob, as Hitler did. But whatever this odd, invaluable, dangerous chemistry was, it has evaporated today. Political speeches are neither elevating nor demagogic; they are dead. Even when politicians take sharply opposing stands on issues, the quality of language and thought on both sides has a staleness that makes the charges and the counter-charges seem part of a single, colorless flow issuing from a common source. The mechanization of speechmaking has come close to destroying the point of making speeches. Taping and recording and the endless repetition of speeches have certainly destroyed any sense of occasion. Television, radio, and amplifiers may make the speaker available to a wider audience, but they also intervene between the speaker and his audience. And the speechwriters intervene between the speaker and his own thoughts. Too many people have got into the act. It seems most unlikely that we're going to find the right man at the right time in the right place between now and November 7th; it will be more a matter of nobody talking to no one about nothing.

JANUARY 29, 1972

THE most appalling result of America's policies in Asia has been the destruction of Asian peoples and Asian cultures, but the most ominous result, perhaps, has been the consistent undermining of our own ends and the destruction of ourselves. This, of course, is a popular point to make. During the recent emergence of Bangladesh, almost every commentator remarked, in one way or another, on the self-destructive nature of our policy. We not only backed a ruthless dictatorship (it was said) but backed an ineffectual ruthless dictatorship. We were not only on the wrong side but on the losing side, too. We defied not just decency but the dictates of power politics. We lost our soul *and* the world. And all this has been said with equal justice of the entire Indo-China war. One reason this point has been made so often is that it's easier to accuse the government of failing to accomplish its own ends (the enhancing of our "prestige," and so on) than to try to hold the government to standards of conduct devised by oneself. Everyone likes a chance to appear more hardheaded than the hardheads themselves. (Some observers, to get extra points in hardheadedness, clearly implied that they would have had no objection to our silence about the massacres in East Pakistan if only there had been some advantage for us in it.) However, there are better reasons for dwelling on this point. A powerful nation that commits terrible crimes itself and condones the crimes of other nations in ruthless, single-minded pursuit of its own advantage and its own interests is naturally a menace to the rest of the world, but in our age a nation that does all this in *spite* of its own interests can be a still greater menace—particularly if it is a nuclear power, as we are. The world should pray that the nuclear powers, if they can't behave with generosity, will at least preserve a lively and accurate sense of their own interests, because their greatest possible interest is also the entire world's greatest possible interest: avoiding nuclear war. In a time when the nuclear powers are indifferent to human life, and are willing to carry out or condone murder on a huge scale, self-interest becomes the last preserve of hope for the race. Selfishness can lead to great crimes, but it can also keep them within certain bounds. It's the self-righteous "selfless" crimes that have no limit. Nuclear war, if it comes, won't grow out of anyone's self-interest (no one has anything to gain)—it will grow out of madness. So if the great powers can't honor the lives of people in other parts of the world, one can still hope they'll learn to cherish their own sweet lives. In Asia, however, we've been pursuing something that dulls us to the pain we inflict on ourselves as well as to the pain we inflict on our "enemies"—something that has started to put us to sleep altogether. In an age when the ultimate calamity is a crime that would combine international murder and national suicide in a single act, these are bad omens.

FEBRUARY 5, 1972

L AST week, the President once again summoned the nation around its television sets to receive a surprise message. Once again, he had secrets to share with us—information about secret trips, secret meetings, secret proposals. We've also learned secrets of a different kind recently, by courtesy of Jack Anderson and Daniel Ellsberg, among others. Their secrets tended to show that the President (whoever the President was) had been wrong and his opponents right. But President Nixon's secrets showed that he was right and his opponents were wrong. "Nothing is served by silence when it misleads some Americans into accusing their own government of failing to do what it has already done," he said, and he also said, "We are being asked publicly to set a terminal date for our withdrawal when we already offered one in private." His point immediately won almost universal acceptance. Senator Muskie, while expressing some misgivings, said, "It's reassuring that we are at last proposing, by a date certain, to withdraw all of our forces in Vietnam." Senator McGovern noted that "at the same time Mr. Nixon was bitterly opposed to the McGovern-Hatfield proposal to end the war, he was . . . offering it to the other side." And the next day most columnists seemed to agree with James Reston's remark in the *Times* that the President's disclosure "clearly puts Edmund S. Muskie, Hubert H. Humphrey, George S. McGovern, and John V. Lindsay in the position of attacking the President for refusing to offer what the President now discloses he has offered long ago." Nearly everyone agreed that the President had now done what his opponents had been asking him to do. *But it isn't true.* His opponents' principal proposals for ending the war were very different from the President's plan. It is a matter of the plainest public record. Thousands of words have been written about these proposals, and they have been embodied in bills before Congress. The McGovern-Hatfield amendment, to mention the most prominent piece of legislation, required the setting of a date for a withdrawal of American forces and an exchange of prisoners six months after the enactment of the legislation. The President's plan calls for a withdrawal of American troops and a prisoner exchange six months after a political settlement with the North Vietnamese. In other words, the McGovern-Hatfield amendment called for a withdrawal with or without a political settlement, whereas the Nixon plan requires a political settlement first, and the settlement he offers is one that all observers—including, no doubt, the President himself—know is unacceptable to the North Vietnamese. These are not superficial or merely technical differences. They are the kind of deep, fundamental differences that have been tearing the country apart over the last decade.

The case of Senator McGovern, whose record on the war has been consistent and straightforward, and who doesn't usually make this kind of slip, is particularly instructive. He wanted to point out that if you believe what the President is now saying, you have to conclude that he was dissembling last year, when his Administration was attacking McGovern and others for putting forward the McGovern-Hatfield amendment; that he was attacking them, and questioning their patriotism, for merely proposing what he was actually doing; and that now, having himself been a party to the secret of the new plan, he was turning around and accusing them of being dupes of the enemy—of having let themselves be "falsely used by the enemy to stir up divisiveness in this country," as he put it in his speech. But in pointing out this inconsistency McGovern neglected to look at the root of the matter— whether the President's secret proposal really was the same as the McGovern-Hatfield amendment—and thus he seemed, for a moment, to join the rest of the world in forgetting his own fine record on the war. No doubt he and others will soon recover and set the record straight again. But McGovern's aberration, together with almost everyone else's, provided a remarkable display of the extent to which American politics has come to be ruled by propaganda. For a moment, the President had achieved what every leader who tries to rewrite history must dream of: he had wiped out his opposition's memory of its own actions. In a way, his television blitz was as impressive a display of Presidential power as the heaviest B-52 raid. It revealed, at the start of this election year, the stunning range of his political resources: his power to commandeer television; his power to dominate the news with pseudo-events, or with real events undertaken for domestic political purposes; his power to undercut the opposition by first withholding and then revealing state secrets; and his power to obliterate the public record with the sheer prestige of his office.

MARCH 25, 1972

THE President's trip to China shows that television coverage opens up what is virtually a new field of action to men in power. With television, a President can draw eyes away from the piecemeal, day-to-day unfolding of policy and focus them on complex, powerful, symbolic events that he can manipulate more easily than he can the world itself. It allows him to act directly on the country's imagination, like a high priest. Major events of this kind, which are designed chiefly for the sake of coverage, are more elusive than events of other kinds. It is not only the results of an event like the China trip that are indeterminate but the very nature of the event. When the excitement has died down, one has to wonder even whether anything really happened at all. As we have turned these matters over in our mind, we have found ourself thinking in more than one voice—in a kind of colloquy. The colloquy revolves around the question of appearance and reality in politics, and goes like this:

FIRST VOICE: The trip was the most unreal, and therefore the most deceptive, event in recent memory. It was a circus put on to enhance the prestige of the participants and divert all of us from their real actions in the world. At a time when action was required, they gave us theatre. Instead of agreements and explanations, they gave us tourism and toasts. (The news-starved reporters raised the art of interpreting official handshakes and official toasts to the level of a new academic discipline.) It was all hints and no commitments. The trip fits into an ominous new American strategy—for widespread but "invisible" continued intervention abroad, with our government phasing out the techniques that attract the public's attention. The new strategy would rely heavily on air power combined with electronic battlefield devices, on the C.I.A. (to conduct clandestine wars, like the one in Laos), on allies and mercenaries (like the Cambodians and the Thais), on donations of matériel, and on the deployment of warships (as in the India-Pakistan war). If troops were to be required, volunteers rather than draftees might be used. At home, the government, instead of seeking support, would encourage indifference. Ideological passion in the public at large would no longer be required, or even desired. Already, the public has discovered that China is an unfriendly but basically reactionary power, like the Soviet Union, and that it is as ready to sell out a revolution (as it did in Bangladesh and is doing in Ceylon) as support one. In the new view, the Great Powers would command the globe like three or four or five giant machine-gun turrets. The China trip set the style for the new international politics. It went a long way toward the Sinification of the American public. It helped get us used to resting content with the pageantry of international relations while leaving the substance to the President and a few experts, who dazzle us from time to time with their startling shifts and unexplained reversals. And while we're watching Nixon and Mao shake hands (live from Peking!) our government is underwriting murder in Southeast Asia.

SECOND VOICE: Your distinction between politically contrived pseudo-events and the "realities," which is indeed often a useful one, has misled you this time, owing to a peculiar circumstance. That is the strangeness and unreality of this country's last twenty years of relations with China, which a high official of the State Department has now gone as far as to call an "aberration." In those years, it was as though the American public wanted to keep the slate on China clear of any information, so that the most hysterical men in our political life would be free to chalk up their worst imaginings there. The President's trip put an end to all this, and to a style of American politics that went with it. And doing so didn't require any of the substance you demand. (In the same period, other people fastened their utopian dreams on China, and their imaginings, too, have now been undercut.) The President's trip *was* a ritual, but it was a beneficent ritual. It was a rite of disenchantment. The hysteria in America and China, which was itself the wellspring of our protracted hostility, and was a potential source of ultimate, global calamity, was calmed in this country, and perhaps calmed in China, too. Here at home, one can already feel a certain lightening in the political mood. To be sure, just before the President's trip a vituperative chorus came out of the White House accusing the Democratic Presidential candidates of, among other things, "aiding and abetting" foreign enemies, but even then the voices seemed to come out of the past. They didn't carry the tremendous coercive weight they once had. (Which enemies? Mr. Nixon's hosts, the Chinese? The North Vietnamese?) Our politics used to be boxed in and confined by charges like these. Now many men in political life, including some of the Presidential candidates, will be able to act with a new sense of freedom, and perhaps lay claim to wider, less fearful constituencies. Whether the President had it in mind or not, his trip can help to liberate new political forces here at home and to move us into a new era.

THIRD VOICE: The question of whether we have really moved into a new era or only done so on television, in the image-world, is crucial. There is no question but that the trip laid to rest the American public's excessive fears of Chinese expansionism, and this is indeed a considerable benefit. Unfortunately, the unreal fears impelled us into a real war and into the quasi-occupation of a province of China. We paid in real blood for our unreal fears. Excuse me. *Are paying* in real blood. The trip has given us relief from our own overheated imaginings, but it has not given us relief from the real war that our imaginings impelled us into. The war continues as an anachronism, and today's bombings are as pale and unreal to us as memories. Has the government found new uses, in new, unannounced policies, for America's war in Southeast Asia, now that the old uses have disintegrated? If this nation has entered a new era, it hasn't yet left the old one behind. Everyone is yearning for the age of peace the President is promising. But we have to hold ourselves back until the old era does actually end. We can't let ourselves enjoy in imagination the fruits of efforts we have yet to carry through to completion in reality. In the present confusion, perhaps the following would be a good rule of thumb: No American may enter the new age of peace until every man, woman, and child in Southeast Asia has entered before him.

APRIL 15, 1972

THE new fighting in Vietnam, which could bring the entire war to its conclusion, finds the United States in a mood of drugged silence. Nearly everybody is behaving as though it all had nothing to do with us. By and large, the Democratic candidates are busy counting up their percentages in the primaries. Since they discovered tax reform, they seem to have forgotten about the war. Their smiles or frowns reflect only the state of their political fortunes. They are like accountants who, absorbed in their figures, have closed themselves off from all life outside. The marchers are quiet, too. They have already proved their points ten times over. Even the Chinese are calmly trading zoo animals with us while we send our five hundred planes over North Vietnam. As for the Administration, it has not said anything substantive about the war in years. Its answer to the "credibility gap" was to stop making statements about its plans at all. That way, it could not be accused of lying. No one knows what it has in mind for the Vietnamese or for us. A final defeat for the Saigon government now seems possible, but no one has any idea whether we would respond by withdrawing or by undertaking further reckless escalations of the war. The country is prepared for neither move. Over the years, millions of people have come to accept the futility of the war. For them, withdrawal and failure seem inevitable and are fully acceptable. But for millions of others, who have not yet grasped the desperately precarious nature of our situation, withdrawal and failure would ram home the full futility of the war in a single thunderclap, as the spectacle of enemy troops in Saigon lit up the then inescapable fact that the ten years of agony and death for Vietnamese and Americans had truly come to nothing. Yet no one in our government has tried to prepare the country for the possibility of such a shock. Nor, for that matter, has anyone in our government done anything to prepare the country for the kind of dramatic escalation that might, in a crisis, be tempting to this Administration as an alternative to complete withdrawal. And nothing, as far as we can see, has been done to negotiate an end to the fighting. It's as though, after a decade of turmoil, we had handed over our fate to the government. And the government, in turn, has handed over our fate to the B-52s. It seems that we're becoming a country that can do only one thing: we can't talk, we can't feel, we can't think, we can only bomb, and bomb again, and then bomb some more. And yet the government and its bombers would shield none of us from the tremendous jolts that could come out of the present fighting in Vietnam. One or two voices have been raised in warning. Senator Kennedy, for instance, has said:

My outrage over the present murderous offensive in Vietnam is matched only by my outrage over the cruel, senseless view at large in the nation today that the proper present policy for the United States is to let the slaughter proceed. How can this nation possibly wash its hands of the blood that is being shed today in North and South Vietnam? It is a tragic sign of how far we have lost our way in Indo-China that the only real debate now under way in the mind of the nation is a debate on the question of whether and to what extent American land, sea, and air forces should be engaged in this incredible new bloodbath. That is not the only question, and if that is the only question we ask ourselves, then we shall never find an answer that can satisfy our conscience. The simple truth is that this test of Vietnamization, with or without American support, is a wholly immoral and unjustifiable test, because it is a test that is being carried out with the lives of men, women, and children. Those dead and dying bodies stretched out beside the road across our television screens last night are the bodies of human beings. We do not have the right—no one has the right—to demand a test like that. What possible justification can there be for a policy that asks such a terrible sacrifice in human life? The conscience of America ought to be demanding a cease-fire, not simply asking our people to accept a ringside seat to watch the slaughter.

In the present atmosphere, Kennedy's voice is like a voice calling from another world—the real world.

APRIL 22, 1972

O UR current bombing campaign in Indo-China is something new in the history of warfare. The Nazis' and Fascist Italians' bombing in support of Franco's forces in the Spanish Civil War—the campaign that lifted the curtain on the age of modern aerial warfare—is the only other instance of a great power's supporting one side in a civil war almost exclusively through bombing. But the present American campaign is really in a class by itself, if only because of its magnitude: our air force over Indo-China is the most powerful ever assembled in a single theatre of war, and the Indo-China theatre is a small one. Moreover, this latest form of intervention in the Indo-China war represents a culmination of our century's tendency toward mechanized killing. In this campaign, the growing American official indifference to human life has come close to perfection, outstripping our performance during the massacres in Bengal, when we were only mute observers and indirect supporters of the killing, rather than mute perpetrators. Nearly all the flaws have been eliminated from the warmaking process. The government has made the invaluable discovery that an air force will go on fighting long after ground troops have balked, especially when there is virtually no opposing air force in the sky. Changes in the way our political system works have removed the public and the Congress from participation. Initially, they, along with the ground troops, were given the role of supporting the war effort, but they were found to be defective elements in the war machine, and were shut out. Newsmen, too, have been shut out, in part because in the massive, indiscriminate bombing of large areas *no one* knows where the bombs are going or whom they are falling on—they simply drop out of sight. And even such meagre information as the officials do have they now withhold, under the pretense of maintaining security. Our new strategy has done away with one of the most fundamental restraints on warmaking. It used to be that those who would kill also had to be ready to die. Even large armies facing small armies knew this and felt it, and, by extension, the societies they belonged to knew it and felt it. There was a feeling of equality in the face of death in wartime which touched both sides and formed the basis for whatever codes of honor have appeared in war. Sometimes, indeed, it formed the basis for paradoxical expressions of brotherhood between opposing armies, such as have regularly appeared in the history of war. The nearness and sureness of death gave war its solemnity, its feeling of great weight for an army or a people. It could not be undertaken casually—not for very long, anyway. But the present policy aims precisely at making the waging of war casual and acceptable. It confronts the innocent and the supposed foe alike with an army of machines, and rests on the assumption that although we don't like to die we don't mind killing. The war that this country's government is waging now is war trivialized. Never has a nation unleashed so much violence with so little risk to itself. It is the government's way of waging war without the support of its own people, and involves us all in the dishonor of killing in a cause we are no longer willing to die for.

APRIL 29, 1972

A T the outset of the Second World War, when Hitler was beginning to murder the European Jews, a joke of sorts circulated in Europe. It went something like this:
A: Hitler is killing the Jews and the cyclists.
B: Why the cyclists?
A: Why the Jews?
This joke applies equally well to our government and the Vietnamese. Why the Vietnamese? The simple truth is that until we thrust ourselves into the picture, there was nothing at stake in Vietnam for the United States. We know now that a Communist regime in South Vietnam would no more have disturbed life in the United States than the regime in North Vietnam did before we attacked it. But the war became more than a war; it became a towering construct of the American imagination. We imagined that there were great dangers for us in the way things went in Vietnam, and then in responding to these false dangers we created real dangers. In fact, in this peculiar manner we have contrived to rearrange the major part of both our domestic and our foreign politics so that they stand or fall with the government of Nguyen Van Thieu.

At home, we've reshaped our national life to suit the war. The outcome of our Presidential election, and perhaps even the survival of our democracy itself, may have been gambled on the performance of the South Vietnamese Army. The headlines are talking about "the stakes in the White House" and about "a test of President Nixon's Vietnamization policy," and newsmen are eagerly reading the results of the current battles as another Presidential primary, in which the tally of killed and wounded replaces the tally of votes.

Internationally, we have arranged things so that the war has repeatedly endangered the peace of the world. Preceding each of our periods of escalation, the government has decided unilaterally to see the hand of one or more large enemy powers behind the Vietnamese Communists—perhaps because of a need to find enemies commensurate with our stepped-up efforts. Then, having imagined the strong presence of other great powers, we have proceeded to take actions that have actually threatened to draw them in. First, in the early nineteen-sixties, we imagined that an international Communist movement was the real enemy behind the North Vietnamese mask. Following our perception of the Sino-Soviet split, the enemy was narrowed down to Rusk's "billion Chinese," and the aim became to "contain" China. Now the Chinese have been forgotten and the Russians have been rolled into view. The President, in an act of seemingly willful misinterpretation, has suggested that the Russians are responsible for the latest North Vietnamese offensive. And in reacting to the offensive by bombing Hanoi and Haiphong and damaging Russian ships he has created the likelihood of a real clash with the Russians.

In any event, if Saigon should fold up—and not even Administration spokesmen are asserting that it won't—the seventy-three thousand American troops remaining in Vietnam might find themselves in terrible jeopardy. If the Administration judges it necessary to bomb Hanoi and Haiphong to "protect" these troops now, what would it do to protect them if they were encircled by North Vietnamese troops? One recoils from thinking about it, but almost any of the escalatory moves that might tempt it could provoke a storm of rebellion here, and a responding wave of repression. Of course, the best way to protect the troops, if that were really the Administration's primary aim, would be not to bomb Haiphong—or to bomb Russian ships, as Senator Goldwater has said he hopes we would—but to bring the troops home. Then they *would* be safe. After all, one doesn't send soldiers into a war zone to "protect" them. One sends them, at the risk of their lives, to accomplish some objective. The objective in this case is insuring the survival of the Saigon government. In the present circumstances, one is forced to ask whether our troops are not being kept in Vietnam precisely because of their vulnerability to attack, in order to give the Administration the pretext for escalation that it has used so freely in justifying the escalations of the last few weeks.

There is a remarkable symmetry between the imaginary perils our government has been battling and the real perils it has unwittingly created. The government thought that world peace was threatened by Communist aggression. Now world peace *is* threatened, but by our own escalation. The government thought that our freedom was threatened by the Communists. Now our freedom *is* threatened—but by the government itself. We need to look to ourselves, but instead, with "Vietnamization," we seem to have turned our fate over to the Vietnamese. Though we have reduced our ground forces, we have not reduced our ambitions. We speak of the current fighting in laboratory technicians' language, calling it a "test" of "Vietnamization," but thousands upon thousands of Vietnamese will never see the results—if they ever wanted to in the first place. They will have been Vietnamized into their graves. Those in our government who support the war are willing to risk everything on the South Vietnamese Army, counting on it to protect us from humiliation and catastrophe. We went to Vietnam to save the Vietnamese, but now we find ourselves asking this small, tormented people to save us. Yet the Vietnamese can't save us. We have put a gun to our own head, and it's up to us, and us alone, to take it away.

MAY 6, 1972

T IME is running out in Indo-China, and events there may be rapidly approaching their conclusion. But in the United States we are transfixed. The responses we have managed to the present crisis have been merely repetitious. The bombers bomb. Demonstrators demonstrate. Senators question Cabinet members. Congress considers legislation against the war. The President gives his speech on the war. Everyone does what he has done many times before, only more feebly. A new political system has apparently come into being in which all these supposedly clashing and disruptive activities have been accommodated into a single, smoothly functioning process. President Nixon's recent speech on the war was like a speech out of the nineteen-fifties. "We will not be defeated and we will never surrender our friends to Communist aggression," he said, lumping Americans and South Vietnamese into a single "we," and lumping all Communist countries into a single "they" capable of concerted aggression. Yet later on he mentions his "historic" journeys "for peace" to the two largest of these same aggressor nations, and goes on to say, "I . . . know that future Presidents will travel to nations abroad as I have on journeys for peace. If the United States betrays the millions of people who have relied on us in Vietnam, the President of the United States, whoever he is, will not deserve nor receive the respect which is essential if the United States is to continue to play the great role we are destined to play of helping to build a new structure of peace in the world." In other words, we have to fight wars with Communist aggressors so that we can simultaneously go on missions of peace to their capitals. After all, how can you be a peacemaker if there aren't any wars to stop? But in another part of the speech the President, after urging us on to victory, suggests that we are not, after all, fighting in Vietnam. He tells us that the South Vietnamese "are now bearing the brunt of the battle" and that "we can now see the day when no more Americans will be involved there at all." But if we are not fighting there, how can we suffer a defeat? And if the stakes for us are as great as the President says they are—if they include, as he puts it toward the end of his speech, "not just peace in our time but peace for generations to come"—why are we withdrawing our troops? We should be sending them in. Be this as it may, while Americans are arguing over whether we're in Vietnam or not, whether or not it's worth it to be there, whether or not we should get out if we are there—even whether or not there's a war going on at all—the North Vietnamese may well destroy the regime in Saigon. If this happens, the crisis that has lurked at the heart of the war all along will be upon us, and we will be in uncharted territory. None of the promises made so far will hold, and no form of escalation will be absolutely out of the question. The President asks us all to be steadfast. Steadfast on a disaster course. In other words, our whole tired crew—with the driver's foot pressed firmly on the accelerator—may be hurtling toward a brick wall at sixty miles an hour.

MAY 13, 1972

AS the United States again draws near to its quadrennial decision about who is to govern the country and how, it strikes us that the dominant note in any sane contemporary political philosophy should be a spirit of conservatism. A conservative is someone who cherishes and wants to protect a people's inheritance, so that it can be passed on undamaged to new generations. In the past, this inheritance was seen, in large part, as consisting of the established political order. In an awed and awesome tribute to the English polity in *Reflections on the Revolution in France*, the conservative Edmund Burke wrote:

> The people of England well know that the idea of inheritance furnishes a sure principle of conservation and a sure principle of transmission, without at all excluding a principle of improvement. . . . By a constitutional policy, working after the pattern of nature, we receive, we hold, we transmit our government and our privileges in the same manner in which we enjoy and transmit our property and our lives. The institutions of policy, the goods of fortune, the gifts of providence are handed down to us, and from us, in

the same course and order. Our political system is placed in a just correspondence and symmetry with the order of the world and with the mode
of existence decreed to a permanent body composed of transitory parts,
wherein, by the disposition of a stupendous wisdom, molding together the
great mysterious incorporation of the human race, the whole, at one time,
is never old or middle-aged or young, but, in a condition of unchangeable
constancy, moves on through the varied tenor of perpetual decay, fall,
renovation, and progression.

But today's conservatives should give their primary allegiance to an estab-
lishment much more ancient, more majestic, and more fundamental than a
government. They should give it directly to nature itself. Burke himself paid
his respects to nature by envisioning society as patterned after it, but he
doubtless never dreamed that nature—the pattern itself—could be threatened.
Today, however, we hold a dagger to the very heart of life.

A conservative in our time should first of all learn to cherish and protect
nature within us, which is to say our human nature. It is threatened by
radiation, which can corrupt the gene pool and destroy the very frame of
man, and it is threatened, of course, by the sheer explosive force of nuclear
weapons, which, if they were used, would be great enough to kill every
human being. Conservatives should also learn to cherish and protect nature
outside us—the land, the sea, the air, our plants and animals, or what we call
the ecosystem—from industrial pollution and, again, from nuclear war. As
Burke saw things, it was an act of intolerable presumption and impudence
for any single generation to destroy, by a revolution, an ancient, established
order that embodied the accretive wisdom of countless generations and to
replace it with a political order based on new and untested ideas of its own.
It was to rob one's heirs of their inheritance. But how much more presump-
tuous he would have found it for a single generation, such as our own, to
imagine that its wants and its political causes might conceivably justify our
jeopardizing not just our inheritance, political and otherwise, but our inher-
itors as well—our sons and grandsons and the myriad unborn generations
whose hopes and achievements we cannot know. This takes truly colossal
arrogance. Is it possible that our generation thinks its own transient conflicts
more weighty than the infinity of the human future?

Yet this arrogance is alive in almost every area of our culture. It dominates
our handling of another legacy from the past—our language. Conservatives
today should be worried about what is happening to language. Common
speech and writing are being drowned out, and the air is choked with voices
that hardly seem to come from a human source, speaking words that seem

to have been composed by the computers and mimeograph machines they issue from. Today, almost every organization has a well-financed team of experts whose job it is to twist words and facts to suit that organization's momentary needs. We are doing to language what we are doing to our natural inheritance. Our language is the fruit of generations of evolution, but we act as though we had made it up ourselves and were the last people who would have to use it. Languages and societies both have a natural "fall, renovation, and progression," and we disrupt this with our impatient, self-centered procedures.

A similar impatience is undermining our laws. Here, the organizations in charge of our enormous new military and economic power, and particularly the executive branch of the government, are the chief source of trouble. Again and again in recent years, they have decided that their supposed needs of the moment—for secrecy, for security, for freedom of action (including freedom from restraint by the public)—are more important than our legal inheritance of rights, so that the law, instead of being a principle of justice that stands above all organizations, including the government, becomes a weapon in the hands of one branch of the government for punishing its enemies. A spirit of conservatism would be helpful here, too.

It should be plain that a true conservatism today would have nothing to do with what now passes for conservatism in the United States. Our "conservatives" follow Burke in respecting the established *political* order but part ways with him in the deeper matter of respecting the *natural* order. And our political order is not in a just correspondence and symmetry with the order of the world. Far from it. Burke knew that there was something in the natural world, in society and also in ourselves, that was best left to unfold and change of its own accord, without our deliberate intervention. Perhaps this is what he meant by nature. But today we rush in everywhere with schemes of destruction and presumed improvement. With respect to the natural order, we are blind wreckers who have nothing to offer in place of what we tear down. Our most powerful institutions of production and war—and the "conservatives" who give them unquestioning support—are forces of extreme radicalism. They have taken it upon themselves to remake, and perhaps to destroy, the legacy not just of generations but of all time. Burke advised his countrymen to "approach to the faults of the state as to the wounds of a father, with pious awe and trembling solicitude," and to "look with horror on those children of their country who are prompt rashly to hack that ancient parent in pieces." Today, a true conservatism, rooted in a new-found reverence not just for the political, or even the social, order but for an inheritance so great that we have scarcely noticed it until recently—an inheritance that is all around us, within us, and is, in fact, us—would ask the state and all other human institutions to approach the whole of creation with the same awe and solicitude.

Is it necessary, this week, to add that Vietnam, where we have turned half a nation into a purgatory (one part prison and torture chamber, one part lunatic asylum, one part whorehouse, and the rest a graveyard), where we have made an assault of unprecedented magnitude on the land, and where, in the process, we have damaged our language with propaganda and under-mined our own laws, is the place where we Americans are hacking away most vigorously at our parent, the Earth? The South Vietnamese government may be crumbling, and with every defeat it suffers our government increases its threats. If the South Vietnamese were to fall altogether and our government were to continue on its present course, Vietnam could become the place where we deliver the final—the nuclear—blow.

MAY 20, 1972

WHEN President Nixon threw down the gauntlet to the Russians and the Chinese by ordering the mining of Haiphong and other North Vietnam harbors, he left the rest of us in an intolerable situation. We found ourselves facing total peril from a position approaching total ignorance and total helplessness. Total peril because we know that if the Russians or the Chinese were to behave as recklessly as our President has done—if they, too, were to define their choices as "immediate withdrawal" of all support, "continued attempts at negotiation," and "decisive military action to end the war," and chose decisive military action—then the next step could be the war that no one would remember. Total ignorance because although almost everyone believes the President has motives and plans he has not disclosed, almost no two people can agree on what they are, and the President himself does not tell us what he is going to do until he has already done it. Total helplessness because over the last decade our democracy has degenerated to the point where the President can make war at any level, from "limited war" to total war, entirely on his own, without the support of the Congress or the people, and because, in any case, the next moves are now up to the other side. We figure in this crisis only as potential victims, not as actors. A peculiar diplomatic incident last week summed up the pow-erlessness—and the degradation—of our position. Just a few hours after our mines in the harbors were activated, a delegation of Russians visited the

White House. The subject was said to be trade, but Ambassador Dobrynin of the Soviet Union and Henry Kissinger also attended. At the end, television cameramen and news photographers were called in. Everyone was smiling. We didn't know of anything to be smiling about, but perhaps they did. What was it? We scrutinized their faces for clues, but we could learn nothing. All we could know for certain was that we had been reduced to the position of those people in the world who must watch for a dimpled cheek or a stern glance in their overlords' faces to learn whether they would live or die.

JUNE 10, 1972

HAVING observed our government's behavior on the international scene during the last few weeks, many Americans must be confused. On the one hand, the government has taken actions that may bring mankind literally incalculable benefit. On the other hand, it has taken actions that risk literally incalculable loss. In one role, we Americans are the savior and protector of mankind, while in a second role we are the mad bomber of Asia. We seem to be living in two worlds—or two historical eras—at the same time. One is the world of the Moscow summit, and the other is the world of Vietnam. The names and the dates are the same in the two worlds, but everything else is different. The policies and actions growing out of each are real—neither can be dismissed as merely camouflage for the other—but they are based on two visions of our times which clash at every point. In the world that dictated our policy at the summit, we are at peace and Russia is our partner in building a new world order—or, at the very worst, she is our "competitor." In the President's words, our flag flies "high in the spring breeze above Moscow's ancient Kremlin fortress." The air is filled with toasts of friendship and the tinkling of champagne glasses. Russia and the United States have agreed to "avoid direct military confrontation." The two nations have joined hands to guarantee that the children of the world—the "other Tanyas" the President spoke of in Moscow—will never again have to die in war. The Cold War is breaking up. The world is now "multi-polar," and scores of small nations are asserting their independence. At home, the President is working, together with Congress and the people, to establish not just a generation but generations of peace. Yet in the world that dictates our Vietnam policy Russia is our enemy. Our men are being killed by forces that the Russians have unleashed. Whole nations are burning, and the air is filled with threats of a wider war. The Russians are brazenly attempting to conquer a country vital to our security. We have been forced to oppose them with a direct military challenge to their shipping. Children are being incinerated *right now*, in the heaviest bombing and the bitterest fighting of the war. The world is divided into two armed camps, and every aggressive move anywhere on the globe—in the Middle East, in South Asia, in Southeast Asia—must be seen as a "Communist" move against the United States. At home, the President is working, alone and in spite of Congress and the people, to perpetuate a war. In one of the two worlds, our leaders are signing joint communiqués with Russian leaders; in the other, the government is rebuking the *Times* for merely reporting what the leaders of North Vietnam are saying. In one of the worlds, the President is calm, wise, farseeing, restrained; in the other, he is petulant, willful, reckless. In one world, we are moving away from the brink; in the other, we are moving toward it. In one world, it's a week for joy; but we also live in the other world, and there is no joy.

JUNE 17, 1972

SOME weeks ago, Senator William Proxmire made public an internal Navy memorandum from Admiral Elmo R. Zumwalt, the Chief of Naval Operations, to Admiral Isaac C. Kidd, the Chief of Naval Material, which read, in part, "Difficulty of achieving these targets during the remaining months of F.Y. [Fiscal Year] '72 fully appreciated. But importance of avoiding shortfall in meeting newly established F.Y. '72 targets to avoid resultant adverse effects on anticipated F.Y. 1973 outlay ceilings dictate[s] need for top management attention." Zumwalt was telling Kidd to step up military spending in 1972 not in order to meet any threat to the United States from an enemy but in order to set the stage for swollen budget demands in 1973. He was saying, in effect, "We've got the money, so let's buy something or they'll think we don't need it." Zumwalt's logic is a paradigm of a kind of thinking that is now fairly common in Washington. Ordinarily, people reason from the need; that is, they first discover something that needs to be done and then look for the means to do it. Zumwalt does it the other way around; he reasons from the means. He starts with the means (the money) and then looks for a need (some new weapons). But, of course, a need that is created rather than just discovered is, by definition, not a need. It's an excuse for doing something unnecessary. When this kind of "need" is answered, the world becomes filled with a great deal of expensive junk. At the moment, a lot of this junk happens to consist of airplanes and explosives. The junk, in

turn, needs a need, just as the money did. It needs threats in order to justify
its existence. Threats have been found. It may even need a war, and we have
a war, too. When the government starts to reason from the means in military
matters, the logic runs backward, and so does the genesis of wars. By and
large, it used to be that a war began when a war aim was perceived. It might
grow out of a desire for conquest or out of fear—it might be aggressive or
it might be defensive—but the war aim was a given, and was the basis for
everything that followed. The war was fought to achieve the war aim, the
army was raised and the weapons were made to fight the war, and money
was raised to pay for the army and the weapons. At first glance, our wars
today have everything wars used to have—taxes, armies, weapons, battles.
But now we begin with the money. Then we make the weapons and raise
an army in order to spend the money, we find a war in order to use the army
and the weapons, and, if our officials then have enough time left over, they
may even figure out some war aims in order to justify it all.

JULY 1, 1972

I N the last few months, we've noticed, the Nixon Administration has been
showing a new concern about the level of excellence—the sheer class—
exhibited in government operations. It came up in a recent interview with
Presidential Assistant John Ehrlichman in which he was asked why the President had been holding so few news conferences. It wasn't that the President
resented the press or that he wanted to keep things from the public. It was
the intolerably low intellectual level of the discussion. "He [the President]
doesn't get very good questions at a press conference, frankly," Ehrlichman
said. "He goes in there for a half hour and gets a lot of flabby and fairly
dumb questions and it doesn't really elucidate very much. I've seen him many
times come off one of those things and go back in and say, 'Isn't it extraordinary how poor the quality of the questions are?' " The whole thing was
simply degrading for a man on the President's level. The new feeling that all
the Administration's activities should be kept on the highest possible plane
also came up a couple of months back when Attorney General Kleindienst,
who was then a candidate for the office he now holds, was defending the
propriety of his involvement in the I.T.T. case. At one point, he remarked,
disdainfully, on the "penny-ante" offense he was being charged with. His
annoyance at being accused of a vulgar, *small* crime was echoed the other
day by the President's press secretary, Ronald L. Ziegler, who described the

recent attempt by five men, allegedly including a Republican National Committee security agent, to bug the Democratic National Committee headquarters as "a third-rate burglary attempt." If someone is going to accuse them of crimes, these officials seemed to be saying, they should at least accuse them of big, classy, first-rate crimes.

JULY 29, 1972

E VERY day last week, we Americans dropped four thousand tons of bombs on North and South Vietnam. On one recent day, in Quang Tri Province alone—an area not much larger than Rhode Island—we dropped twenty-five hundred tons of bombs, with three or four times the blast-damage force of the atomic bomb dropped on Hiroshima. That is what the war has come down to. In this year's Presidential election, as in the last two Presidential elections, the country will be brought face to face with the question of the war, but it is a changed war now, and a changed country. The country has been brought to the point of exhaustion by the war. It is an exhaustion of sensibility, however—not physical exhaustion. Most of us find it more tiring to think about the war than to wage the war. Thinking about the war takes special effort, after all these years. On the other hand, waging the war is easy. All you have to do is to go on with business as usual. This is enough because the war has become part of America's business as usual. The war has inertia on its side. In a strange reversal of the usual order of things, it requires inaction to fight the war and action to stop fighting it. And because it takes so little for most of us to go on with the war, we sometimes get the feeling that someone else is waging it, or that *no one* is waging it—as though the computers and the B-52s could wage it by themselves. Yet in fact it is no one who is killing the Vietnamese but we ourselves. If we are not killing them, who is? Some people go as far as to maintain that *the war is over.* But what has happened is only that its shape has been changed to fit the public mood in the United States. For the Vietnamese, the war is in its most punishing phase. Throughout their country, a sequence of events is proceeding that spells annihilation for ordinary people. The Vietnamese we oppose launch an attack, and their shells fall on the towns. The Vietnamese we support flee. Then we Americans make our contribution: we blanket the whole area with an inconceivable volume of every imaginable kind of munition short of nuclear bombs. Then our Vietnamese, if they are able, return and loot the remains. So towns that put their trust in us and our clients are punished three times over: they are abandoned, then incinerated, then sacked.

But if the war is the only reality for the Vietnamese, who are living with it, it is almost wholly unreal to us Americans, who are supplying most of the explosives. This is partly because what we are doing in Vietnam isn't like war as we have known it in the past. War is fought against an enemy, but who is the United States' enemy in Vietnam? The North Vietnamese cannot harm us now and never will be able to harm us. They can just barely harm the force we are using to destroy them. The enemy can hardly be the Chinese, who, we are told, will soon be flying about in American 707s. And surely it isn't the Russians, whose Party Chairman now drives a Cadillac given him by President Nixon. Wars involve risks, but in what is happening in Vietnam the risks to most Americans are nil, and the combat casualties of those in the theatre of war are regularly lower than the casualties resulting from accidents. For Americans, Vietnam is less a battlefield than an open pen that we fire into at will as the people flee in masses from one side to another. War is a contest, a murderous competition, but for Americans in Vietnam there is no contest. The people we are killing are unable to pit their arms against our arms. Instead, they have pitted their willingness to suffer and die against our willingness to torment and kill. Our strategy is to punish them until they can no longer endure the punishment and must give up. This is the logic of the torture chamber, not of the battlefield. Wars call for sacrifices, but few people on the home front are being asked to make any. Those who lose their sons don't find that the burden of their loss is being shared in any way by the rest of us.

All in all, the American endeavor in Vietnam is more like a factory than like a war. It's a war in which the assembly line ends in the villages of Vietnam. None of the Americans participating are ever reminded that they are involved in anything out of the ordinary—not the scientist who designs the weapons, not the worker and the executive who manufacture them, not the taxpayer who pays for it all. And, at the end of the line, the pilots who deliver the bombs to the Vietnamese villages are as undisturbed as milkmen delivering bottles to the doorsteps of American homes. There are all kinds of factories, and the American machine in Vietnam is a death factory. We are its workers and its consumers, our ships and planes are its moving parts, and the Vietnamese are its raw materials. In this new guise, the war has become so much a part of our lives that we scarcely notice it any longer. In a way, those who claim that the United States is no longer active in Vietnam are right. The war cannot now be seen merely as something we are doing; it is what we are.

I N recent years, the national debate over the war and over foreign policy in general has been framed, as often as not, as a clash between idealism and realism. Political commentators are already framing the coming election in these terms, with President Nixon being seen as the realist and Senator McGovern as the idealist. The opposition between these two viewpoints was most clearly drawn, no doubt, by Machiavelli—himself a realist if there ever was one—who wrote, "The way men live is so far removed from the way they ought to live that anyone who abandons what is for what should be pursues his downfall rather than his preservation; for a man who strives after goodness in all his acts is sure to come to ruin, since there are so many men who are not good. Hence it is necessary that a prince who is interested in his survival learn to be other than good, making use of this capacity or refraining from it according to need." He also wrote, with a kind of frankness that is virtually unknown today, "You must recognize that there are two ways of fighting: by means of law, and by means of force. The first belongs properly to man, the second to animals; but since the first is often insufficient, it is necessary to resort to the second. Therefore, a prince must know how to use both what is proper to man and what is proper to beasts." Princes of many kinds, bestial and otherwise, may have found Machiavelli's distinctions useful in pursuing their aims. But we Americans seem only to confuse ourselves when we frame our debates in these terms. The distinction between realism and idealism, to be of any use, rests on a number of other distinctions, which are getting harder and harder to make. For one, you need to be able clearly to distinguish your own interests from other people's interests, so as to benefit yourself at other people's expense if you are a realist, or, if you are an idealist, so as to benefit others at your own expense. But in the most important matters today, our own and other people's interests overlap to an ever-increasing extent, so that when we hurt them we end up hurting ourselves, too, as we have done in the Vietnam war. You need also to be able to distinguish between what is real and what is fantasy. But many of the "harsh realities" we have been facing up to over the last decade, although they seemed harsh enough, were not real; the world Communist conspiracy we are supposed to be fighting in Vietnam is an example. Finally, you need to be able to distinguish between the possible and the impossible. It might be said that in Machiavelli's world there was a paucity of means, so a prince had to be particularly careful not to exhaust them in hopeless undertakings. But today we have a superfluity of means, and have to be careful *not* to accomplish many dangerous things that are well within our grasp. These may be some of the reasons that, in practice, we have shown ourselves incapable of making a clear choice between a realistic policy and an idealistic policy in any given matter. One would be hard put to it to decide whether we got into the war, for instance, out of an excess of idealism or out of an excess of realism. If anything, we've had an excess of both. With us, either seems to give rise to its opposite. On the one hand, we have the managerial and academic people behind the government scenes who take a professional pride in their suppression of natural feelings, or what they consider their "toughness"—the Pentagon Papers are an example of their work—and, on the other hand, we have the political men out in the open who build their careers on high-sounding phrases and grandiose promises.

Machiavelli wouldn't necessarily have objected to this state of affairs in itself, for he counselled, "One must know how to mask this [bestial] nature skillfully and be a great dissembler. Men are so simple and so much inclined to obey immediate needs that a deceiver will never lack victims for his deceptions." But the elements of Machiavelli's machinery of coercion and deception were co-ordinated and controlled to achieve some large end. In contrast, the elements of the machine we have assembled seem to be perpetually malfunctioning in such a way as to accomplish some unexpected, unwanted end. When we lie, the first people we fool are likely to be ourselves. When we turn beastlike, the first things we devour are our own limbs. When we put forward ideals to cover up self-interested moves, we end by believing in the ideals and letting them entrap us in impossible undertakings—and then, to justify these, we may point with pride to our own self-deception, and maintain that the brutality of our actions is redeemed by the purity of our motives. So instead of having a ruthless, efficient machine that serves our interests we have a ruthless, berserk machine that harms our interests— a two-headed monster at whose bidding the practical, "realistic" managers, cut off from normal human impulses, run amok in a bureaucratic darkness while our spokesmen disgrace themselves before the public with a sentimental and scarcely credible idealism.

The answer isn't to step up the idealism and cut back on the realism, or vice versa. In discussions of public policy, simply to identify any purpose as an "ideal" tends to discredit it. Just by mentioning ideals you awaken echoes of their opposite—the uncontrollable realities. What we need now may be not to promise, or to do, amazing new things but to hold ourselves in check. Perhaps instead of a new set of ideals we need a new sense of limits. The word "idealism" has come to suggest a straining after the impossible. In a time when our foresters are setting forest fires in Vietnam, and our meteorologists are busy making storms, and our bombs are equipped with television cameras, what we need to strain to do is to keep the impossible from occurring.

OCTOBER 14, 1972

ALEXANDER Solzhenitsyn recently wrote, in his speech accepting the Nobel Prize for literature, "Violence, less and less embarrassed by the limits imposed by centuries of lawfulness, is brazenly and victoriously striding across the whole world." In 1972, the primary representatives of victorious violence on the world scene have been the terrorist and the bombardier, each of whom has been having extraordinary success in extending the domain of political violence into new regions. Yet these eminently contemporary figures are the agents of seemingly opposite contemporary trends. The terrorist is an agent of the trend toward politicizing every aspect of life. He wants to bring war into the living room and the bedroom—not to mention the airport, the airplane, the ocean liner, the university, the office building, and the public square. He is so obsessed by politics that distinctions—between political life and private life, between the soldier and the civilian, between the adult and the child—have vanished from his mind. Daily life becomes his enemy. The family picnicking on the grass, the schoolchild at his desk, the elderly couple out for an evening stroll—all are his foes and his potential victims. His program is to charge all innocent, ordinary things with uncertainty and fear, so that people everywhere must live with the possibility that any sports event may turn into a massacre and the morning mail may blow up in their faces. The bombardier, on the other hand, has become the chief representative of a trend toward depoliticizing. Whereas the terrorist is white-hot, the bombardier is cool. The Arab guerrilla is wholly possessed by his cause, but the B-52 crewman may hardly give a thought to what ends he serves. He may hardly consider himself at war. And the people at home who send him on his missions can also remain unconcerned. His way of fighting takes the sting and the passion out of war, both for himself and for his country. Yet the bombardier, like the terrorist, is an eraser of boundaries, both legal and national. Women and children are massacred by the bombs of both of them. So the terrorist, agent of hysteria, and the bombardier, agent of apathy, arrive, in the end, at the same point. Some people today are more inclined to inveigh against hysteria and the brutal, face-to-face murders that it makes possible; others prefer to inveigh against apathy and the "impersonal" killing that *it* makes possible. The truth is that both states of mind are murderous.

Of course, the extension of violence into all departments of life was largely accomplished decades ago. The terrorist achieved his masterpiece in the universal, undiscriminating terror of the Hitler and Stalin regimes, and the bombardier achieved universal scope for his variety of terror with the invention of nuclear weapons. And yet, as Solzhenitsyn notes, in recent years there have been new breakdowns of the boundaries that protected us from violence. There once was a time when violence was seen as a means of last resort. Men employed it to get what they wanted after talking had failed. Violence then was usually directed toward some particular, concrete end, such as crushing the resistance of an enemy. Now we employ violence in a different way: we begin with violence, and we use it not so much to accomplish a particular end directly as to prove a point to a third party. Violence has become our method of communication. The terrorist calls his violence "symbolic." Its aim is not to bring the oppressor to his knees, or even to weaken him directly, but, rather, to "educate," or to politicize, the world by making headlines with spectacular explosions and murders. Almost any explosions and murders will do. Consider the recent killings at Lod Airport, in Israel. In that episode, Japanese gunmen killed, among others, a number of Puerto Rican Protestants on a pilgrimage to the Holy Land. This was meant to aid the cause of Palestinian refugees. But how could the deaths of Puerto Ricans at the hands of Japanese help the Palestinians? According to the logic of the terrorists, it taught the world some sort of "lesson" about the desperate, insane resolve of the Arabs not to stop at anything, no matter how unrelated to their cause, until their demands were met. It was as though, in their frustration at not being able to strike effectively at their real foe, Israel herself, they had taken the innocent people of the world hostage. These victims, at least, were easily accessible to them. And the lack of discrimination in the choice of victims has gone even further—to the point where the connection between "revolutionary acts" and the particular revolutions they are meant to advance is often so tenuous that the act affords no clue to the identity of the revolutionary group or the nature of its cause. For instance, a while back a bomb went off at the New School for Social Research here, yet the people at the New School were simply at a loss to know who their foe had been. Had it been anti-Castro Cubans? Or pro-Castro Cubans? Had it been Puerto Rican nationalists? Or a group opposing the war? Or a group favoring the war? In instances like this, the survivors of the attack must wait for the scrawled note in the mail letting them know who is claiming "credit" for the bloodshed.

And even then they are sometimes left in the dark, for a number of groups may vie in claiming credit for crimes they did not commit.

In the case of the bombardier and those who dispatch him on his missions, a similar logic has come into play. They, too, are not out to accomplish anything directly so much as they are out to prove a point. The bombardier's violence, too, is symbolic; that is, it is carried out more for the sake of appearances than to accomplish concrete ends. His bombing is undertaken as a demonstration to third parties of our "toughness" and our "resolve." A memo in the Pentagon Papers, for instance, describes our aim in Vietnam this way: "However badly SEA [Southeast Asia] may go over the next 1–3 years . . . we must have . . . been tough . . . gotten bloodied, and hurt the enemy very badly. We must avoid harmful appearances which will affect judgments by, and provide pretexts to, other nations . . . regarding U.S. policy, power, resolve, and competence to deal with [its] problems." Interestingly, among the nations most often mentioned as those we are trying to impress with our toughness is Egypt—a nation we tend to hold accountable for the activities of the Palestinian terrorists. So it emerges that we are engaged in a global shadow war in which all the victims are proxies. The guerrillas kill scores of innocent people at airports in the Middle East, and we retaliate by killing scores of innocent people in Indo-China. Just as the Palestinian guerrillas, who are unable to get at the source of their difficulties, the nation of Israel, kill Puerto Ricans instead, we, who are unable to strike at our presumed real adversaries, China and Russia, must content ourselves with killing Vietnamese to show our power and resolve. And the victims of our bombing, including the villagers of Vietnam, Laos, and Cambodia, are as bewildered about our purposes as the people at the New School were about the purposes of the presumed revolutionaries who bombed them. What do the villagers of Indo-China know of the arcane geopolitical reasoning of our experts? To explain ourselves, we, too, must resort to little notes delivered after the fact—in this case, the millions of propaganda leaflets we drop over Indo-China explaining why the bombs have fallen. For Vietnam in itself is no more a threat to the United States than the Puerto Rican pilgrims were to the Palestinians. As for our direct dealings with the Chinese and the Russians, we find it more expedient to stick to friendly, televised summit conferences and grain deals.

The violence of the terrorist and the bombardier has broken the final restraint—the limits and the direction imposed on violence by its own purpose. This kind of violence does not single out a particular foe but treats us all as foes. And whether we are threatened by the bombs that fall from overhead or by the bombs that come from the underground, we are all held hostage by every determined fanatic who has some point to prove. What is the real message of all this symbolic killing? When the connections between violent acts and the causes they are meant to promote are as tenuous as the connection between the massacre of Puerto Rican pilgrims and the plight of Palestinian refugees, and as tenuous as the connection between the bombing of Indo-China and our competition with the Russians and the Chinese, then it may be said that the acts are without specific content. What is left is only the willingness to kill—it no longer matters whom or for what reason. Perhaps that is the real message, sent out over and over, in so many forms. To take human life is undoubtably a fearsome thing. The political powers in the world wish to be feared and taken seriously. They prove their seriousness by killing. By killing, they show that, whatever it is they mean—and this becomes harder to discern with every day that passes—*they really mean it*.

So the messages fly back and forth—every one with a bomb enclosed.

OCTOBER 28, 1972

T HE framers of our Constitution were marvellous cynics when it came to power and the love of power. They saw no chance of eliminating selfishness and ambition from the political scene, and so they adopted clever stratagems for harnessing these qualities to achieve constructive ends. They gave political men wide scope in our democracy. They gave them the whole turbulent, disorderly stage of democratic politics. But they sharply limited the governmental power to be won on that stage, and, what is more, they divided up such power as could be won so that even the most successfully ambitious men always found themselves pitted against other successfully ambitious men. In a time like ours, when the Constitution seems to be unravelling, bit by bit, before our eyes, the wisdom of these arrangements is particularly clear. For in recent years powers ordinarily held separate in our system have shown signs of fusing into a single, overwhelming, potentially repressive force. Just within the last few weeks, the executive branch, having wholly taken over the warmaking power from Congress, has made a bold assault on Congress's powers of appropriation by proposing a bill that would give the President the power to cut spending anywhere in the budget. At the same time, the executive branch has pushed legislation that would weaken the jurisdiction of the courts in the matter of school busing. Congress, in the meantime, has challenged the Supreme Court in other matters, most notably through the crime bills. And even the Court itself—that weak sister among the branches of the federal government in the game of usurping new powers from the other branches—is exercising such feeble illegitimate influence as it can muster: an aide to Chief Justice Burger is discovered over on Capitol Hill lobbying for the weakening of a bill to provide legal protection for consumers, in order to keep the courts from being burdened with too heavy a load. Meanwhile, the membranes that are meant to seal the government off from illegitimate influence by other centers of power in the society have grown steadily more porous. Money flows into campaign coffers at an unprecedented rate from corporations, and the favors flow back from Congress and the President. Military procurers, instead of protecting the taxpayer, increasingly defraud him by entering into lucrative partnerships with industrial contractors. And the military secures its position with Congress and the President by extensive lobbying and by its own system of favors, thereby completing the circle.

Throughout these upper reaches of our society, power, like a river that has overflowed its banks, has been spilling out of the channels prescribed for it by tradition and by law. As the duties, rights, and restraints of positions of responsibility blur and wash away, men at every level of our hierarchies are dreaming of new powers and new fields of activity. Executives of I.T.T. begin to talk among themselves of overthrowing a government in Chile. Officers in Vietnam inaugurate a secret bombing campaign on their own authority. Officers at home get busy spying on American citizens. F.B.I. agents and other security agents, not content with merely detecting political misbehavior, start to encourage it and provoke it, the better to make arrests. The Justice Department, restless within the bounds of law enforcement, tries its hand at politics and bends the law to serve electoral purposes. And as roles blur, in the law-enforcement agencies and elsewhere, the very definitions of power, law, and crime also blur, and eventually disintegrate. A man caught breaking into the Democratic National Headquarters with bugging equipment reasons publicly that he has done nothing wrong, because he committed his crime while he was in the employ of the "top lawman" in the land—the Attorney General. It does not occur to him that if the top lawman orders crimes to be committed, he is acting no longer as the top lawman but as the top lawbreaker. In this man's muddled brain, the role of "the law" has become to sanction crimes. Moreover, in this bewildering new atmosphere even ordinary criminals have lost sight of their proper role. They have lost track of what crime—*their* business—is, and have strayed into legitimate business.

It is only in an atmosphere like this—an atmosphere in which everyone is minding everyone else's business and neglecting his own, an atmosphere in which nothing goes through the proper channels, because the proper channels have been destroyed—that the latest and most serious abuse of official power could have occurred. We are speaking of the recruitment, apparently by high White House aides, of a clandestine, sometimes armed force that was sent into the field to commit crimes against the Nixon Administration's political opponents, including Democratic candidates for the Presidency. In the last several years, we have seen examples of the political use of some law-enforcement agencies, but this is the first time we have seen the organization of an entirely new force accountable only to its political masters. It could turn out to have been an important step in a gradual extinction of our democracy. An incident reported recently in *Time* shows how quickly things can develop. According to *Time*, Bernard Barker, one of those captured at the Democratic National Headquarters, had earlier recruited nine Cubans and assigned them to beat up Daniel Ellsberg on the steps of the Capitol. This they attempted, with only modest success. "Our mission is to hit him— to call him a traitor and punch him in the nose. Hit him and run," Barker is said to have told his hired thugs. It's a lesson in how swiftly the terrifying changes can come once the formal restraints on the uses of power break down.

NOVEMBER 4, 1972

LAST week, we had a letter from a friend of ours, who, like so many other people, has been kept in something like low spirits for almost a decade by the war in Vietnam. "I get service from a cable-TV outfit," he wrote us. "One of its offerings is a channel with the Associated Press wire service on it. On the screen, you see the news going by on the ticker tape. For sound, there's a wholly unrelated program of music. The viewer, though, can't help seeing and hearing the news and the music as one thing, and the results turn out to be strange and unsettling. An item like 'MOTHER AND SON KILLED AS THEIR CAR COLLIDES WITH TRUCK' moves down the screen while a Brahms symphony plays, or you read 'B-52S MAKE RECORD RAIDS IN INDO-CHINA' while you listen to a Beatles song. But the problem isn't an occasional clash between a particular song and a particular news item. It's that there has been some hopeless incongruity between the whole spirit of the news recently and the spirit of music itself—any music. Last Thursday, something magical seemed to happen. I flipped on the A.P. station, and the ticker tape on the screen read, 'THE WHITE HOUSE . . . PRESIDENTIAL AIDE HENRY KISSINGER SAYS "PEACE IS AT HAND." ' They were playing a Burt Bacharach song, and for once

the music sounded right. Later, there was Joan Baez singing John Lennon's
'Imagine.' That fit, too. There were more songs, and they all sounded right.
It seemed that after years of unfailingly surreal juxtapositions the music
programmers couldn't go wrong now. They switched to classical, and this
was even better. There was a Beethoven piano concerto. Then it was a Vivaldi
concerto announcing the good news—here was news worthy of Vivaldi's
trumpets. At last, the news and the music were truly one thing, and the results
were blissful."

Peace is at hand, and one can only be grateful. Yet there's a hidden sting in
it. There never was anything for the United States to gain in Vietnam; nor
was there any chance of our attaining even the mistaken aims we did set
ourselves. And, indeed, as we appear about to leave the war, we have gained
nothing, attained nothing, save the peace itself. Any agreement to end the
war is joyful, but the plain truth is that the agreement we are heading toward
now is the outcome that has been in the cards from the start. It's the outcome
that has been painted on signs at countless demonstrations. It's the one that
President Nixon should have accepted four years ago, when he was elected
(as the Democrats point out), and it's the one that President Johnson should
have accepted eight years ago when *he* was elected (as the Democrats do not
point out). And it's the one we will have to accept at some future time if by
some chance we do not accept it now. What it is, when all is said and done,
is a unilaterally determined and, in effect, unconditional American withdrawal
from Vietnam. All parties to the agreement certainly know this to be so. But
the language of the agreement makes it seem otherwise. The fighting stops.
Within two months, we withdraw our forces and get our prisoners back. That
is the straightforward part. That is the *real* basis for our rejoicing. But what
then? Well, the Vietnamese themselves will work that out—the same Vietnamese who have been slaughtering each other for the last several decades.
But now, according to the terms of the agreement, they will stop slaughtering
each other, and a virtual utopia will bloom at their conference tables. In this
section of the agreement, the framers have allowed their descriptive powers
full scope. Democratic liberties, free elections, reunification, full international co-operation: it's all there in impressive detail, along with an assurance
that the agreement will be "strictly" adhered to—under the supervision of
an international control body. In his famous recent press briefing, Henry
Kissinger remarked, with some amusement, that the arrangements were so
intricate that only one person in the United States government really understood them, and he noted that graduate students of the future would no
doubt enjoy studying their complexities. The graduate students had better

get to work quickly, for it seems likely that not one of the contracting parties expects much of this to actually come to pass. In fact, of all those concerned, it may well be only the American public that is supposed, for a short time, to take it all seriously. For the temporary conviction that these things may come to pass is the "honor" for us in the phrase "peace with honor," which we have heard so often of late. Except in deference to us, neither of the Vietnamese parties probably counts these provisions for much. They know that what really matters is that, after we leave, the North Vietnamese and the Vietcong together will be, by all accounts—including American accounts—incomparably the most powerful force in Indo-China, and that sooner or later, one way or another, they will do what they have been trying to do for more than a quarter-century, international control bodies notwithstanding. Both sides frankly acknowledge this. Thieu has said of the North Vietnamese willingness to sign an agreement, "Their cunning scheme is to beg for a cease-fire now in order to keep their troops in the South to prepare for another offensive in the future." And the North Vietnamese, in their statement announcing the agreement, went on to say, bluntly, "Our people are determined to fight shoulder to shoulder with the fraternal peoples of Laos and Cambodia and inflict a total defeat on the U.S. imperialist aggressors and their lackeys," and they added, for extra emphasis, "We will win!" Mr. Kissinger calls these declarations "rhetoric," but it may well be this rhetoric that spells out the long-term fate of Indo-China. Peace is at hand. But it is not more than peace. It is not "peace with honor," however the word "honor" may be construed. It is not victory. It is not "peace for a generation." It's just peace. There's gladness enough in this, without supplementary claims. We entered the war deceived and fought it for a decade under a series of delusions. We should at least enter the peace with our eyes open.

NOVEMBER 11, 1972

A S we go to press this week, the voters are preparing to go to the polls, and it seems worth noting, just before the decision comes in, that the choice described by both candidates as "the clearest choice in this century" has become in the eyes of most voters something like the murkiest choice in this century. The candidates, instead of steadily growing in presence and in stature as the campaign has proceeded, have seemed to shrink and fade away. The President, apparently as a matter of conscious policy, has virtually disappeared from public view, reducing himself to little more than a voice on the radio. In public, he is represented by dozens of figures called "surrogates," rather as if he were a character in a science-fiction story. Senator McGovern, on the other hand, seems to be everywhere at once, but, for reasons that quite defy analysis, his voice has not seemed to carry and be heard, and even many of the enthusiasts who helped him to victory in the primaries now seem bewildered by his campaign. The contest has taken on an elusive, unreal aspect—Don Quixote tilting against the Invisible Man. The issues, too, have blurred and faded. Two of the most important ones have simply been withdrawn from the forum of public consideration. The war is being held suspended, in what may be a state of calculated irresolution, and the issue of political sabotage and espionage surrounding the Watergate affair cannot be fully joined until after the election (when trials will begin), because of a Presidential decision to maintain silence on the charges. An election is supposed to be an occasion for judgment and decision, but this election has been made into an occasion for postponement and deferral.

It is perhaps not surprising, then, that the opinion polls, which appear to have virtually decided the election in advance, report that the voters are losing interest even as Election Day approaches. The nation's mood is frequently described as apathetic, but it seems to be something worse. There's a sourness in the air, a sense of stubborn withdrawal. According to the opinion polls, President Nixon does well compared to Senator McGovern, but it is *only* when he is compared to Senator McGovern that he does well; the electorate gives him a poor rating on his performance in many areas when it considers him on his own. A few weeks ago, we happened to have a conversation with a farmer in Minnesota, and his views struck us as representing the new mood perfectly. He told us he had once been a Republican but then had become fed up with the Republicans and switched to the Democrats. Then he had become fed up with the Democrats and switched to Wallace (before Wallace switched back to the Democrats). We asked him why he had supported Wallace. "Well, I knew he couldn't win, and I wanted to vote for someone who was going to lose," he told us. We asked him whom he was going to vote for in the coming election. "Whoever looks like he's going to lose," he said. "One of those fellows is going to be in the White House, but I'll be damned if it's going to be with my support."

We speak of mandates at election time, and the word "mandate" implies approbation and assent, even enthusiasm. But this year there are few signs of assent or approbation, let alone enthusiasm, whether for President Nixon or for Senator McGovern. Perhaps the answer is that unless a campaign attains a certain level of reality there simply is no mandate to be won from the voters. It's a sobering thought for whoever wins this strange, phantom election of 1972.

Meanwhile, we read that someone in our government has designed an interesting new plan to send advisers to South Vietnam. . . .

NOVEMBER 25, 1972

I N a recent interview, President Nixon said, "The average American is just like the child in the family." It was a remarkable way for an American President to express himself. The *Times* called it "authoritarian," and it was that, but for the exact parallel one has to look still farther afield: it was Confucian. The President went on to say of the average American, "You give him some responsibility and he is going to amount to something. . . . If, on the other hand, you make him completely dependent and pamper him and cater to him too much, you are going to make him soft, spoiled, and eventually a very weak individual." The President also said he was worried about "those of us who basically have a responsibility of leadership not recognizing that above everything else you must not weaken a people's character." Certainly not. But neither should our leaders seek to discipline or strengthen it. In America, a person's character is his own business, and it is not up to the government to shape it, whether through pampering, or through punishment. A President may, it is true, help set the country's moral tone by the force of his example, but he cannot influence it by direct action. That kind of action, such as the issuing of executive orders, must be reserved for more tangible ends. Take welfare, for instance. The President describes the welfare problem as a matter of character and morals, and in his interview he observed that "this escalation of the numbers on welfare . . . is a result simply of running down what I call the work ethic." Yet it has been in the Nixon years—years in which "the work ethic," far from having been run down, has had constant encouragement at the highest levels—that we have seen the most dramatic rise in the welfare rolls. For when it comes to welfare it is not "the work ethic" that counts for most, it is *work*—opportunities for jobs and training for jobs—and in this area the Administration, like earlier Administrations, has yet to find any answers. The welfare program is meant to supply a livelihood to those who can't otherwise find one—not to build character. If the welfare problem has a moral dimension, it is to be found not in the "character" of the luckless people in the welfare hotels but in the character of the rest of us and of the politicians who have backed away from the sacrifices and efforts that alone offer the hope of a solution. Or take the matter of crime. Here, too, we are offered moralizing, along with symbolic action, instead of the far-reaching and probably costly measures that might actually bring us some relief.

The President speaks of putting an end to "the whole era of permissiveness." The idea seems to be that the government, besides cutting down our allowance ("goodies" is the President's word), is going to stiffen our punishments. But how can a President, who has enough trouble putting an end to particular social ailments, put an end to a "whole era"? President Nixon looks to the Supreme Court to do the job, and promises more "conservative" appointments. But if morality cannot be legislated, it cannot be appointed, either. The Supreme Court, which is not, after all, a junta, will be powerless, even with a new "conservative" cast, to curb a wave of crime, just as the "liberal" Court that preceded it was powerless to cause one. Indeed, if the Court is truly conservative, and so is exceptionally respectful of judicial precedent, its power to effect large social changes will be all the less, whatever those changes might be. The federal government cannot order up a new era as easily as that. For the average American is not a child—not a soft, spoiled child, not a chastened, obedient child. Nor is the government his parent or the guardian of his character and morals. The average American is a grown man or a grown woman. It is *he* who is the guardian—the guardian of his own morals, and the guardian, too, of the government he elects to serve him.

DECEMBER 9, 1972

WHEN the President came to our city the other day, he heard his old friend Norman Vincent Peale praise him from the pulpit as "one of the great peacemakers of history." Now, it is true that the President has talked of peace incessantly. He has extolled the benefits of peace. He has promised a generation of peace. His advisers (by referring to our "peace-time economy" and the like) have implied that we are already at peace. He has told us, through his deputy, that peace is at hand. He has travelled all over the world in the name of peace. He has done everything, in short, but the one thing he must do if he is to deserve the title of peacemaker. He has not made peace.

When the President himself tells us of his efforts to bring peace to the

world, he usually lays the greatest emphasis on his trips to Moscow and
Peking. And, indeed, it may well prove that at some future date, in one part
of the world or another, war will be avoided because of developments set in
motion by the President's trips. But the effect on the war that is with us here
and now seems to have been just the opposite. One might have thought that,
inasmuch as the war in Indo-China was conceived as a front in the Cold
War—a front, that is, in relation to Russia and China—the friendly atmosphere of the trips would constitute a reason for ending the war quickly.
Instead, what seems to have happened is that the President enlisted the co-
operation of these two Great Powers in the war's continuation. For if fear
that these powers might enter an expanded war once operated as a check on
our warmaking, that check now seems to have been removed. The Chinese,
by receiving our President in their capital not long after we had supported
an invasion of their next-door neighbor Laos, appeared, in effect, to acquiesce
in our action. And the Russians, by entertaining the President in Moscow
shortly after he had offered them the extreme provocation of barring their
ships from the harbors of their ally North Vietnam, appeared to remove a
further check. So, whatever the long-term effects of the trips may have been
for a future world peace, the immediate effect was an expansion of a war.
Although mankind as a whole may have benefitted from the restraint shown
by Russia and China, since the danger of war between the Great Powers was
modified, the peoples of Indo-China were made to suffer more, since the
acts of restraint had the effect of sanctioning a wider war on their soil—a
wider war that has continued with unabated intensity to this day. It is as
though, as a price for good relations with us, the Chinese and the Russians
were willing to allow us a freer hand in Southeast Asia. And when they did
so, the war, which had until then been largely the responsibility of the United
States, became, in a sense, an arrangement sanctioned by international agreement, albeit tacit agreement. The Great Powers, having failed for so many
years to bring peace, had, in a rare show of "international coöperation,"
reached a sort of agreement to continue a war. The result has been that in
the year and a half since the President first announced his trip to China what
we've had has not been a stable peace so much as it has been a stable war.
It is as though by tacit international agreement the Great Powers had decided
to turn Vietnam into the sink of the world—where the rest of us, living in
peace ourselves, could vent what is suspicious, brutal, warlike, and vile in our
natures. So Dr. Peale's description of the President as a peacemaker was, at
best, premature. Naturally, we all pray that it was not premature by much,
and that the President's trips will help swiftly bring peace in Indo-China,
and that they will prove, one day, to have helped make other parts of the

world safer, too. But until this happens we must judge that their only immediate effect has been to make the world safer for war.

JANUARY 6, 1973

WAR may seem like an odd place to look for scruples, since wars apparently represent the breakdown of all scruple; yet the history of war holds as many restraints and inhibitions as the history of peace. Many of these sometimes seem odd and quirky. For instance, in our century we have felt more comfortable using bombs than using gas, and we have felt better about killing with bullets than about killing with germs. And although no one has maintained that the lives of women and children are worth more than the lives of men, we particularly want to spare the women and children in war. War may also seem like an odd place to look for justice, but a sense of justice can survive there, too. A sense of justice is grounded in the mental operation by which a person puts himself in someone else's shoes—most particularly a suffering person's shoes. Justice is bound up with equality, and the reason is that to imagine yourself in someone else's shoes you have to imagine him your equal—to recognize that he is as much loved by his family and friends as you are by your family and friends, that he is as able to suffer as you are able to suffer. You must acknowledge that he is as irreplaceable as you know yourself to be. In short, you must acknowledge that he is a man like you. And because you and he are equal, the most primitive law of justice is "An eye for an eye, a tooth for a tooth," and not "Two of his eyes for one of my eyes, ten of his teeth for one of my teeth." And not "One thousand of their lives for one of our B-52s." The bombing of North Vietnam offends our sense of justice. Justice wants adversaries to be equal or nearly equal. It abhors a big man's beating up a child. And when we perform the mental operation of putting ourselves in someone else's shoes, we don't want to find ourselves staring up helplessly at waves of B-52s, just as we don't want to find ourselves strapped to a rack with the torturer approaching. As a nation, we seem to fail utterly to acknowledge that the Vietnamese are people like ourselves. Indeed, we make them disappear from our view even as we kill them, and they lack the means to strike back and so force us to recognize that they are there. We first erase them from awareness and then erase them from the face of the earth.

Perhaps many of our century's wartime scruples (which, it must be said, have been more talked about than honored) have to do with a sense of justice.

For instance, we have a special aversion to killing the wounded or sick in hospitals. We are more protective of the ailing, the dying, and the half dead than we are of the healthy and whole. It is because they are helpless and cannot strike back. They are unarmed men. With them, the inequality in power is beyond argument. They are already threatened from within by wounds or germs, and to threaten them also with bombs seems to impose an unbearable heaping up of misfortune. That is why when, in the midst of Christmas shopping, we heard that our bombers had destroyed the Bach Mai Hospital in Hanoi it came to some of us as the cruelest news of all in a week of cruel news: the most helpless people in a helpless country were dying at the hands of the world's most powerful country using its most powerful machines. It was an event that illuminated the monstrous character of the entire campaign. The disproportion of it—and the injustice—had become total.

JANUARY 13, 1973

I N recent weeks, the war in Vietnam has led the United States into a new relationship with the rest of the world. When the terror bombing of Hanoi began, world opinion—that amorphous institution made up of whatever voices have the strength and the freedom to make themselves heard—seemed, after several years of silence, to reconstitute itself for the occasion. Heads of friendly countries voiced their objection to our bombing and to our whole war policy. The Canadian House of Commons voted unanimously to condemn the bombing. The governments of France, Denmark, and Finland arranged to send funds for medical supplies. So did many private organizations, including the World Council of Churches. Throughout Western Europe, the most highly respected publications likened our actions to those of the Nazis. Boycotts against American ships were proposed in several countries, and one was carried out in Australia. Harold Wilson cancelled a lecture tour of the United States because of "strong feelings" against the bombing. Some governments said nothing, but almost none offered approval or support. As might have been expected, it was in the democratic, not the totalitarian, countries that the deepest revulsion was expressed. There had been waves of protest before, but this was something of greater weight than protest. The world appeared to have reached that degree of near-unanimity of feeling which makes up a prevailing historical judgment that will stand for decades to come. It was as though the war had lasted so long that historical judgment was delivered on it even before it was over. This shift of opinion was the end, not the beginning, of a debate. Decent men all over the world had declared that our war policy had moved beyond argument.

There were several reasons this particular escalation of the war had such a decisive effect. In the first place, it had once been possible for an onlooker to suppose that our government believed that in fighting Vietnamese it was actually fighting "Communism," a force that included such large and credibly menacing powers as Russia and China, but after the President's cordial and friendly visits to Russia and China it became inescapably plain just who our adversary really was: it was only little Vietnam. The true disproportion of the war stood revealed. And since we had nothing to fear and nothing to gain from such a tiny, remote power, even self-interest no longer served as an explanation of the war. Vietnam began to look like a forsaken land where a lunatic giant appears and, having shot up everyone in sight, shoots himself. Also, whereas we had undertaken other escalations in response to real or imagined moves by our adversary, this one we took unilaterally and without any military pretext. We went from the smiles and jokes of the peace talks to the bombing with perfect nonchalance, like one of those teams of torturers who alternate between ingratiating themselves with their victim and beating him up. Finally, since we no longer had large numbers of troops in the south, the excuse that we were "protecting our withdrawal" could not be advanced. In short, the war had been stripped of all its disguises. And the Administration, seeming almost to acknowledge that the debate had ended, and that any justification it offered could only add to the offense, offered no arguments or justifications. The war was now being fought not only without reason but without rationalization. In these circumstances, the world saw the bombing for exactly what it was. It was murder—murder with "no comment."

But just at the moment when the world was finding its voice and uniting to express its horror at the war, the United States seemed to be slipping into a world of its own. In the past, if some Americans had been the world's pre-eminent warmakers, other Americans had been the world's pre-eminent protesters against the war. But at the moment when the world was awakening, the American people as a whole, who are supposedly in the driver's seat of the machine that is crushing Vietnam, were nodding at the wheel. Then, as the Ninety-third Congress got under way, there came some stirrings, and now the country seems to have arrived at a moment of decision—to be poised between a national life of full-time wakefulness and a national life of full-time somnolence.

From the start, our war in Indo-China—even as it took millions of us to a land thousands of miles away—has tended to cut us off from the world. It sent us running all over the world but held us paralyzed in isolation. It held us in a world of our own hallucinatory obsessions, which has now swollen to the point of blotting out the real world altogether. And the real world, for its part, watches in dismay as the United States, which has only to look up for a moment to find, and to rejoin, a world of eased tensions, returns with obsessive fury to hacking away at the bloody mess at its feet which is Vietnam. We went to Vietnam to save the Vietnamese, but the Vietnamese we were saving were imaginary. The real Vietnamese wanted us to leave them alone. Now we are out to save the world, to build a "stable" world, a "generation of peace." This time our beneficiaries are the peoples of the entire world, and once again our beneficiaries don't want our help. Our characteristic vice in the war years has been not so much to defy the world as to deny it, not to see it at all. Now when the Swedish government protests our actions we tell it not to send us its new ambassador. We put him, and his country, out of our sight. In the long run, a nation that encloses itself in a shroud of secrets and lies cannot stand free intercourse with the world. We started by blotting out the truth about our actions in the world, although some of our own people tried to get the message through. (The trial of Daniel Ellsberg started last week.) Now the entire world is trying to tell us the truth about ourselves, and it's the world's turn to be blotted out. We can't make other people close their eyes to what we're doing, but we *can* make them disappear by firmly shutting our own eyes. A recent event at the Pentagon suggests how things can be blotted out. Mr. Jerry Friedheim, the Pentagon spokesman who had been saddled with the job of explaining the bombing to the nation, was asked about the reports that American bombs had hit the hospital of Bach Mai, in Hanoi. He refused to confirm the report, and went as far as to question even the existence of the hospital. He said, "I don't know what the other side may refer to as the Bach Mai Hospital, if indeed there is one." And he was right, of course. There *was* no Bach Mai Hospital.

FEBRUARY 3, 1973

L AST Saturday, at seven o'clock in the evening, the nation, led by President Nixon, marked the end of the war in Indo-China with bell ringings, church services, and a moment of silence. The talk from official quarters was not merely of peace but of a generation of peace, as though we were ushering in a new golden age. But while we were ringing bells, and praying in silence, bombs were being loaded onto American planes on bases in Asia, and before the first twenty-four hours of the "peace" was over, we had flown over a hundred air strikes against targets in Laos and Cambodia. Far from there being a generation of peace, there wasn't even ten minutes of peace. It left us wondering how many times the United States was to celebrate the end of the Indo-China war before the war ended.

In Vietnam, fighting also continued, but our troops and planes were mercifully out of it. And, much as everyone would like to see a generation of peace, an end to the American combat role is all that most of us ever really expected or asked for from this peace. This much has come—at least to Vietnam—and it has come for the best of reasons. It has not come because of Great Power diplomatic triumphs, nor has it come because the United States has attained its objectives in South Vietnam, and it has not come, either, because the United States was defeated in Vietnam. It has come because the American people as a whole rejected this war and wanted it over. Millions of Americans simply loathed the war. They were of all ages and from all walks of life, and were by no means restricted to members of the peace movement. There were very few bellicose or enthusiastic supporters of the war. Most Americans, perhaps, tolerated it uneasily for a while, but many of them did so not because they believed in the war but because they believed in the government and the government said it knew things they did not know, or because they wanted to support the President. These people were put in the position of having to unlearn their trust in their leaders in order to learn the truth about the war. Millions learned that lesson. When it is all far behind us, it may finally be decided that this was a war started by the government and ended by the people. But for the moment this fact is disguised. One reason is that the government took so many years to respond to the public's signal. The public mood of disillusion with the war crystallized sometime around the spring of 1968. Its political manifestation was President Johnson's decision to limit the bombing, start the negotiations, and not run again for the Presidency. The stage seemed set for an end to the war. Then the four-year delay began, and the strain it placed on our political system and on the public's confidence in that system was so great as to constitute an entire fresh tragedy for the country. The public's mood moved from disillusion with the war to disillusion with politics in general. In the last week, one of the most striking signs of the general disillusion has been the refusal of a large portion of the public to believe that the war is ending even now. The willingness of these people to believe the announcement of the end of the war—or, probably, to believe any large piece of news—is one more casualty of the war.

The people's central role in ending the war has also been disguised by another unexpected peculiarity in the events of the last week: the President's manner of presenting the peace to us. The people's will was that we leave Vietnam. The President, when all is said and done, is the people's instrument. In leaving Vietnam, he was doing the country's bidding, and this is all as it should have been. But even as the President responded to the popular will in his actions, he seemed in his words to deny it and to be ashamed of it. He refused to acknowledge our rejection of the war. Instead, he congratulated us on our steadfastness in supporting the war, and assured us we were leaving now only because our aims had been achieved—because we had attained peace "with honor." That is to hide our country's light under a bushel. The American people were not steadfast in this cause, and it is a fine thing. We are actually leaving the war without attaining our war aims, and this is to our credit. It is too late for jubilation and congratulations. But hope is reborn with this peace. It lies not in the fact that we fought the war but in the fact that we are, finally, putting an end to it.

FEBRUARY 17, 1973

DURING the war years, it often seemed that Americans on opposite sides of the war issue had developed greater bitterness toward each other than any American had developed toward the Vietnamese foe— almost as though the war were not really the issue that was dividing us but only one irritant in a purely private quarrel among ourselves. And now that an American withdrawal from Vietnam appears to be finally almost completed, it has indeed turned out that our quarrels with "the enemy" have been easier to resolve than our quarrels among ourselves. The peace has come, but we Americans remain embattled. To the North Vietnamese foe we are promising gifts—as we should be doing. If the figures that are being bandied about on the amount of aid we are ready to hand over are correct—figures ranging from two and a half to four and a half billion dollars—we'll have to send the B-52s back over Hanoi after all, this time to drop bales of money. But to Americans who refused to fight the war we are promising punishment. While the Vietnamese who were shooting at our troops are cashing their United States checks in Hanoi as they prepare to get on with taking over the South, the American draft evaders and deserters, who opted out of the shooting, will remain in exile, for the President has said that they must pay a price, and the price is a "criminal penalty." The American people have emerged from the war exhausted, but the American authorities have emerged from the war with a chip on their shoulders. They are returning home from their inglorious foreign adventures with wounded pride, with little disposition to face the truth about it all, and with old scores to settle. It will be the job of the American people now to calm these edgy, defiant, war-trained leaders and gently but firmly draw them into peaceful ways. During the war, some radical groups had the slogan "Bring the war home." And the war did come home. Now we have a peace, and we must bring the peace home.

II. THE WAR COMES HOME

APRIL 28, 1973

WE were in Washington in the momentous days before and after
the Watergate story broke open and the walls around the White
House—walls of silence, deception, and denial—came tumbling
down. We arrived in a grim and worried town a week or so before the
President released his aides to testify before Congress. All in all, the past few
months had been a confusing time in the headlines. In Cambodia, American
planes were at work turning one more country into a desolation of casualties
and refugees; at home, the citizenry had been displaying its outrage at the
price of red meat; and on Capitol Hill prominent men of both parties were
announcing that the United States Constitution was threatened. This last
was a matter that some people seemed to see as a quarrel between politicians—
a wrangle strictly local to Washington—rather than as something of general
interest. Moreover, in the public eye all these events—the boycott, the
bombing, the battle for the Constitution, and the then still-simmering Watergate story—were apparently unrelated, like the acts of a three-ring circus.
It was as though Americans were living not in one nation but in several,
which were not so much divided against each other as disconnected from
each other. In this slack, dispiriting atmosphere, a growing number of legislators had been sending up fearful warnings. Senator Edmund S. Muskie,
not a man renowned for reckless overstatement, had warned of "one-man
rule," and so had Senator George S. McGovern. Senator John C. Stennis—
no hothead—had worried publicly from his hospital bed about the erosion
of the powers of Congress, and, speaking of the war power, had declared
that "the fabric of our Republic . . . cannot long withstand the strain of asking
citizens for the ultimate sacrifice without permitting them to participate in
the decision of whether to make that sacrifice." Senator J. William Fulbright

had expressed fear that we might "pass on, as most of the world has passed on, to a totalitarian system." In the press, it was becoming popular to refer to our Constitutional government as an "eighteenth-century-system." Remarks like these sent a chill of real fear down our spine. Yet not only were the warnings evidently failing to stir the country but they were failing, it sometimes appeared, to stir even the men who were issuing them. The country's listlessness sometimes seemed to have reached the very men who were trying to rouse the country out of it. At the beginning of last week, the country seemed to be sliding into a dangerous stupor. By the end of the week, it seemed about to revive and to reorganize itself around one issue—Watergate.

When we got to Washington, we went first to the Capitol, to talk with Senator Mike Mansfield, the Senate Majority Leader, who has spent thirty years in Congress, serving in both the House and the Senate. He welcomed us into the Majority Leader's office—an ample eighteenth-century room with complex gilt-edged molding on the ceiling and walls—and poured us a cup of coffee. There were cookies and brownies on a low table in the center of the room. We sat down across the table from our host. Senator Mansfield holds his chin upraised, and his gaze often seems fixed on something high in the distance. His expression is perfect, unreadable poker. The answers to the questions we asked came back loud and clear, with astonishing promptness, in a high, flat voice speaking short, brisk sentences without any hemming and hawing.

We asked Senator Mansfield about the state of the Constitution.

"It comes down to two fundamental issues," he said. "One is impoundment. The other is executive privilege." The President, of course, had not yet made his announcement. "There is some room for impoundment, but not to the tune of twelve billion dollars. The President is entitled to some executive privilege, but it certainly doesn't apply to all present and former employees. There is no Constitutional ground for that."

We asked whether, in his opinion, this was a full-scale Constitutional crisis.

"Not yet. It could come to that, and it will if these actions are not reversed."

"Are we really headed in the direction of one-man rule?" we asked.

"The trend is in that direction. But Congress has only itself to blame for having its power diluted. It handed its power over to the President on a silver platter. It gave away its war power several decades ago, and now, because of this last war, it's waking up to the fact. It's finding that power is easy to give away but hard to get back."

It struck us that here was one possible explanation of why Congress sometimes seemed muted even as it delivered dire warnings. Presumably, it's more difficult to get indignant at yourself than at some other culprit. We went on to ask, "If there is a threat of one-man rule, doesn't that mean that we are in danger of losing our republican form of government?"

"No. I wouldn't say that," Senator Mansfield replied, with his usual alacrity. "Right now, the balance of power is dangerously tilted in the direction of the executive. If the trend continues, the Constitution will become null and void and worthless."

"But doesn't that mean that we will lose the Republic?" we asked. "Wouldn't we then have lost our liberty and everything that goes with it?"

"I can't envisage those things in the United States. The Congress is waking up now. We have a suit against impoundment in the courts. We have leg-islation started on executive privilege and impoundment. Even if the Con-stitution becomes, shall we say, weakened, I can't see us losing our liberty. Of course, it's true that the media are under attack, too, and this increases the sense of uneasiness."

"Then there's no real danger of the Constitution's collapsing?"

The Senator answered with a declaration of personal conviction. "I still have great faith in the Constitution, in our institutions, and in our freedoms: the freedom of speech, the freedom of assembly—peaceful assembly, that is." He raised an admonitory forefinger. "I guess it's just an enduring faith I've had all my life. If I lost that faith, it would be time for me to resign as a senator."

"But if we lose the Constitution—" we began, but the Senator interjected "We won't lose the Constitution!" and rose to his feet.

We next started in the direction of the law firm of Covington and Burling, on Sixteenth Street, just a few hundred yards from the White House, for we were to meet John Sherman Cooper, the former Republican senator from Kentucky, there; he had retired from the Senate several months earlier, and was now practicing law. But first we stopped in at the Everett McKinley Dirksen Senate Office Building, where three subcommittees were holding joint hearings on the subject of executive privilege. At this particular session, as it happened, Attorney General Richard G. Kleindienst had asserted unlim-ited executive privilege for all two and a half million employees of the executive branch, and had just told the senators that if they had any objections they could impeach the President. Now, with Kleindienst still in the witness chair, the committee members had, to their evident surprise, wandered into the subject of impeachment. Senator Sam Ervin pointed out that if Congress couldn't call witnesses from the executive branch, it probably couldn't get the evidence for an impeachment, to which Kleindienst replied that no evidence was needed—only the votes of enough senators and representatives were necessary. Ervin then pointed out that the Chief Justice of the Supreme Court presides over an impeachment trial, and would be likely to require some evidence. Kleindienst replied that Congress could then impeach the Chief Justice. Earlier, he had said that if they didn't like aspects of his own behavior they could impeach him, too. The senators were visibly shaken up and embarrassed by all this talk of impeachment.

We continued on our way to see Senator Cooper. When we arrived, he showed us into an office adorned with photographs, most of them of the Senator in the company of Presidents. Senator Cooper is a tall, slender man with a gentle, almost shy manner. We asked for his views on the Constitutional questions before the country. As it happened, he said, he was preparing a speech on just that subject, and he asked us if we would like to hear some of the ideas as he had sketched them out. We said we certainly would.

Senator Cooper's view of the country's recent history turned out to be a kindly one. There were no villains in it; indeed, Senator Cooper spoke hardly a word that could be construed as direct criticism of anyone at all. The whole atmosphere was agreeable, in contrast to the conversation about impeachment in the Senate hearing room. Senator Cooper began by reviewing the performance of recent Presidents. Truman's period was one of "high hope, generosity abroad, and confidence in our role as guardian of the world's security." Eisenhower was "much loved and respected, probably universally respected." Kennedy "brought new spirit to the country, and probably to the whole world." Johnson opened up new opportunities for disadvantaged people here at home. On Vietnam, "his advisers misled him." President Nixon, Senator Cooper said, is probably "the hardest worker" of them all, and is also "an excellent student." Furthermore, he "may be the most *determined* President." Turning to the question of the war power, the Senator noted that in the nineteen-fifties Congress gave over its power willingly and not even the press raised any objections. "The bilateral treaties all had the same language. If an ally was attacked, we would go to its aid but would do so 'in accordance with Constitutional processes,'" the Senator noted. "Now, in my judgment the Congress's only real power in this business lies in the power of the purse. The war-power legislation can't do it very well. It allows the President to go in for thirty days without approval. That's enough. Once the troops are in and get fired on, the national honor's at stake, and the President assumes his responsibilities as Commander-in-Chief. You can only cut off the funds. Of course, Congress is reluctant to do that." The Senator laughed. He saw impoundment as an "inchoate area," for which it would also be difficult to

frame effective legislation. Both the impoundment issue and executive privilege might prove to be non-litigable areas as well, and the courts might
simply decline to hand down rulings.

We asked Senator Cooper whether he would care to comment on the
Watergate story.

A look of distaste and uneasiness passed over his face, and he said, "Too
much has been said about that already."

We remarked to Senator Cooper that he did not offer much hope of
recourse in any area.

"Well, there is some question whether this system is meeting its objectives,
and more effort must be made in these areas I have been speaking of. But
I'm optimistic. I believe that the majority has common sense. And I believe
also that the courts, which really are the backbone of our system, will protect
the delicate balance between the other branches from getting too far out of
line."

Just around the corner from Covington and Burling is another law firm—
Clifford, Warnke, Glass, McIlwain, and Finney. Its senior partner is Clark
Clifford, who was a close adviser of Presidents Truman, Kennedy, and Johnson, and who finally became Secretary of Defense under Johnson. That day,
he had testified at the hearing we'd attended, but not until after we had left.
We learned later that Senator Ervin had described Mr. Clifford's presentation
as "the most total and succinct statement I've ever read on executive privilege."
We met Mr. Clifford in his offices in the late afternoon. He introduced us
to Miss Mary M. Weiler, who has been his secretary for forty-five years, and
then he showed us into a long, spacious, dimly lit office. There were Oriental
scatter rugs on top of wall-to-wall carpeting, and, behind his desk, a row of
windows with the blinds drawn. Mr. Clifford is a distinguished-looking gray-
haired man with something delicate and precise in the set of his mouth.

Mr. Clifford offered to show us his view, and parted the slats of one blind.
In the foreground, and below us, was the White House; in the back was the
Washington Monument. We asked Mr. Clifford about the mood in Washington and in the country. He answered us in soft-spoken, measured sentences:

"This country has traditionally rested on a deep sense of decency and
compassion and on a respect for freedom. But it's not being led in that
direction now. Recently, we saw a drive to help the nation's unfortunate. But
that is changing. There was an attempt to strengthen the rights of the individual. Now that's all gone. Instead, we're being guided by a driving ambition to make the country more powerful. Power, armed might, a reputation
for 'toughness'—these are the goals with which the present Administration

seems to be replacing our old purposes. And the new aims are being pushed forward with proved public-relations methods of salesmanship. In the process, I believe, deception has been practiced. Even our prisoners returning home are encouraged to sound a sales theme. No public-relations detail is overlooked in these campaigns. I find it cold, pragmatic, and chilling."

We asked whether he took seriously the warnings about the nation's losing its system.

"I'm not prepared to say we're about to lose it, because I still think the American people will wake up to the enormity of what's been going on. The Watergate case may help in this respect."

"What *has* been going on?"

"It is the centralization of governmental power in the presidency. The executive branch is engaged in a planned campaign to denigrate the legislative branch and in a planned campaign to malign the press. The press has grown muted already. It feels obliged always to give 'two sides' to every story. This is an entirely new concept in journalism. The intention is to shake the people's confidence in Congress and the press, so that in the end they will trust only the President. If we Americans aren't careful, we could end up controlled and regimented to an extent never realized before. President Nixon has a vision of America which encompasses his statement that 'the average American is just like the child in the family.' A child has to be led, and President Nixon sees himself as that leader. An American way of life that we older people have known and taken for granted is beginning to seem not secure at all. This is the first time in twenty-five years that *fear* has become a recognizable, vital force in Washington. It is the fear of retaliation against anyone who attempts to impede this march toward the Administration's goals. Sometimes one can even see a startling resemblance between these developments and similar developments in countries where one-man rule has developed."

The next day, Senator Barry Goldwater made his statement: "The Watergate. The Watergate. It's beginning to be like Teapot Dome. I mean, there's a smell to it. Let's get rid of the smell." The issue, he said, was "Can you trust Dick Nixon?" In retrospect, his statement appears to have been the first intimation that this story, which many people had thought to be one that *should* shake the nation, actually *would* shake the nation.

On the same day, Representative John B. Anderson, of Illinois, the Chairman of the House Republican Conference, made his statement: "The Attorney General has thrown down the gauntlet. If this Congress is to preserve even a semblance of integrity and independence, it must act immediately to nullify the sweeping claim of executive power asserted by the Attorney General."

• • •

The morning after that, Senator Cooper got in touch with us and said he would like to add that not only did the three branches of the government have to maintain their delicate balance but "the people also have to be able to maintain their trust in the government as a whole."

A few days later, we called on Senator Muskie in a small auxiliary office he keeps in the basement of the Capitol. Among the senators who had spoken of the danger to our system, Senator Muskie had shown himself to be one of the most strongly aroused. At the hearing on executive privilege, it was he who had most persistently drawn out the Attorney General's testimony, and it was his questioning that had clarified the full, sweeping implications of the executive-privilege claim. We had noticed flashes of real anger in his questioning. In addition to having warned earlier of one-man rule, he had spoken at the hearing of proposed legislation that would restrict the flow of information from the government as leading us toward "the silence of democracy's graveyard." The familiar tall figure welcomed us into his office. He was looking trim and vigorous in a blue suit and a red tie—fresher and more robust, we thought, than when we had last seen him, on television on the campaign trail. A couple of weeks before, we knew, he had offered the one-man-rule speech to television on behalf of the Democratic leadership of Congress in rebuttal to the President's recent nationwide speech in which he announced a ceiling on meat prices and went on to attack Congress for its budgetary policies. The networks had turned Senator Muskie down. We asked the Senator about that rejection.

"It's clear now that television is a critical instrument of enormous power which can be a great influence in shifting power from one branch to another. And this occurs without any Constitutional amendment or any decision on the part of the people. Congress has now developed a system for designating spokesmen to answer the President, but the networks won't put us on the air. Yet if it's established that *one* branch of the government—the executive branch—alone has the right to speak to the entire nation, and therefore *for* the entire nation, depriving the other branches of that right, then we've taken the step: the system has broken down."

We asked him what he thought one-man rule might look like in America.

"You don't have to look down the road," he said. "You can look at what's already happening. Probably the man in the street isn't worrying about executive privilege or impoundment directly. But Watergate may get him worried. You know, I was giving a speech near Galveston, Texas, the other day—not the most radical place you can think of—and the people in the audience were asking how the President had got so much power. I answered, 'Because *you* people gave him that mandate; a man like him shouldn't be given such a mandate,' and there was a wave of applause in the room."

"But how can the people grasp the seriousness of the situation when the Congress refuses to reassert its own power?" we asked.

"Don't forget where the power comes from," he said. "It's from the people. And if Congress loses access to the people through television and the other media, then it's powerless to mobilize the people's support and to win the battle of public opinion. And when Congress is cut off from popular pressure it can be mobilized by other pressures—the interest groups. The President can organize opinion. For instance, he was able to organize opinion on the war. He simply comes out the winner in the P.R. race."

Here, it occurred to us, was another possible answer to the question of why the country, and even the Congress, seemed so muted. Communication between Congress and the people had been disrupted by Presidential pre-emption of the main channels of public access. It was in the nature of Congress not to speak or act boldly, or even to reassert its Constitutional power, until it had received a strong signal from the people. It did not have the executive's capacity for initiating elaborate public-relations campaigns to influence opinion. And without greater command of television Congress was cut off. It was only talking to itself—or, worse, discrediting itself as a disruptive element, disturbing the great calm of the Presidential consensus.

We mentioned some of this to Senator Muskie and asked if the term "one-man rule" had a frightening import for him.

"If I went as far as to say that all this could one day lead to a Hitler or a Stalin regime, that would be regarded as unfair or inaccurate—as a little too much. Look what happened to McGovern when he merely *mentioned* Hitler. I suspect that things like the Kleindienst testimony are giving people an idea of what *could* be, though. It wasn't just what he said, you know; it was his attitude. So casual and arrogant. When he sat there and said, 'You do not need facts to impeach the President,' he was saying that the impeachment of the President is a *political* trial." Senator Muskie struck his fist in his palm. He was speaking with strong feeling now. He continued, "And if that is so, why, then, *any* trial could be a political trial. If you look at things that way, then *facts* mean nothing, *legality* means nothing, and *legitimacy* means nothing; only *power* means anything—power employed by the man in charge for *political* ends. This has been the thinking behind authoritarian government since the world began. And in this Administration everything seems to come down to political power. This was the most frightening part of the testimony to me— even more frightening than the part about executive privilege itself. The whole idea behind our system is that power is divided. But now the President can even make war *all on his own*. He announces that the war is over, says that he's won, and then he goes right on, with no color of authority. Experience tells us that when power is concentrated it is not likely to be used for the benefit of the great masses of people. And the least fortunate are always the first to suffer. This is the lesson learned by the makers of our Revolution. It's the basis of what we've practiced for two hundred years, and I don't want to see it lost."

We thanked the Senator, and went over to the Justice Department, where we were to meet Donald E. Santarelli, an Associate Deputy Attorney General who was just about to take on a new job—head of the Law Enforcement Assistance Administration. The Justice Department is a five-story, block-square building with office numbers running into the thousands. Here and there on the corridor walls of this large bureaucratic building are framed photographs of other large bureaucratic buildings (as if the building itself had put up photographs of its building friends). When we arrived in the anteroom of Mr. Santarelli's office, we found it in something of an uproar, with files being sorted and packed for the move to his new job. Shortly, he came out and invited us into his office. Mr. Santarelli is a thin, restless-looking man in his mid-thirties with an authoritative, booming, rapid-fire voice and a set of expansive, vigorous gestures to go with it. We had the impression of almost a superabundance of energy. On one wall of his office there were photographs with inscriptions by L. Patrick Gray, the Acting Director of the F.B.I., and Attorney General Kleindienst. An American flag stood behind his desk. We knew that Mr. Santarelli had had a hand in drafting many of the Nixon Administration's crime bills, and we asked him to tell us something about the job he was leaving.

"This is an idea shop," he told us, putting his feet up on his desk. "We work on concepts, develop them, delve into them." He gestured broadly toward piles of paper on his desk. "What you see before you is thoughts. We don't handle cases; we work on the large picture. 'Give me a plan,' the President says. Or 'Here's a concept. Flesh it out. Give me some options.' This job didn't exist in its present scope before this Administration. It was developed by the President for me."

"How does it all work?" we asked.

"Well, we might start with an analysis. Then it might turn into a combination of any of the following—a Presidential speech, a legislative package, a press release. We'll develop the idea at each stage. Of course, there's a lot of interface. I work closely with the White House staff. Our office devised a system to reform the administration of justice in Washington. In 1951, there were only two thousand one hundred felony prosecutions in Washington a year. Now there are four thousand two hundred felony prosecutions. We have more than tripled the number of felony judges. But none of these things got as much attention in the press as some relatively unimportant legislation such as no-knock and preventive detention."

"How did you first get in touch with Mr. Nixon?"

"I was working on the Hill as special counsel to the Senate Judiciary Committee, and I was one of the few staffers on the pro-prosecution side up there. Most of the guys were pro-defense."

"But how can there be such a thing as a pro-defense side and a pro-prosecution side in a situation like that?" we asked.

"There shouldn't be, but there is. I was prosecution-oriented. Anyway, that was the President's program: to 'strengthen the peace forces' against those concerned exclusively with defense."

We went on to ask Mr. Santarelli for his reflections on the Constitutional questions that were on our mind. As a point of departure, we gave him an article in the April 23rd *Newsweek* to look at. It was by Kevin P. Phillips, a former campaign aide to President Nixon, and was called "Our Obsolete System." Phillips suggested that the system of balancing governmental powers against each other was a mistake conceived by Montesquieu. "Our Constitution freezes Montesquieu's mistake in legal concrete," he wrote. "Congress's separate power is an obstacle to modern policymaking. . . . In sum we may have reached a point where separation of powers is doing more harm than good by distorting the logical evolution of technology-era government." Phillips suggested, as a remedy, calling a Constitutional convention to abolish the separation of powers and perhaps establish a parliamentary system. We asked Mr. Santarelli what he made of all this.

"I don't agree with his proposal," he said. "But I like the substance of his concepts. His main point is that the separation of powers is obsolete in modern decision-making, and I agree. They didn't have modern affirmative-decision-making in the eighteenth century to the extent that we do. They didn't need such hurried, precise decisions. They didn't have the kind of dynamic national purpose that we have now. The balance of power turns every issue into a great political power struggle, and obscures the business of actually running the country, of reaching national goals."

We asked our old question—was there a Constitutional crisis?

"We're living in a very historic time," he said. "You can see the manifestations everywhere. This is a time of great changes. The legislative branch, which was pre-eminent, has gradually lost power to the judiciary and the executive."

"How do you mean, the judiciary?"

"I mean the so-called judicial revolution—the Supreme Court rulings in favor of civil rights and criminal rights. All that is changing now. But the liberals gained power by it. They benefitted. The strengthening of the judiciary—or the judicial usurpation, as I would call it—was an unbalancing element."

"And the executive?"

"The executive branch has gained power. It was *inevitable*. Its basic design is geared for efficiency; it has adopted management tools—computers, executive techniques. Congress fell behind, and now it is fussing in a stew of its own making. An unpopular war has given Congress a toehold again, and it's taking up things like executive privilege. But executive privilege isn't a legal question; it's a political question. That's the key thing. Don't be fooled. These battles are basically political. Each age defines the Constitution for its own needs. It's evolutionary. I'm sounding like Ramsey Clark here. The Clarkian view takes the Fourteenth Amendment as very flexible and accordionlike, but if you so much as mention changing the Fourth Amendment, against unreasonable searches and seizures, in order to bring it up to date with modern prosecution needs, you find it's locked in stone. That's natural. If you're on the side that's gaining power, you praise the changes. If the changes mean you lose power, you bitch about them."

"Which are you doing?" we asked.

"I'm mildly praising."

"But this isn't exactly a strict-constructionist viewpoint," we observed.

"No, sir. That's a misnomer. The Constitution is flexible. Period. Your point of view depends on whether you're winning: 'My side won! I'm happy!' If you're against busing, you think an anti-busing amendment should be in the Constitution; if you're for busing, you complain that the Constitution is being wrecked. The Constitution isn't the real issue in this; it's how you want to *run the country*, and achieve national goals. The language of the Constitution is not at issue. It is what you can interpret it to mean in the light of modern needs. In talking about a 'Constitutional crisis' we are not grappling with the real needs of running the country but are using the issues for the self-serving purpose of striking a new balance of power. Times are changing now. The Constitution is flexible." And then he added a remark that no one we had recently spoken to in Washington would have fully disagreed with. "Today, the whole Constitution is up for grabs."

• • •

While we had been talking with Senator Muskie and Mr. Santarelli, the President had been telling the nation of "major developments" in the Watergate story.

A short time later, we ran into Senator Fulbright in the Dirksen Senate Office Building. He was on his way to a vote, and he invited us to ride with him in the little subway car to the Capitol. News of the President's Watergate announcement was just reaching Capitol Hill.

We asked Senator Fulbright how large he thought the stakes of the dangers he had referred to were.

"*If* we don't turn things around, *if* we throw over the Constitution and establish executive rule, then, in the long run, we might expect the same kind of ruthless tyranny that you had under Hitler or Stalin. Don't expect some sort of simple, *benign* dictatorship. This country never goes halfway. That's not our style. We go all the way. You've seen what we did in Vietnam. Our capacities are great. We can display great compassion and show great concern over one little girl, perhaps, or maybe a dog. But we can be ruthless and savage, too. It was when we got the idea that we are a chosen people that we went wrong. We're really just the same as everybody else. We're all people, and, given certain conditions, we'll do certain things." When we arrived at the Capitol, Senator Fulbright went in to vote and asked us to wait outside the Senate chamber.

He came out again, and invited us to ride back with him to the Senate Office Building. "I just want to add one thing," he said in the subway car. "I want you to know that right at the moment I am feeling better about the prospects of avoiding these terrible things than I have for almost ten years. The Watergate case is regrettable, of course, but, looking at the turn it seems to be taking now, I have hopes it may serve to draw people's attention to these other threats, which have been building all those years. It may bring people to the limit of how much they're willing to take."

The next morning, we woke up in a different Washington—perhaps in a different country. Watergate had blown sky high. Everyone we had interviewed in Washington, whatever his politics—and we, too—had seen an executive branch in the ascendant over the other powers in our society. Now, at a stroke, all this was altered. A staggering reversal of fortune had taken place. The wall of executive privilege was down. And when we all saw what was inside, it was almost enough to make us wish it could be put back up. The executive campaign to undermine and discredit the press had itself been undermined and discredited. Executive moves to take over congressional powers had been checked—at least for the duration of the present Administration. Indeed, all across the board the executive reach for new powers had been blocked. For the whole country had now had a shattering glimpse into that "technology-era government" in whose name Congress and the other institutions of our democracy were to hand over their powers to the executive. Now the Congress, the judiciary, the press—even Common Cause—found themselves in positions of renewed authority and strength. Senator Sam Ervin, Judge John J. Sirica, the Washington *Post*, and John Gardner had been heard. All the former accused were suddenly in the judges' seats (It can be hoped that these judges will act *with* pity.) The president of the Newspaper Guild was calling for a "public apology" to the press from President Nixon. An entire style of governing had been buried. Scenes of recent weeks—of the Attorney General discoursing on impeachment, of the President lashing out at Congress as "irresponsible," of Administration officials lecturing the country on law and order—had overnight become part of a closed chapter in our history. This Administration's drive to change the face of our national life had not, it turned out, been an effort to bring our eighteenth-century principles and institutions in line with the twentieth century; it had been a sheer grab for power, ending with a cover-up of a second-story job on the political opposition. The news was tearing an entire Administration apart, but at that moment in the spring of 1973, for the first time in many years, the old eighteenth-century system looked to be alive and well.

MAY 5, 1973

T HE cracking of the Watergate case illumines and reaffirms the greatness of the American form of government. The slow unfolding of the case has been a gruelling course of study for the entire country, in which we have been shown once again, as in a high-school civics course, why we are a republic and why we must remain one. It has not been, however, a lesson in the strength of public opinion. Something that must be faced is that the public, like the President, was not much aroused by the Watergate case for a full ten months. The public had not ruled out the possibility that high Administration officials were involved in planning and then in covering up the incident. Rather, a large portion of the public believed these things to be true, but, in a striking reversal of its traditional response to governmental corruption, it did not care to pursue the matter any further. This was, one hopes, the nadir of public opinion as an institution in our national life. When public opinion has lost the will to compel a thorough investigation into the apparent subversion of a Presidential election by officials of the Administration in power, it has been neutralized as a voice in the basic affairs of the Republic.

What finally did break the case was the force of sheer truth in a system that is as helpless to deny the truth as it is to deny public opinion when public opinion is aroused. In the last few months, we have seen the power of truth, acting almost in spite of the public mood, turn our political life upside down. In effect, the public was dragged from a willful ignorance by the truth. In Hannah Arendt's words, "truth has a despotic character." The truth is that which *compels* our minds' assent. And in a democracy certain forms of truth do more than compel our minds' assent; they compel us to act. In a democracy, we are not permitted to seek out the truth about our affairs and then to ignore what we learn. When evidence of murder comes to light, indictments must be brought and a trial held. Our system is arranged to make such action reflexive. We must hold the trial whether we want to or not. In sermons, political speeches, and the like, truth and justice are often given a favorable mention together with other ideals, such as compassion and decency. But these other ideals are a different matter altogether. We may be exhorted to decency, but whether we follow the exhortation is, by and large, up to each of us. Decency and compassion belong to the large category of ideals which float above our heads as a reproach to our actual behavior. Truth and justice, on the other hand, are rooted as powerful forces in the heart of our political system. They have shaped and determined the fundamental structures of our institutions. Thus, the system of justice is the mechanism whereby certain forms of truth compel us to act. In a democracy, we are free to do many things, but we are not free to ignore the truth. It holds the system itself, and our individual liberty, hostage. In the end, it is by virtue of this power of truth that our nation consents to march to the tune of a piece of paper—the Constitution.

The history of the Watergate investigation is not a story of mounting public pressure but, rather, is a story of successful efforts to consolidate widespread public suspicion of wrongdoing, which the powers of society felt free to ignore, into hard legal evidence, which no one—not the press, not Congress, not the courts, not the President, not even the public—felt free to ignore. The question was finally put to the public in its most demanding form. It was no longer "Are you willing to forget about the bugging of one party's headquarters by another?" It was "Do you support apparent efforts on the part of high officials in government to obstruct the course of justice in order to hide their own wrongdoing?" The question was now whether we wished to throw out our system of justice. And our answer was no.

While the press, Congress, and the courts were busy developing evidence in the Watergate case, the principals, apparently, were busy covering their tracks. But a cover-up, although it may be an effective strategy for dealing with a deadened public opinion, is a poor strategy for coping with the law. The chief difficulty is that covering up a crime is itself a crime. The attempts to destroy evidence leave more evidence, which must also be covered up; thereby leaving still more evidence, and so on, until scores of people have become implicated and the few original traces of evidence have grown into a mountain of evidence. Of course, the ordinary criminal does not have the resources to make this mistake. Certainly no ordinary person suspected of wrongdoing would ever have the opportunity that John Dean had to run the investigation of crimes in which he was a possible suspect; in this case, it seems, the investigation *was* the cover-up. In fact, it is only the executive branch of the government that could ever really attempt a cover-up on such a grand scale. Because of the tendency of evidence to mushroom in cover-up cases, the plotters soon find themselves driven to make the maximum effort. And the maximum effort is nothing less than to try to intimidate, paralyze, or suppress all the major organs of possible truth-telling in the society, which is to say the press, the Congress, the courts, and even private individuals. In the months before the Watergate case broke, just such a campaign was going into high gear. The press and television (particularly publications or stations that had dwelt long on the Watergate story) were under heavy attack, the Congress was denied the right to any information whatever from the executive branch, and the courts were blocked from further investigation of the case by an underzealous prosecuting arm of the Justice Department. The cover-up of a crime had expanded into a systemic crisis.

The men of this Administration had succeeded in taking control of public opinion. They had been able to blanket the airwaves with propaganda, to fix polls, to persuade millions to forget their own experience in the war and accept a public-relations version of it, and to win a landslide election. But they had forgotten about the law. For under the law, even though you have the millions on your side for the moment, just one person in possession of the truth and willing to talk can bring the whole elaborate show to a dead halt. No landslide could bury one bit of what John Dean, Jeb Magruder, or Martha Mitchell might tell the Washington *Post* or a grand jury. Men who could wipe countries off the face of the earth at their own discretion, or blow us all to extinction, were powerless if Martha Mitchell reached for the phone. She might be ridiculed, but she could not be "silenced." She could not be made to disappear. These men had forgotten that in a true republic it is a fact that, as Solzhenitsyn has said, one word of truth outweighs the whole world.

MAY 19, 1973

AS the days pass, it becomes clear that the Watergate affair is bringing about a sweeping transformation of American politics. Never before has an upheaval of this magnitude come upon us so swiftly. One week, a political commentator was wondering whether Watergate might not turn out to be a "political plus" for the President. Two weeks later, he was wondering whether it might not force the President's resignation or impeachment. Only a month ago, the executive branch of the government seemed poised to take full control of our nation's affairs. The opposition had been surrounded and penned in, and was being disarmed; Congress had been shouldered aside; a few more appointments to the Supreme Court promised to bring the Court into line; the President and his public-relations advisers had pre-empted the major channels of public discourse, so that while other voices were still free to speak they could not make themselves heard. The executive had lowered a curtain of secrecy around itself. And, although the public still did not quite believe it, the men in the White House had deeply compromised the electoral system. Their well-made plans of self-aggrandizement and usurpation were unfolding smoothly in every area. Then, in an instant, the advancing executive machine went entirely to pieces, as though someone had touched a secret spring at its back. There had been no bold campaign by an opposition camp; there had been almost no speeches, and not one demonstration. Rather, a few intrepid investigators had uncovered a few facts, and the incredible collapse began.

Where a moment earlier the men of the executive had been spreading out unchecked across a clear field of action, now a whole jungle of prohibitions and laws had sprung up around them. In a flash, all their strengths had turned to weaknesses; the dynamics of self-aggrandizement had been converted into a dynamics of self-destruction. The telephone calls to powerful friends that had once protected them now increased their jeopardy. The coverups that had kept the investigators at bay now led the investigators in deeper. All the moves designed to strengthen the White House position were now expediting its undoing. Each well-laid plan emerged as a damning conspiracy, and the better co-ordinated it had been, the easier the investigators now found it to follow the links from one conspirator to another. The group's cohesion had been perhaps its greatest strength, and as soon as one man deserted, suspicion seeped into every relationship and they all began to desert. A frightful metamorphosis had taken place, as though a curse had been laid on the whole group overnight. Where once silence had been so efficiently preserved, there were dozens of voices broadcasting not only the damaging truth but also any rumors or lies that might help each person save his own skin by putting his former colleagues in peril. Where once fanatical loyalty had been the rule, there was betrayal in equal measure. The ruthlessness that these men had directed outward was redirected toward one another. Each man became both the blackmailer of his old friends and the victim of blackmail by them. The same momentum that had carried these men to the pinnacle of their power was now carrying them back down to their ruin. Even the weapons they had used in the open were blowing up in their hands: in a striking parallel to the "black propaganda" they had been so fond of (propaganda with which they attempted to discredit their foes by making them appear to have uttered damaging statements), their own techniques of vituperation against the Congress and the press rebounded to their disadvantage in the changed atmosphere. And even the arguments by which their supporters had attempted to shore up the President's position turned against him: the supporters had hinted broadly that we should not press too hard for the truth, because we could not afford to have a crippled President in the White House, but when a good part of the truth had come out, and the President *had* been crippled, the argument that we could not afford to have a crippled President in the White House weighed in on the side of his stepping down. Once the fact-finders had brought out their facts, the opposition had only to stand on the sidelines and watch what the executive branch of the government would do. A few people moved quietly in the direction of the truth, and the great bully overthrew himself.

It could not have happened five years ago. In those days, the fate of an Administration in such a case would certainly have been decided along the old, "polarized" lines. The liberal Democrats would have been in the vanguard of a full-scale assault on the President. At their backs would have been "the kids," in armies of millions in the streets. Republicans and conservative Democrats, fearful of weakening a President in wartime, would have rallied to the Commander-in-Chief, and at their backs would have been the military and the police. The United States would have been lucky to emerge from the ensuing strife as a Constitutional republic. But the kids have stayed out of these recent events altogether. Having checked the progress of an unjust war, they have retired to their campuses and left the new job to elder dragonslayers—men like Senator Sam Ervin, Senator Barry Goldwater, and Judge John J. Sirica. Their weapon has been an intimate knowledge of our Constitutional system—not a strong point with the kids, and, for that matter, not a strong point with the men of the present Administration. And once the underbrush had been cleared away by the inquiries it was not the liberal Democrats but the conservative Republicans who became the chief advocates of a full showdown. It was good ethics for the Republicans to do this, and also good politics. Republicans have no wish to be married to Watergate in the public mind for the next thirty years.

We were warned when the revelations began that if they were to implicate the President directly and thereby force us to take steps to remove him from office, the country might bog down in "mutual recriminations." A few years ago, such a warning would have made sense. But in recent weeks what has materialized before our eyes, far from being scenes of mutual recrimination, has been a succession of undreamed-of reconciliations. We have seen the President's press secretary, Ronald Ziegler, apologize to the Washington *Post*. We have seen Barry Goldwater join with liberal Democrats to call for an independent prosecutor. We have even seen President Nixon congratulate the men of the press and the judiciary (though not of the Congress) who set the stage for his present troubles. Watergate has brought us together. The deeper truth, though, is that we simply are no longer the divided nation we once were. What is there to divide us? For the public, the war is over. (One solemnly trusts that soon it will also be over in fact.) The rigid mindsets that embittered ordinary people against each other have dissolved. The discord of the nineteen-sixties ended several years ago, and now the manufactured discord of Administration propaganda and provocation has been ended. To be sure, the scene around us is not one to gladden the heart. The neglected work of a decade that was half turbulence and half torpor has piled up on the doorstep of the public: a public that may lately have been undivided but has also been dead to the world—a public lost, for the moment, to public affairs. Now, though, a prevailing atmosphere of compulsion has been lifted from the country. The Congress is getting up off its hands and knees and onto its feet. (Its first job will be to put an end to the bombing in Cambodia and Laos.) The men on television are blinking awake; their frozen "objective" expressions are giving way to smiles and frowns. According to the latest polls, the public has begun to stir. The rule of fear has been broken. We may be exhausted, but we are free.

MAY 26, 1973

W ATERGATE has given new impetus to the country's long-standing debate over the merits of "the system." Since the term became popular, about ten years ago, it has merged at least two meanings that should have been kept distinct. On the one hand, it has referred to the system of guaranteed freedoms and governmental checks and balances which is spelled out in the Constitution. On the other hand, it has referred to the "system" that people saw around them. This system was at first felt to be a monolithic structure, made up of the country's most powerful institutions and groups, that controlled all our lives and did not respond to the needs or wishes of the people. In later years, this second system began to crystallize into outright Presidential rule. Watergate has at last made the distinction between the two meanings inescapably clear, for it has restored the Constitutional system and discredited the Presidential system. In the nineteen-sixties, it seemed to many Americans that you had to accept the two systems as one or to reject the two as one—to support both the Constitutional system *and* the Vietnam war, for example, or to reject them both. The legislators in Washington and the armies of dissidents in the streets, divided as they were on most matters, were united, by and large, in this mistake. They became assailants of "the system" and defenders of "the system," when there were actually two systems. The failure to make the distinction meant that the central issue of the time, which was to prevent the one system (the Constitutional system) from being superseded by the other system (the monolithic Presidential system), was obscured. The authorities in many instances supported the Constitution in name while ignoring it or sabotaging it in fact. The young rebels tended to dismiss it in name while acting in a way that happened ultimately to strengthen it in fact. The spirit of the Constitution was alive in the hearts of some of these young people, but it wasn't alive in their words.

The Constitution has emerged surprisingly whole from this decade of turmoil. Today, Americans are saying, almost unanimously, that the uncovering of Watergate was a triumph of our Constitutional system, and it was. Still, it was not *our* triumph. When we congratulate ourselves on our success, or congratulate the men of the press or the men of Congress or the men of the judiciary, or congratulate the public, we spread the credit too wide. Any credit to contemporaries goes not to the press as a whole but mostly to the Washington *Post;* not to Congress but mostly to Senator Sam J. Ervin, Jr.; not to the judiciary but mostly to Judge John J. Sirica. Only these few, and a handful of others, properly used, and thereby saved, our system. The rest of us still have our medals to earn in the battle of the Constitution. In the decades of Presidential power, the members of the rival institutions learned servile habits, and now that they have been released from intimidation, the question is whether they will be able to stand on their own feet or whether the long years of subservience have bent them permanently into a crawling position. This time, the country was saved without them. And, great as the contribution of the intrepid few among us was, the few were given the strength of thousands by the long arm of the Founding Fathers reaching down across two centuries to save us all. We were all reaping benefits from a system that too many of us had failed, in recent years, to understand or support. It was a rescue operation from the eighteenth century, and our own contribution was minimal. In a sense, we didn't save the system—it saved us.

JUNE 2, 1973

I N its opening stages, the Watergate affair has shaped up as a very special kind of political struggle. So far, it has not become a clash either of parties or of ideas. Rather, it has been a clash of facts. Recollection has been pitted against recollection, document against document. In the years leading up to Watergate, the country had come to live in a world of Presidential facts. The facts-according-to-the-President, which were incessantly repeated virtually word for word by his growing legion of surrogates and amplified throughout the country by the many organs of public communication, had succeeded in overriding all the other sources of facts put together—had succeeded, that is, in overriding what used to be known as "the facts." Others might speak, but soon they would be discredited with organized campaigns of slander, or pressured behind the scenes into silence, or simply drowned out by the White House propaganda. The Presidential facts were crowding all other facts off the stage. Like the President himself, they had become sovereign.

The actual facts, when they are not interfered with by any single, overpowering influence, flow from innumerable sources, and although some may be introduced into the world self-servingly, they soon escape the control of their sources and join a body of reference that serves us all equally and impartially. The Presidential facts, on the other hand, remain under the President's control and always serve him. Like the members of his staff, they have no independent status. They were called into public service by him and can be dismissed by him. He is the Great Father of all facts, and he can eliminate them at will. The actual facts belong to all of us, but the Presidential facts belong to the President. In his world, various kinds of facts are wiped out by special moves. Facts that have been exposed as false, for instance, are rendered "inoperative." Actual facts that were once acknowledged by the President but are now damaging to his needs are attributed to his having "misspoken himself." And, finally, actual facts that a White House official has not acknowledged and does not wish to acknowledge but that have been brought out into the open are disabled when they run up against the official's shield of "deniability." The President, as befits his rank, is armed by all but impervious deniability. Compared to the Presidential facts, the actual facts are durable and permanent. Presidential factuality requires that the public short-circuit its memory, since new facts are constantly overriding old ones. The public must be trained to live in a feverish Now in which the unveiling by the President of his latest "surprise" on all three networks simultaneously is so vivid that it effaces everyone's recollection of all previous surprises. When peace is at hand for the third time, the public must forget the first two occasions. The Presidential environment, because it requires constant uprooting and erasing of the known record, is radical and disturbs the people. The factual environment, by contrast, is conservative and reassures them, because although it, too, may change swiftly, each change grows out of what went before and is connected to it. Sometimes the President may feel that he has to reach beyond the recent past and perform an operation on a more distant period. Here, also, the suppression of actual facts may be called for, as when the Administration attempted to block publication of the Pentagon Papers, or the invention of false ones may be needed, as when White House men attempted to defame the memory of John F. Kennedy by faking State Department cables implicating him in murder. And so, while the White House is attempting to throw a man in jail for life for revealing certain true stories, because, it is said, that information would hurt our country, it may at the same time be smearing the reputation of our country with stories that are even more hurtful and are not true. The actual facts are many and complex, and anyone may add to them or have access to them. The Presidential facts are generally simple and few. They compose a hermetically sealed world in which a few events ("my speech of August fifteenth," "my statement of April twentieth") and a few phrases ("peace with honor," "law and order") are drilled into the minds of all of us with monotonous persistence. In recent years, no matter what the subject—whether Vietnam, say, or inflation, or the "big spenders in Congress"—these facts were pre-eminent. The Watergate affair has changed that, along with so many other things.

Now the President has no sooner released his version of the affair than it disintegrates before our eyes. Each statement must be followed by another, longer one, until by this time the statements are running into thousands of words. The President's words have lost the power to compel our assent when our own knowledge, deductions, and hunches indicate that the actual facts are otherwise. Breaches have opened in the protected factual world in which the President had enclosed first himself and then all the rest of us. Nor has authority been claimed by any other single voice. Rather, authority has reverted to where it belongs—to the multiplicity of contending voices that have always kept our country informed in the past. The many traditional wellsprings of information have been unclogged and are flowing freely. The backed-up information of half a decade of our history is spilling out, and, after a long drought, the nation is suddenly awash in news.

JUNE 9, 1973

WHEN James W. McCord, Jr., according to his testimony, declined to obey a clandestine White House instruction that he plead guilty at the trial of the Watergate burglars, a White House emissary warned him, "Everybody else is on track but you. You are not following the game plan." If there was one thing the Nixon men could not stand, it was someone who refused to follow the game plan. Another of the Watergate defendants, Bernard L. Barker, had a better idea of what was required of him. On being asked at the Senate Watergate hearings what he thought he had been put up to when he was told to break into the Democratic National Committee Headquarters, he answered, "I was not there to think; I was there to follow orders, not to think." Later, speaking of his superior, E. Howard Hunt, Jr., whom he greatly revered, Barker said, even more self-effacingly, "I was part of Mr. Hunt's image." Last summer, the country had a long look at another piece of the Administration game plan, in the form of the Republican National Convention. What was presented as an outpouring of spontaneous enthusiasm for the President turned out—when a script fell into the hands of the press—to be a three-day display of carefully staged, minutely controlled political theatre. Every word, every gale of laughter, every patter of applause, every cry of enthusiasm had been planned and approved at the White House weeks before. Even instances of uncontrol had been planned, for at one point the script indicated cheering and applause so vigorous that the chairman's gavel blows—also indicated in the script—would fail, for an allotted time, to bring order.

With the Watergate revelations flooding the news, the country is learning about still more pieces of the Administration game plan. The full extent of the staging and manipulation is still unknown, but what we have already learned throws a great deal of the rest of the record in doubt. Settled or forgotten questions open up again. We know that the 1972 election was heavily sabotaged. The Administration, far from sincerely struggling against the influence of long-haired radicals, was pushing them to the center of the stage. Far from working to subdue them, it was hiring replacements for their depleted ranks to create disorder at the Conventions and elsewhere, the better to divide and conquer the electorate. One unkempt young man is reported to have been hired to sit in front of the White House wearing a McGovern button. And if the real radicals were not committing enough crimes the F.B.I. encouraged them to commit more, and taught them how. The Nixon men were flooding the mails with fake letters. They sent them out to the people under the names of opposition candidates. They sent them *from* the people *to* the candidates, and to the press. They even sent themselves fake letters. False information was leaked to the press; phony ads were put in the newspapers; phony samplings were sent in to the polls. Doubtful scenes from earlier periods float out of memory: Nixon, just before the 1970 elections, standing up to face a mob of "demonstrators" in California, then making an angry televised address; the hardhats attacking demonstrators in New York, then receiving an invitation to the White House; the P.O.W.s stepping off the plane with words of praise for the President on their lips—words that he now repeats in his public addresses. Nothing in the Nixon years has been quite what it seemed to be. Much of the public record, from which we all take our bearings, was a deliberate sham. People and institutions that were thought to be acting independently turn out to have been acting under orders. Americans, more and more, were falling in with the White House game plan. And the script of this plan was not just for a political convention, or even for an election; it was for the whole political life of the nation. As one revelation follows another, a factual seasickness sets in. Half a decade of our history spins before our eyes and then dissolves.

JUNE 16, 1973

I N recent weeks, attempts have been made to simplify the shapeless,
shifting, growing thing called Watergate down to a single straightforward
question: Did the President himself participate in a crime? The President
asks us to believe he did not, and pleads that he was unaware of his subordinates' wrongdoing, and when Watergate was only an incident, a Presidential
plea of ignorance at least was a sensible defense, since it left the President open
to nothing worse than a charge of negligence. But now that Watergate has
assumed the proportions of a national catastrophe the question of his knowledge loses its pre-eminent importance and his plea of ignorance takes on a
wholly different character. For if Mr. Nixon was unaware of orders that his
assistants were giving to the Securities and Exchange Commission, the F.B.I.,
the Justice Department, the State Department, the Department of Defense,
and the C.I.A. on matters that, by the President's own account, were more
important than any others to the security of our nation and to the peace of the
world, then he is telling us that under his Administration the United States has
been led not by its President but by a handful of grim oligarchs using a gullible
President as their front man. In effect, the President is telling us that the three
lawful branches of our government were supplemented and to an important
degree subverted by a hidden fourth branch, composed of the men on the
President's staff. He seems to be confessing not to negligence but to a virtual
abdication of his office in favor of these men. The Congress found the rule of
Mr. Haldeman and Mr. Ehrlichman—men holding positions not mentioned in
the Constitution—barely tolerable when it thought they were exercising their
unprecedented power in accordance with strict Presidential instructions. To
discover now that in the most important matters they had been acting in defiance of the President would be, in some ways, more of a shock than to discover
that the President had ordered the Watergate bugging or its cover-up. The
alibi, that is, turns out to be more frightening than the crime.

JULY 9, 1973

S OME politicians have been known to claim that when they walk into
a crowded room they can tell at a glance who their friends and enemies
are. Apparently, this was not the case with the Nixon men. They kept
a list. Last week, a White House "enemy list" was revealed at the Watergate
hearings. It included scores of newsmen, businessmen, religious and educa-

tional leaders, actors and actresses, labor leaders, and political figures. They were to be tormented by every federal agency that could be bent to that purpose, including the Justice Department, which was to look for opportunities to prosecute—and thus perhaps to imprison—them. Just a few days before the country learned who the Administration's enemies were, it was given an extensive look at one of its friends. He was Mr. Leonid I. Brezhnev, the Secretary-General of the Communist Party of the Soviet Union, and we watched a euphoric President toasting him almost nightly in champagne. At one time, of course, many Americans had been taught by Mr. Nixon and others that if this country had any foes in the world the leaders of the Soviet Union were surely among them. Now it was as though, having taken the welcome step of making friends of the Russians, the Administration had been working overtime to create enemies at home to take their place. Some of these "enemies" it provoked into hostility, some it imagined, and others it hired. As it happened, just as it was gearing up to face "the revolution," the revolution, such as it was, was fading. (One of the more frequently repeated myths to arise out of the Watergate affair is the notion that the Nixon Administration assembled its secret-police apparatus in response to mounting disorder on the left in this country. Actually, the influence of the left, which reached its peak in about the spring of 1968, was already declining by the time President Nixon came to office.) However, the preparations went forward. It now appears that the men of the Administration could not rid themselves of the idea that a raggle-taggle conspiracy made up of hippies, newsmen, intellectuals, and fashionable partygoers, and funded by a few minor left-wing powers, such as Cuba and Algeria, was posing a threat to the survival of the American government. When this conspiracy could not be established by the C.I.A. and the F.B.I., they insisted on its existence anyway, even to each other, and went on governing the country as though the conspiracy were real. And where the supposed threat could not be discovered they manufactured it themselves. With the left wing on the wane, they sometimes found it necessary to employ suitable-looking young people to pose in the role of the domestic menace. On many occasions, life must have become quite confusing at the White House. In one instance reported at the Watergate hearings by Dean, the President became angered upon spotting a lone protester with a sign across the street from the White House, and an aide ordered him removed. Dwight Chapin, the President's appointments secretary, reportedly set off to get some "thugs" to do the job. (He seems to have been restrained, however, and the Secret Service apparently carried out the mission.) But on another occasion, it has been reported, the Administration itself hired an unkempt young man to sit outside the White House wearing a

McGovern button. The idea was to discredit Senator McGovern. In such cases, there was a danger that the Administration might send out some of its thugs to beat up others of its thugs; or it might write down the names of some of its own impostors on its enemy list. Nevertheless, the President apparently preferred having the phony demonstrator in front of the White House to having the real one there. When he looked out on that particular member of the supposed subversive conspiracy to undermine the American form of government, he could reassure himself that, in this case at least, the conspiracy was his own.

JULY 16, 1973

S OME observers, after getting over their shock at discovering that something called an enemy list was being kept at the White House, have taken comfort in the list's evident sloppiness. A number of friends of the President were on it, and the name of former Secretary of Defense Clark Clifford was misspelled ("Gifford"). The nation may have been heading in the direction of a police state, these observers argue, but at least it would have been an inefficient police state. They should take no comfort in that thought. Though the absence of any clear distinctions in the selection of people placed on the enemy list has some amusing aspects at first glance, it is in reality one more of the frightening things about the list. It is a great mistake to think that totalitarian regimes attack only their foes. Inefficiency, particularly in the form of indiscrimination in punishing political enemies, has been a virtual hallmark of twentieth-century totalitarianism. Totalitarian terror may begin with the singling out of a handful of supposed "subversives" (or "wreckers," as they were originally called in the Soviet Union), but it expands by degrees into every sphere of the lives of ordinary people, and soon reaches into the circles of the terrorizers themselves, who end by putting each other's names down on their enemy lists and shooting each other. In the purges in the Soviet Union during the nineteen-thirties, for example, the Communist Party, in whose name they were being carried out, was more heavily purged, perhaps, than any other group in the society; indeed, it very nearly succeeded in wiping itself out altogether. And now it is interesting to note that the Nixon men, as they made their first exploratory steps down the path toward totalitarian rule, began to wiretap each other almost as soon as they began to wiretap the opposition. One official rationalized Henry Kissinger's decision to wiretap his own aides with a pretty little piece of totalitarian logic: Kissinger had them bugged not because he mistrusted them, the official suggested, but because he *trusted* them and, being so certain of their loyalty, knew that their trustworthiness would be reaffirmed when it was put to the test of the taps. In President Nixon's White House, then, to be tapped was a favor, since the tangible proofs of your loyalty provided by wiretap logs would increase your stature with the President and his most important aides. Of course, in a world in which you are tapped because you are trusted and tapped because you are mistrusted, no one escapes tapping.

Totalitarian indiscrimination, flowing, as it does, from an irrational and blinding fear, which knows no boundaries, is indeed "inefficient" in the narrow sense that it leads to the wholesale punishment of "innocent" people, including people who are completely uninvolved with politics. But this inefficiency is highly efficient in a broader sense, for by punishing people virtually at random a totalitarian regime keeps everyone, and not just its enemies, in a state of fear. Totalitarian indiscrimination gives the regime a reputation for an in-human, godlike ruthlessness that ignores not only ordinary human moral distinctions but even the twisted distinctions put forward in the regime's own propaganda. That is why, when a police state is forming, anyone who fancies that he can win safety by allying himself with the regime is fooling himself. In many cases, it is the friends of the regime who turn out to be in the greatest danger of all, as the Nixon loyalists who have had their phones tapped or have discovered their names on the enemy list are beginning to learn. They are finding out what the Southeast Asian peasantry has known for a long time now: that American terror, like all other outbreaks of terror in our time, does not make fine distinctions. In our country, as elsewhere, once the police break down your door and start shooting, it isn't of any help that they can't spell your name.

JULY 30, 1973

I N the course of the Watergate hearings last week, the Senate Select Committee on Presidential Campaign Activities stumbled across some news of surpassing strangeness. The Committee and the nation learned that in the spring of 1971 President Nixon, acting on an impulse that has not been fully explained, secretly ordered that every conversation he held in the Oval Office, in his office in the Executive Office Building, and in the Cabinet Room in the White House be automatically taped by means of bugs and phone taps placed in the rooms and connected to tape recorders, and that every telephone conversation he held in certain other rooms, in the White House and at Camp David, be tapped and taped as well. According to the testimony, this system was not under the control of the President, who was thus not able to conduct any business in the wired rooms out of earshot of the machines. In other words, the President, in an act for which there is no known precedent in history, placed his working life under round-the-clock self-surveillance. The most secretive Administration in our history has proved to be threatening us with a surfeit of disclosure—if not now, then at some future date, when the doors of the Nixon Library are thrown open. The people who claimed executive privilege for the lowest clerk of the federal bureaucracy turn out to have had no idea of the meaning of privacy. These withdrawn men turn out to have been secret exhibitionists. While they were stopping up leaks, they were arranging the deluge. While they were trying to suppress the Pentagon Papers, they were preparing the White House Tapes. They had a peculiar notion of democracy: leave the present generation in the dark but reveal everything to generations of the future. Between the one purpose and the other, they had work enough to keep their shredders *and* their tape recorders going full time. While the shredders were tearing it all up, the tape recorders were taking it all down. Now it is up to the rest of us to figure out what this entire episode means.

It goes without saying that surreptitious taping is dishonest and is unfair to anyone who is unaware that he is being taped. And since the President taped just about every statesman and major politician in America and the rest of the world, we have learned that for more than two years virtually the entire business of the President of the United States was conducted under false pretenses. But if the taping was harmful, in its unfairness, to those with whom the President did business, its effects on the President himself were still more disturbing. According to one witness before the Watergate committee, the tapes were made for "posterity." If this is true, then the President had arranged to live every moment of his working life with an audience of future millions looking over his shoulder. This seemingly reclusive man had in reality banished all privacy for himself. The issue once again, as with nearly everything relating to Watergate, has to do with freedom. This time, it is not Constitutional freedom. It is simply the freedom to be oneself. It is the unconstraint that comes with privacy. A President, possibly more than any other person, needs the walls of silence that restrict some of his words to a close circle, and he needs, too, the merciful oblivion that swallows up most mere conversation. The loss of these protections is a loss of freedom. If all his words are to be carved in stone, then he has lost the privilege of speaking unreservedly, of doubting and wondering aloud, of saying reckless or foolish things, of trying out farfetched ideas, of allowing for the tentative and chaotic talk that often precedes important decisions or precedes the formulation of the few words a statesman may utter that *should* be carved in stone. By placing himself under the reign of tapes, he censors and stunts his words and deeds at the source and cuts himself down to a cramped half-man. But America cannot afford a half-man in the Presidency; we need a free, whole man. Some observers have gone as far as to say that the taping has a totalitarian flavor, and they are right, yet the chief victim of the taping has been none of those who visited the President or spoke to him on the phone but the President himself. He has placed himself in the position of a political prisoner who lives in a cell in which a light burns all night and a guard keeps watch through a one-way mirror in the door. He is not the average tyrant. In fact, he made himself the first victim of the totalitarianism that he and the luckless men of his Administration now seem to have been putting together for the rest of us. This self-reduction may account for some of the difficulty that the President and his aides have had in understanding what the rest of us were complaining about when we said we didn't want to live under twenty-four hour surveillance. It may also account for their insistence that the Watergate bugging was an "incident" that was being "blown up" by the press. After all, it was a lot less than the ordeal the President had prepared for himself. This latest revelation of fantasy in the White House may cast new light on much that has happened in the past five years. It seems that, after all, the President's main object was not to oppress us. Never a passionate lover of freedom, this most powerful man in the world had worked out a way to oppress himself, and, having discovered what was, by his lights, the good life, he wanted to share it with the whole country.

AUGUST 6, 1973

IN March of 1969, Secretary of State Rogers, testifying before the Senate Foreign Relations Committee, said, "Cambodia is one country where we can say with complete assurance that our hands are clean and our hearts are pure." At that moment, with Secretary Rogers' knowledge and assent, we were, the public has now learned, bombing the neutral country of Cambodia; the Administration was keeping our illegal bombings (a total of more than a hundred thousand tons of bombs dropped) secret from Congress and the American people; and the Pentagon was falsifying the records of our raids. In a military parallel to Watergate, the White House presided over a crime—

the illegal bombing of a neutral country and the taking of uncountable lives—and then over a historically unprecedented cover-up. In what can now be recognized as the style of this Administration, it acted lawlessly, it acted in secrecy, and it lied. Yet one cannot doubt that Secretary Rogers really thought that our hearts were pure, that his heart was pure, just as one cannot doubt that former Attorney General Mitchell was speaking sincerely when he said he did not feel that in the Watergate affair he had done anything "mentally or morally wrong." In fact, one of the most persistent themes at the current hearings is the theme of innocence. "I was just a messenger." "I was a conduit." "I took the bag of money from here to there, but I didn't know whom it was intended for or why." "I made the telephone call, but I didn't know what the message meant." "I typed the memo, but I didn't read it for content." "I assumed that if the instructions came from the White House what I was doing must be authorized and legal and proper." "I trusted my superiors." "My subordinates were carrying out my orders with a zeal that I did not anticipate." "It was a matter of national security." "I listened to my own tapes, and I found myself innocent." And, in a sense, all these people *are* innocent, just as we are all innocent. We did what we did because, one way or another, by whatever moral maneuvering, through whatever intricate transactions we could make with our consciences, we thought that what we were doing was right at the time. It is sad that we must be judged by others rather than by ourselves.

Ten saints gather on a village street, and talk and do whatever else it is they have to do, and then go their separate ways, leaving behind them a corpse.

SEPTEMBER 17, 1973

H ENRY Kissinger is a prodigiously intelligent, articulate, talented, witty, captivating, and imposing man. He is quite unlike most of the people President Nixon surrounded himself with in the White House. He has style, he has intellectual finesse, he has warmth and humor, he speaks the English language, he is without pretension, he is not mean-spirited, he seems instinctively drawn to telling the truth, and he clearly wants to serve his country well. He also appears to have a historical vision, shared by the President: that by maintaining our military pre-eminence and by standing fast wherever we think we are challenged, as we thought we were in Indo-China, we may avoid a nuclear confrontation with, first, Russia and, second, China, and thus preserve a relatively peaceful world for many decades. Now he has come before the Senate Foreign Relations Committee as the President's choice for Secretary of State. In the questioning that took place on the first day of the confirmation hearings, last Friday, the senators displayed a mixture of admiration, respect, and bewilderment. Obviously, Kissinger was not a man to be lightly rejected. Yet there was a profound uneasiness in the air. It was as if two Henry Kissingers sat before them in the hearing room: the Henry Kissinger who had the highest possible qualifications for the post to which he had been named—who had the makings of a great Secretary of State—and the Henry Kissinger who had been intimately bound up with the conduct of our foreign affairs for the past five years. It was as if a third man, too, sat before them: President Nixon. For if the President had an alter ego on the world stage it was Kissinger. The actions of the two men could not be separated. Together, for five years, they had dictated our foreign policy. To confirm Henry Kissinger as Secretary of State was to ratify what he had done, and what the President had done, for those five fateful years. And what had that been? Together, they had established relations with China, improved our relations with Russia, and successfully completed the first phase of SALT— and for these immense achievements most Americans are grateful. Together, also, they had planned the undisclosed bombing of Cambodia in 1969 and 1970; they had initiated the unauthorized wiretapping of members of Kissinger's staff and of newsmen in 1969; they had planned the invasion of Cambodia in 1970; they had planned the use of American air power to support the invasion of Laos in 1971; in 1971, too, they had "tilted" in favor of Pakistan in the India-Pakistan war, though at the time Pakistan was carrying out mass murder of Bengali subjects in East Pakistan; in early 1972, they had planned the mining and blockading of North Vietnamese harbors; later in 1972 they had planned the "Christmas bombing" of North Vietnam—all this done in secrecy, and without congressional consent. The senators, in effect, were being asked to ratify a series of actions that should never have taken place without their approval, and that most of them had abhorred and protested. Try as they might, the senators could not escape this nightmarish five-year history. While the President and the men of Watergate were, it now appears, undermining our democratic system of government in domestic affairs, the President and Henry Kissinger were undermining the system in foreign affairs. Last Friday, Kissinger gave the senators assurances that he would mend his ways. There were even subtle overtones of remorse. But what the senators were forced to pass judgment on was a whole new way of government: how we had been governed in recent years and how we would be governed from now on. They had to think about the dark side of the Kissinger record: how he, together with the President, had violated the Constitution, defied Congress, and contemptuously ignored the will of the nation's people. The senators were presented with a dilemma. They could have this charming, brainy, penitent-seeming man as Secretary of State if they would forget the last five years of history, including the millions of victims of an un-Constitutional and unnecessary prolongation of a war, and if they would overlook the curious fact that the nominee had by no means been joined in his expressions of regret by his present and future superior, the President. In happier times, Kissinger—the same man, with the same extraordinary qualities—might have walked into the hearing room with a record that was unmarred. Today, Kissinger is not so fortunate. After five years of close collaboration with President Nixon, after acting with him in secrecy and without the legal and moral sanction of Congress or the American people, he walked into the hearing room with a burden that must be anguishing both to him and to his judges. One could only look on in sorrow as the senators, the President, and Henry Kissinger faced one another in these tragic circumstances.

OCTOBER 15, 1973

IF only it were a social law that ridiculous events were never dangerous, America would have nothing to fear from her government at the moment. For although the gravest events may be in the offing—although prominent observers have been saying for weeks that both the President and the Vice-President might well be forced to leave office within the next few months—the fact is that our affairs have an inconsequential, weightless feel that is hard to shake off. Perhaps the problem is that they fail to correspond to some fixed notions we have about what great events should be.

Great events, including great disasters, should be seen to affect the fate of millions, but when we watch the President and the Vice-President, the one running to the courts and attacking Congress, the other running to Congress and attacking the courts, we have the illusion that only the fates of the embattled men on our screen are involved, and a national crisis is reduced to the dimensions of a comic-strip drama. Great events should inspire great passions, and some commentators and officials have, in fact, made reference to a "nightmare of division" and "an orgy of recrimination," but actually nothing of the kind has occurred. The nation, as far as one can tell, has been attentive but calm—even placid. It judges the price of food to be more important than the crisis in Washington. One almost has the feeling that if the public were to decide that the President had to leave office, it would still find food prices more important. Whatever the meaning of such a mood may be, it doesn't look like the stuff of a national upheaval.

We are in the habit of thinking that great events take the form of great contests, but these great events have taken the form of a strange anti-contest, in which the contestants do not battle each other but, rather, enter the ring and start to beat themselves up. The way it looks from the outside, the winner must be the one who knocks himself out first. It is a contest of weakness, a contest of will-lessness. A year ago, the executive branch seemed to have gathered almost all governmental power into its own hands, and Congress seemed hardly able to give away its powers fast enough. No sooner had it handed over the last vestige of its war power than the House of Representatives was rushing across to the White House to hand over the spending power, in the form of a budget ceiling that would enable the President to cut any part of the budget he wanted to cut in the name of economy. At that point, Congress seemed a sure victor in the contest to defeat oneself. Then, this spring, the President began to give it serious competition. The White House began to tear itself to pieces. (This is the only sign so far of any "orgy of recrimination.") In a mere matter of months, it had all but knocked itself out. Not only had the men in the White House been up to their necks in indictable offenses but they had been getting the evidence in order for the prosecutors. Charles Colson had been writing up an incriminating memo listing all the other incriminating memos he could think of in the I.T.T. case. Howard Hunt and Gordon Liddy were making sure of getting photographs of themselves at the scene of their abortive burglary of the office of Daniel Ellsberg's psychiatrist. John Ehrlichman was taping phone conversations that seemed to incriminate him as well as his colleagues. And President Nixon, leaving nothing to chance, was getting it *all* down on tape. Faced with this self-destructive display, Congress began to show some strength. It set up a select committee to investigate campaign abuses. But by the end of the summer it seemed to be back on its own self-destructive track. It decided that the hearings would be cut short. It approved one questionable executive appointment after the next. It maintained its near-perfect record of failing to override Presidential vetoes. But the White House, too, had unexpected reserves of weakness to draw on. The Vice-President came under suspicion of impeachable offenses. A rift opened between him and the President, and the executive branch of the government dissolved into a chaos of warring factions.

Finally, in great events we expect to find that everything is larger than life. But in this, too, the current events disappoint us. For the Watergate atmosphere is one that diminishes not only the nation's leaders and institutions but the nation's calamities as well.

OCTOBER 22, 1973

THE day after Vice-President Agnew resigned, we tuned in to the Watergate hearings and found, of all things, the large, humorous, melancholy face of Senator George McGovern's "political director," Frank Mankiewicz, on our screen. We realized that we had more or less forgotten that there had ever been an opposition in the 1972 election. Mankiewicz's testimony brought back some aspects of the opposition's campaign. Asked to "state briefly" his "role" in the campaign, he listed a few duties—he had "travelled with the Senator," he had been the main "inside man"—and then, with a smile, gave up the attempt. McGovern's campaign hadn't been as structured as the Nixon campaign, he reminded us. Mankiewicz came before the Watergate committee with clean hands. He had nothing to apologize for, and he did not choose to be combative. A relaxed, genial atmosphere spread through the Caucus Room. Majority Counsel Sam Dash read a few memos written by Patrick Buchanan, President Nixon's political strategist for 1972. "McGovern is our candidate. . . . McGovern is the one," Buchanan had written—as though the McGovern campaign had been run by a subcommittee of the Committee to Re-elect the President. "Let him have his run at the nomination," one memo recommended. Buchanan seemed to have had more ideas for clandestine tactics to use against the Democrats in their primaries than the Democrats had for open tactics to use against each other. He wanted the Republicans to promote black candidates in the Democratic Party. The way Buchanan saw it, this would help divide and defeat the Democrats. He also suggested that the Republicans act to promote a fourth party, on the left, which would siphon off votes from the Democrats. When Mankiewicz heard these memos and others in the same vein, he remonstrated that the Democrats, too, had had something to do with their campaign, and that although Buchanan's efforts to foment disorder in the Party had had considerable effect, the Democrats had not simply been tools of the White House. But Sam Dash, as though to affirm that the McGovern campaign had been nothing more than a figment of Patrick Buchanan's imagination, referred to Mankiewicz as Mr. Buchanan at one point, and later referred to him as Mr. McMinnoway. Michael McMinnoway had been one of the Nixon spies. Mankiewicz took it all in a spirit of resignation. "I'd rather be called Buchanan than McMinnoway," he said, with meek humor. The television cameras panned the room. Where once there had been hundreds of newsmen, there were empty tables. The McGovern campaign had not managed to command the nation's attention in 1972, and didn't command it now. At the end of the afternoon, as Mankiewicz rose from the witness table, the chairs around him were empty. No one rushed up to him to ask him questions or to congratulate him. The news was all elsewhere. Outside the empty, paper-strewn Caucus Room, the capital was reeling from the Agnew resignation. And the case of the tapes was moving forward. For Mankiewicz, it was all over. The fate plotted for him in the White House had befallen him: he was out of power. But his honor was intact. Now, in courtrooms and prosecutors' offices all across the country, the Nixon Administration was moving steadily closer to the much harder fate it had unknowingly prepared for itself.

OCTOBER 29, 1973

AUTHOR'S NOTE: On Saturday, October 20th, President Nixon ordered his Attorney General, Elliot Richardson, to fire Archibald Cox, the special prosecutor appointed to look into wrongdoing in the White House. Richardson refused, and Nixon fired him. Nixon then gave the order to the second in command at the Justice Department, Deputy Attorney General William Ruckelshaus. Ruckelshaus also refused, and Nixon fired him, too. Nixon now delivered the order a third time, to Solicitor General Robert Bork, who fired Cox. These events, which later came to be known as the Saturday Night Massacre, unleased a flood of protest around the country that led finally to the impeachment proceedings against the President.

FOR nearly a decade, a question has been haunting our national life. It is whether the Republic will live or die. The question has been asked in countless forms. May newspapers print whatever they wish to print, and the people read whatever they wish to read? May the people assemble without fear of injury or loss of life? Must senators and others always support the President in his difficult decisions? Are the people to be treated like children or like adults? To what extent does the government have the power to check up on what the people are doing? To what extent do the people have the right to check up on what the government is doing? How do we spend our money? When do we go to war? Who decides? The question arose on the battlefields of Vietnam, and it hung in the air over the battlefields of America. Lieutenant Calley posed it for us in one way, Daniel Ellsberg posed it in another. Several times, we came near to paying with our Republic for our war. The question loomed in city streets, in precinct houses, in congressional hearing rooms, in courtrooms, at the summit in Moscow and Peking. Now, in the coming days and weeks, the nation must give its answer. The President has dismissed the man charged by Congress and the Attorney General with discovering any wrongdoing in the White House. The potential defendant fired the prosecutor and defied the judge. For the moment, those guilty of crimes in the Watergate cases are beyond prosecution. And since the President, by the same stroke that removed him from the law's reach, took personal control of the law—forcing two Attorneys General from office before he found one willing to obey his commands—every innocent person in the country is endangered. For the machinery of law enforcement has been transformed wholly into the political—even the personal—instrument of one man. On this occasion, as on many others in recent years, the President has flouted the law. He has not merely broken the law; he has overthrown the law. But this time, since his lawbreaking seems to remove a threat to the very survival of his Administration in office, it is not just this one act but the continuation of the Administration itself that has become lawless. The question of whether the Republic will live or die has now been decisively posed in this form: Will we remove a lawless Administration from office or will we submit to illegitimate rule? The question has probably been put in its *final* form, and may not be asked again. When the President launched the country into the worst Constitutional crisis in its history, he explained that he had done it to avoid a Constitutional crisis. But it was not a Constitutional crisis that the President wished to avoid—it was the Constitution. The problem we all face now is not how to avoid a Constitutional crisis but how to resolve one. And the only resolution the President has left to us, unless he resigns, is for Congress to begin consideration of impeachment proceedings.

The country surveys a scene of devastation. The wreckage of American institutions lies all around us. Any future under the present leadership is unthinkable. The point of no return has been passed, and the country has no choice but to take the first, dread steps toward putting its house in order.

NOVEMBER 5, 1973

AUTHOR'S NOTE: While the Saturday Night Massacre was occurring, Israel was fighting the Yom Kippur War with Egypt and Syria. On October 20th, a cease-fire was agreed upon. On October 24th, Soviet General Secretary Leonid Brezhnev urged the United States to join the Soviet Union in sending peacekeeping forces to the Middle East to enforce the cease-fire, and stated that if the United States did not reply, he would consider acting alone. Taking this as a threat of unilateral intervention, President Nixon placed American forces on worldwide alert.

L IKE many people in the country last week, we spent the hours of the worldwide American military alert next to our radio and television set. The President's televised news conference was, of course, one of the moments of greatest anxiety. The President wore a broad, fixed smile as he made his way to the podium. Once he was there, however, his countenance became solemn. He made a long opening statement on the Mid-East crisis and on the subject of a new special prosecutor. Then, replying to a question, he informed us that the nation had just been through "the most difficult crisis we've had since the Cuban confrontation of 1962." His use of the past tense was odd but welcome, since in his opening statement he had somehow forgotten to announce to the public that the hour of peril had passed or had not passed. As he spoke, the alert was still partly on. Then the President said that, the extreme gravity of the crisis notwithstanding, we had all just experienced a reassuring episode in the new politics of détente. He and Secretary Brezhnev had exchanged "firm" notes, and had understood each other perfectly, owing, in part, to their personal acquaintance. (We couldn't help recalling that the firm notes had been supplemented by the even firmer troop alerts, including, in this country's case, an alert of the Strategic Air Command.) During the questioning, the smile returned. But the words were angry. The President launched his bitterest attack on television and the press to date. He said that he had been subjected to the most "outrageous, vicious, distorted reporting" he had experienced "in twenty-seven years of public life." "When people are pounded night after night with that kind of frantic, hysterical reporting, it naturally shakes their confidence," he said. (The *News* headline the next morning was "SMILING NIXON TAKES ON MEDIA.") A reporter in a back row asked the question that was uppermost in everyone's mind: Had the domestic crisis surrounding Watergate influenced his actions in the international crisis? The President acknowledged a connection between the two matters. "Even in this week, when many thought that the President was shell-

shocked, unable to act [because of Watergate], the President acted decisively,"
he said. In other words, Watergate had damaged his prestige—had left many
people thinking there was a shell-shocked President in the White House—
and the confrontation with the Soviet Union had, in his view, repaired it.
This is by no means the same as saying that he had taken dramatic action
in the international crisis *in order* to recoup his losses in the domestic crisis;
nevertheless, he indicated, this would possibly be the happy result. A week
earlier, he had referred to the connection between the two crises from the
other side; he had instructed Special Prosecutor Cox not to seek any further
evidence from the White House by court action, in order to avoid a Constitutional crisis "at a time of serious world crisis." At that time, he had called
for an easing of the domestic crisis in order to strengthen his hand abroad.
And, just as he now called the alert a decisive action, he had said of his order
to Cox, "It is necessary to take decisive actions that will avoid any possibility
of a Constitutional crisis." A President with a penchant for decisive actions
had taken two in one week—one in the foreign realm and one in the domestic
realm. In the course of doing so, he had merged the two crises into one.
Watergate, that uncontrollably spreading thing, had become entangled with
the apocalypse. Now Donald Segretti and his obscene letters and stink bombs
were mixed up with the armies clashing in the Middle East, and what Bebe
Rebozo had done with Howard Hughes' hundred thousand dollars was mixed
up with what the B-52s carrying the hydrogen bombs would do, and the
survival of all of us rested on how these matters mingled in the mind of our
beleaguered, angry, smiling President.

NOVEMBER 12, 1973

SIXTEEN months ago, five men (in case anyone hasn't heard) were caught
in the headquarters of the Democratic National Committee carrying
wiretapping equipment. Whom could they have been working for? The
country awaited evidence. In one man's pocket were consecutively numbered
hundred-dollar bills that were soon traced to the Committee to Re-elect the
President. In another man's pocket was a notebook that contained the entry
"W. House." One of the men turned out to be the chief of security for the
Committee. It became known that a Committee counsel had planned their
action. Could it have been the Committee to Re-elect the President that the
men were working for? The President said he thought not. The F.B.I. thought
not. The Criminal Division of the Justice Department thought not. And the

public thought not. Six months passed. The men were indicted and convicted. As far as the public knew, they had committed their crime for no reason and had been paid by nobody. Then, four months later, in what has turned out to be one of the great understatements of world history, the President announced "major developments" in the case. Soon it became apparent that the men *had* been working for the Committee. And that the entire top echelon of the President's staff for domestic affairs as well as most of the top people in the Committee to Re-elect the President had been busy for most of a year trying to conceal this fact. But had the President known of the cover-up? The public awaited further evidence. And soon it came. The President's former legal counsel reported that the President had known. The former acting director of the F.B.I. told of warning the President about the possible implication of White House aides. The deputy director of the C.I.A. reported that he had been ordered in the President's name to call the F.B.I. off the evidentiary trail. The President's campaign director said that the President had never asked him what was going on. At the same time, a mountain of other dismaying information was piling up. The public learned of the sabotage of Presidential election campaigns, of the secret, Presidentially approved Tom Charles Huston plan for an illegal domestic espionage agency controlled by the White House, of the secret use of the United States Air Force in Cambodia, of public money poured into the President's private property, of extortion and influence-peddling on a grand scale, of politically inspired prosecutions and politically inspired reprieves. And while all this evidence about what the White House had done in the past was coming out, the White House went to pieces before the public's eyes. The White House staff was scattered to the four winds. The Cabinet was thrown into disarray as its members rushed from post to post. The Vice-President fell. And now the special prosecutor on whom the nation's last hopes for justice rested has been fired; the Justice Department has lost its Attorney General and its Deputy Attorney General; and millions of people at home and abroad believe that when the President called a nuclear alert he was toying with the survival of mankind in order to protect his own survival in office. Again, the public awaits more evidence. We find ourselves in an atmosphere that has no precedent. In broad outline and in fine detail, the portrait of misrule is complete. Yet many of us still decline to "prejudge" the situation. The very fact that for sixteen months we have failed to judge the situation and to take corrective measures has come to seem like evidence that nothing is seriously wrong— for if we are in serious trouble, why have we not acted to save ourselves? Meanwhile, the national life turns to farce. A second-rate detective story— that of the tapes—installs itself at the heart of our national affairs. It is as if, unwilling to take measures ourselves, we had turned our fate over to a tape recorder. Our tragedies repeat themselves to the point of absurdity. (The man now on his way to Capitol Hill for confirmation as Attorney General would be—if we count Acting Attorneys General—our sixth in two years.) But, even with talk of resignation in the air, many of us avert our eyes from all this and go on searching for evidence—evidence that can only prove for the thousandth time what we already know. Hypnotized by investigations, we have not, as a people, found the will to press for a resolution. Even in our extremity, we wait, it seems, for evidence that is more than evidence, as if some final memo or tape from the White House could free us of our obligations, and make for us the solemn decision we must now make for ourselves.

DECEMBER 3, 1973

L AST week, shortly after the Dow Jones industrial average fell more than twenty-eight points in a single day, and shortly after we had seen a smiling, vigorously gesturing, rapid-speaking President telling a group of editors at Disney World, "I'm not a crook," we picked up our issue of *U.S. News & World Report* and turned to the "Tomorrow" section—the typed yellow "Newsgram" near the front of the magazine which, with copious underlinings, gives the reader "a look ahead from the nation's capital." The news coming into the *U.S. News* offices from the future was basically good. The latest bulletin revealed that "some Americans worry that *today's troubles*—political, economic, and international—signal start of a *decline* by the U.S. as world's *leading power*," and went on, "There's no doubt that it's a time of *adjustment*— some of it painful. But fact remains that this nation *is still No. 1* by nearly any measure. What's more, Americans *should stay on top for years*." As evidence, the "Newsgram" noted, among other things, that *"diplomatic clout* backed by plenty of *military force*" had helped us obtain a cease-fire in the Middle East, and that the dollar was regaining strength. Some of the good news for us consisted of bad news for our allies: "Nations that have been *gaining ground* on the U.S. are running into the same problems facing this country's businessmen— inflation, pollution, labor unrest. *Japan* and *Western Europe* are prime examples." It would be some time before *they* were No. 1, anyway. There was other reassuring news, too: *"Beginning to spread* in Washington in mid-November: belief that worst of the Watergate crisis is *over*, that heat on the President is *dissipating.*"

The news about this nation's No. 1 status and the news about the President's status went together. President Nixon, after all, was the first President in our history to make remaining No. 1 a national goal. He had continued the war in Vietnam for four years to keep us No. 1. His people had waged the dirtiest, most expensive campaign in our history to keep the Presidency out of the hands of a man who in the President's view hardly cared whether we were No. 1 or No. 10. Oddly, though, it was under President Nixon that our people first began to doubt whether we were No. 1. Before the United States was a world power, people did not doubt whether we were No. 1—they *knew we weren't* No. 1. And in the early days after we became a world power, our people were quietly confident, on the whole, of our strength—some were even a shade embarrassed by it—and few talked about it very much. The boasting and the doubting began at the same time.

The "Newsgram" also reported a strong feeling that "forcing the President out of office *won't help*," and "could even *make things worse*," as far as our remaining No. 1 was concerned. As we looked over the news, it seemed to us that his staying in might also make things worse. He was in the midst of "Operation Candor," and one Republican governor, intending a compliment, had summed it up perfectly when he said that the President, in his efforts to be candid, had achieved "a great deal of verisimilitude." But, whichever way things turned, the "Newsgram's" final piece of news was unchallengeable: "For some time . . . life in the U.S. *may not be the same* as it has been."

DECEMBER 10, 1973

THIS winter, as the nation sits in its dimmed, chilled living rooms watching the comet Kohoutek, which is due to appear in our heavens soon (it will be our finest Christmas ornament in this darkened season), and pondering the impeachment of the President, it may also want to reflect upon some statistics that the President reviewed the other day in his speech to the Seafarers International Union, and his comments on them. "There are only seven per cent [actually, five and a half per cent] of the people of the world living in the United States, and we use thirty per cent [actually, thirty-three per cent] of all the energy," he said. "That isn't bad; that is good. That means we are the richest, strongest people in the world, and that we have the highest standard of living in the world. That is why we need so much energy, and may it always be that way." In other words, as we turn our thermostats down, perhaps we can warm ourselves with thoughts of how

much colder it's going to be for those people in other parts of the world
who have to make do with the fuel that is left over. In the same speech, the
President reaffirmed his commitment to Project Independence 1980, which
would allow us to become independent of outside sources of energy by 1980.
The thirty-three per cent of the world's energy we would be using would
then be *all ours*. And in a crisis, of course, no one else could have any of it.
Among those who would have to fend for themselves are Western Europe
and Japan. Together, they consume twenty-six and a half per cent of the
world's energy, and the President has not announced any project that would
ever enable the United States to supply some sixty per cent of the world's
energy. And here is where not only Project Independence 1980 but any
notion of complete economic independence—or, for that matter, any notion
of complete independence in any area at all, including the military area—
breaks down. To begin with, Europe and Japan are allies of the United States,
and whether or not we are "independent" in fuel, they cannot be—and the
truth is that if they cannot be, we cannot be. The fundamental significance
of the Arab nations' oil embargo, as distinct from the global fuel crisis, is
that now the Arabs can, if they choose, bring the economies of Europe and
Japan to something like a standstill. And our fate—economic or any other—
is far from being independent of that of Europe and Japan, as two world wars
and the Depression have taught us. For this reason, world politics, particularly
a peace settlement in the Middle East, has more to do with resolving our oil
crisis than any Project Independence ever will. The newly recognized global
limits of natural resources, of which the fuel shortage is only one manifestation, force us and the Arabs and the Europeans and the Japanese and all
the rest of the peoples on the planet into dependence on one another. In
the last analysis, the rationing we need is global. (The Arabs have *their* idea
of equitable rationing: cut off all our oil.) The day when the five and a half
per cent of the world's people who live in America could decide how much
of the world's resources they would use is over. Nor will boasting, about our
appetite endear us to our suppliers—the other nations of the world. The
inseparability of oil from diplomacy and war is only one example of the new
interdependence. Consider the recent debate in this country over whether
to make any new trade privileges for the Soviet Union conditional upon a
relaxing of a Soviet emigration law that has prevented Soviet Jews from
leaving for Israel. Just as the Arabs are now attaching political conditions to
the flow of Arab oil to the United States and other nations, many senators
wish to attach political conditions to the flow of American wheat and computers to the Soviet Union. Were both the Arabs and the senators to succeed
wholly in their aims, Soviet Jews would be perfectly free to go to Israel, but

there wouldn't be any Israel for them to go to. There is no need to equate, or even to compare, the Arabs' motives in regard to the Middle East with the senators' aims in regard to the Soviet Union to see that global politics and global economics are now entwined inseparably, and that no Project Independence can ever disentangle them. However, the lesson our planet should learn is if we should not arrange our economic needs wholly to suit our political needs, neither must our political needs always give way to our economic needs. We do not want a totalitarian world with all the trains running on time, any more than we want what we have now—a feuding, anarchic world that can blow itself up at any minute. But, whichever way we turn, hopes of total independence for any nation are only fantasies.

That this is so is grim news. The loss of independence is real and it is deplorable. The idea, for instance, that we in this country might acquiesce to some extent in the Soviet Union's repression of Jews or of anyone else in the Soviet Union because of the Arabs' decision to cut back on the West's oil is even more distressing than the idea that we would acquiesce for the sake of advancing détente and the chances of the world's survival. And yet if, as many Americans are now suggesting, we use our economic leverage on the Soviet Union to induce it to influence the Arab nations to relax the oil embargo, can we use that same leverage to force a change in the internal policies of the Soviet Union, particularly when the change we want is one that infuriates the Arabs? These are elaborate calculations, but they are the ones that will determine the shape of the future—at least until the world sets about its neglected business of establishing ways of facing our common predicaments in common. There was a time when the notion of a world order was thought to be a utopian vision. We can see now that, in many respects, it is a hellish necessity. As for man's old dream of the world's becoming one, that, whether we like it or not, occurred years ago.

DECEMBER 17, 1973

T HE Big Lie is a strategy for concealing the truth by putting forward a story so audaciously false that it disarms ordinary skepticism, which is ready to cope only with petty distortions and deceptions. The White House, in its Watergate maneuverings, has apparently adopted another strategy: that of the Big Snarl. Instead of putting forward a single, easily grasped false story that routs all other stories, including the complex true story, from the field, one who resorts to this strategy puts forward—and then often retracts—numberless clashing, mutually cancelling stories, so that before long the integrity of all the facts and the logic of all the justifications are destroyed beyond reconstruction. Instead of hiding in simplicity, one takes refuge in hopeless complexity. Instead of advancing a phony story that pushes aside the truth, one assails the very idea of a single truth and effaces from the public mind the memory of what truth is. In this way, a public figure can in effect shred a bothersome issue while working to debase public standards to the level of his own conduct. In recent weeks, such deterioration has been spreading in our political life. It has shown up, for instance, in some new ideas about two basic elements of politics—confidence and candor.

Several weeks ago, at the time of the nuclear alert, Secretary of State Kissinger appealed to the press and the country to show confidence in the Administration. "It is up to you, ladies and gentlemen, to determine whether this is the moment to try to create a crisis of confidence in the field of foreign policy," he told an assembly of newsmen. He also said, "There has to be a minimum of confidence that the senior officials of the American government are not playing with the lives of the American people." The implication was that the public and the press were hurting the country by losing confidence in the President. And certainly it was true that a minimum of confidence must exist. But the Secretary had seemingly forgotten where confidence comes from. Having confidence in the government is not a duty of citizenship, like paying taxes. No such obligation could ever be met, because confidence is a state of mind and cannot be willed. A person looks at what his government is doing, and either he has confidence or he doesn't have it. If he doesn't have it, he can fake it but he can't manufacture it. In matters of public confidence, it is on the government that the obligation falls.

Candor is one quality that officials must have if they wish to win confidence. But it is a much simpler quality than anything the White House currently has in mind, to judge from the Operation Candor that has been under way recently. Candor is sometimes painful, but it is rarely laborious. No "operation" is required. A "counter-offensive" won't help. Perhaps what the White House now has in mind is not candor at all but something quite different: credibility. Credibility is the modern version of candor. Candor entails truthfulness, but credibility does not. Credibility is the public-relations version of truthfulness. It is the truth's "image." And, like any other image, it can be manipulated and faked. Probably none of us should be surprised when politicians offer us credibility instead of the truth; what is odd is that the audience sometimes seems to be satisfied. For example, one Republican governor was heard to remark admiringly after a meeting with the President, "He was very believable today—more believable than I've ever seen him before." It wasn't quite that the governor *believed* the President; it was only that the President had been *believable*—credible. Instead of asking "Is it true?" people were asking "Is it credible?" Observers were saying that the President had "helped himself" by his operation, although the observers did not believe him themselves. All over the country, Operation Candor was being reviewed like a new musical comedy. It seemed to be accepted that the President's candor, like the confidence that the Secretary of State was urging the rest of us to display, was an act—something forced or faked, which could be judged, like the skill of an actor. In this vision of our political life, it would be not only the performers but the members of the audience who would be actors. The President would perform and we would applaud. He would pretend to tell the truth and we would pretend to believe.

JANUARY 21, 1974

O VER the last decade or so, two standard reactions to bad news seem to have developed in our country. One reaction is "It didn't happen," and the other is "They all do it." In the early Vietnam years, when the bad news about the war was just starting to come in, the tendency was to react in the first way. In those days, since the citizenry still had what politicians often call "faith" in our institutions, we tended simply to reject the bad news. It was not until about five years ago that the second reaction began to emerge. The historical moment when "They all do it" eclipsed the theme of denial may have been the indictment and conviction of William Calley. On that occasion, the public tended to believe, simultaneously, that there had been no massacre of innocents at My Lai and that there were massacres of innocents in all wars. In the press of the day, the theme "They all do it" took the form of the statement that all wars are equally brutal. A modish pessimism about human nature itself was revived for the occasion. Now the Watergate disclosures appear to have buried the inclination to believe "It didn't happen," and "They all do it" reigns supreme. (The President, who seems to grasp such changes instinctively, has gone to considerable lengths to spread the idea that Presidents before him engaged in illegal wiretapping, took questionable tax deductions, and secretly taped conversations. He seems to be saying that all Presidents did what he has done.)

The two standard responses—the one denying abuses, the other seeing them as universal and probably eternal—seem to be at opposite poles, but the fact that they often crop up at the same time and on the lips of the same people (for instance, the President's "I didn't do it"/"They all do it" defense) is a clue that the public, in its heart of hearts, means the same thing by both of them. Rendered roughly, the meaning is something like "Go away!" The man who sees no massacre and no Watergate and the man who sees massacres and Watergates as the inevitable lot of all societies in all times have one thing in common: neither of them can be expected to take any action. If "they all do it," only a fool would exert himself to stop them. There would be no need even to take the trouble to try to distinguish between people who did it and people who didn't. What's more, one might reason, "If they all do it, maybe I can do it, too." And if "they all do it," that leads on to a still more attractive idea: that "they" are responsible for everything, and "we" are responsible for nothing. The conviction that the energy crisis (which is going to change our lives for the indefinite future no matter what games the oil companies may be playing with the present shortage) is the product of a corporate or governmental conspiracy is only the latest example of the spreading half-baked shrewdness that sees the conspiracy of an omnipotent "them" behind every headline.

The world of undiscriminating cynicism, where no one is trusted and nothing is believed, is in many ways a comfortable one. Every citizen enjoys the automatic right to a sly, knowing, and superior attitude toward all authorities but has no obligation to do anything about them. What is the use of changing one for another when they are all the same? In this world of cynicism, the people complain about the authorities the way they complain about the weather. Everyone grumbles, but it leads to nothing. Politics is everyone's cross and no one's responsibility. "They're all crooks," the people say to one another, and go about their business. This state of mind is new to us in the United States. But it is all too familiar to anyone who has spent some time in Eastern Europe or in South America, or in any of the countless other places in the world where people have lost the bold, sometimes innocent spirit of the free and adopted the easy sophistication of the powerless.

JANUARY 28, 1974

THE papers last week brought us news of the loss of a piece of American history and the restoration of a piece of Russian history. The piece of American history—what President Nixon said to his chief of staff, H. R. Haldeman, on June 20, 1972, three days after the Watergate break-in—was short, but it was crucial. The fate of an Administration seemed to hang on how it disappeared. For the moment, all we have left is an eighteen-and-a-half-minute hum. The piece of Russian history—what happened to tens of millions of people in forced-labor camps in the first several decades of Soviet rule—was long, and also crucial. In neither country did the authorities show any eagerness to hear any of this news. The Soviet authorities called Alexander Solzhenitsyn a "traitor" and suggested that he get out of the Soviet Union. A campaign of letter-writing against Solzhenitsyn on the part of the "public" was organized by the authorities. Letters flooded into Soviet television stations. (We, too, have now had experience with officially inspired letter campaigns to television stations. The difference is that in Russia the television commentators and the authorities are one and the same, whereas here the men on television still cling to a measure of independence.) About the Watergate news the Soviet authorities have nothing to say. Like Solzhenitsyn's book, comment would hurt détente.

Our authorities likewise blame the bearers of the news for the tidings they don't like. They tell us that the Watergate news that has been inundating us for the last year is the work of television, the press, and political enemies. On Solzhenitsyn *they* have no comment. But whereas Solzhenitsyn is all but suffocated in the totalitarian murk of the Soviet Union, and can be made to disappear at any moment, we still breathe the air of freedom, and can think and act without reprisal. Even Solzhenitsyn is in certain ways sustained by our freedom. His voice can be heard because there is a part of the world where independent voices are still allowed to speak out and public discourse is not yet dominated entirely by the well-amplified voices of the authorities sending themselves messages of support. And not only are we in the free countries the last forums for independent voices—we are the repository of the world's culture and known history. We are the keepers of the record. (In China last week, the authorities took out after Schubert and Beethoven.) One of our obligations is not to let gaps appear. For the moment, the gap in this nation's part of the record is only eighteen and a half minutes long. In the Soviet Union, the gap is decades long. There Solzhenitsyn, at the peril of his life, has rescued the memory of millions from darkness. Here, where the going is still easy and action is still possible, we let the erasers of the record continue with their work. If they are permitted to go all the way, there will be no record left, here or anywhere else. An American Solzhenitsyn, should we be lucky enough to have one, would have nowhere to make himself heard. The gap then would swallow us all, and the global hum could go on for centuries.

FEBRUARY 4, 1974

T O anyone who happens to be interested in the varieties of facts and alleged facts, the White House scandals have turned out to be an inexhaustible source of new and striking specimens. There have been "offensives," "operations," and other military maneuvers carried out by means of facts; there have been facts that disintegrated as soon as they were looked at; and there have been facts that broke down like cars on the road and became inoperative. Last week, we all had our first introduction to still another species of fact—the Unrevealed Fact. Senator Hugh Scott said on television that he knew of facts that would "exculpate" the President. But Scott wasn't saying what the facts were. The distinguishing mark of the Unrevealed Fact is that it is launched into the world in an incorporeal state. Two days later, Vice-President Ford picked up Scott's theme. He, too, knew of the amazing facts. But Ford, unlike Scott, had not himself inspected them. "I haven't had time to read the information," he explained. Ordinary facts are straightforward things. An Unrevealed Fact acts upon the world circuitously. It is known only to a few initiates, who then bring the rest of us the good or bad news. Ordinary facts are brash. Unrevealed Facts are shy and mysterious. But they can be powerful. They can permeate the atmosphere with their occult influence. The ones that Senator Scott has seen are alleged to have the power to move a mountain of wrongdoing and release the whole nation from its torment. They could do for our President what almost a year of information in the public realm has been unable to do. The facts on the record betray him, but the Unrevealed Facts exculpate him, and he stands blameless in their miraculous, forgiving glow.

FEBRUARY 11, 1974

I N the days before the State of the Union Address last week, there was a good deal of curiosity around the country about what the President might say. Ordinarily, the occasion is one in which the Union becomes briefly visible and audible in the form of the officers of all three branches of our government assembled under one roof. The President speaks, and the rest applaud, and we the citizens are reminded that, when all is said and done, we are one nation. This year, of course, with the Congress considering impeachment of the President, there were special problems. At the appointed hour, we turned on our television set, and soon it became obvious that there would be no State of the Union Address. The President was speaking, and the officers of the other branches were there, but the Union remained concealed. Intense discomfort was written on the faces of the men and women in the audience, as though they wished they were somewhere else. The President, too, looked as though he wished he were elsewhere. He began by describing the state of the Union five years ago. It had been poor. There had been burning cities, campus riots, war, crime, drug addiction. Now things were better. The President continued to make a series of proposals. Time slowed. At one point, the President seemed to falter and to gasp for breath, as though he could not go on. And why should he go on? The words were without weight or importance. ("The time has come, therefore, for a major initiative to define the nature and extent of the basic rights of privacy. . . . I shall launch such an effort this year at the highest levels of the Administration. . . . There will be no recession in the United States of America.") From time to time, a cheer went up from a small band of people somewhere in the House chamber. It was a particular kind of cheer, and we recognized its special sound from other occasions. We had first heard it, perhaps, from the people at the Republican National Convention of 1972 who shouted "Four more years!" on cue. We heard it again when Gerald Ford was nominated for the Vice-Presidency at the White House. It was hoarse and loud, and went on too long. The second the President completed his prepared text, a number of senators and representatives made for the podium to escort him to the exit, but they were premature, and had to be brought back. The President had a "personal word" to add. "One year of Watergate is enough," he said. For a moment, he got into the details of his defense. He would cooperate with the House Judiciary Committee in its inquiry into impeachment, but only up to a certain point. And then he said, "I have no intention whatever of ever walking away from the job that the people elected me to do for the people of the United States!" He seemed to liven up as he made his declaration, and he smiled. It was what he had come to say. A part of his audience gave him an ovation, and a part remained seated.

Until this moment, a shaky pretense had been kept up that what we had been hearing was a State of the Union Address. But now the occasion was revealed for what it was: a purely personal transaction. All year, the President had used the powers of government to protect himself. He had invoked the special privileges of his office; he had fired the man he appointed to investigate him; he had programmed his assistants and his Vice-Presidents to launch nationwide "offensives" against his opposition; and he had taken refuge behind the foreign policy of the United States, telling us to keep our eye on what was happening abroad and to forget about Watergate. Now, in his address, he made his defense before the entire government and the entire nation. Given his predicament, and his unwillingness to resign, it no doubt had to be that way. In the meantime, as the senators, representatives, Cabinet officers, and Supreme Court justices sat and listened to what was not a description of the state of the Union but a disguised legal brief, it seemed that one man had borrowed the whole Republic and all its officers and converted it to his private, idiosyncratic ends.

FEBRUARY 18, 1974

W HEN the energy crisis dealt its first sudden blows to the world's economy, there were not a few people who believed that a "return to the simple life" might be here or in the offing. Visions of cozy rural communities, with "old values" fully restored, and of quiet cities filled with cyclists and pedestrians floated before their eyes. A bracing austerity, it was said, would bring the world to its senses. Now that many people are giving thought to the simple life, we decided to make a quick check of a few of the world's nations to see how it is coming along.

In Peking this week, the eye and ear were assailed by the stirrings of a new national "campaign." In China, when the newspapers, the radio, television, and the loudspeakers in the factories and fields drop their standard propaganda and begin to pound out a single new theme, the Chinese know that a campaign is under way. The lives of millions will be changed—although the Chinese do not yet know how—and the life of the nation may be overturned. The last major campaign was the Great Proletarian Cultural Revolution—an event in which Mao Tse-tung and his colleagues unleashed bands of angry youths against all levels of the Party and governmental bureaucracy. After some months, normal daily life was completely disrupted, and after three years the Cultural Revolution was abandoned. The new campaign is cryptic in its aims. It has no name as yet. The nation is to "criticize" Confucius, Schubert, Bee-thoven, and Lin Piao. This campaign is all the more obscure in that none of its principal targets are among the living. No one knows precisely what it is that Beethoven and Schubert stir in the human breast, but the Chinese authorities somehow sense that that's the thing they want to stamp out.

In Moscow this week, a recently launched campaign continued, but its targets were the living—notably, the author Alexander Solzhenitsyn. The aim here is no mystery. In his recent book, *The Gulag Archipelago, 1918–1956,*

Solzhenitsyn has revealed a large part of the truth about the past of the Soviet regime, and the authorities wish to discredit both the author and his revelations. Not long ago, his ex-wife joined in the campaign. Russian viewers of television, although they are not allowed to read the book, allegedly write to the Soviet authorities expressing their outrage at its contents.

We turn now to the United States. The preoccupation here is not with writers and artists, whether living or dead. Here it's the Devil that absorbs us. President Nixon had a few slighting words to say recently about "professional criers of doom and prophets of despair," but the people who are lining up around the block to see *The Exorcist* were not listening. The experts are not sure why so many people want to see a film about a little girl possessed by the Devil. At least one or two experts think that minds are beginning to collapse under the weight of our day's insoluble problems. "My janitors are going bananas wiping up the vomit," the manager of one theatre where the film is playing reports. The Devil is on people's minds at the White House, too, where he is suspected of having erased eighteen and a half minutes of tape, according to the President's chief assistant, General Alexander Haig. However, not everyone is carried away. The press, on the whole, has taken a "balanced" approach to the Devil. *Newsweek* opined that "it is probably just as well . . . that the fad will inevitably pass, for the Devil's realm is dotted with pitfalls." One clergyman, upon hearing of a supposed exorcism, declared that the problem had not been the Devil at all. That idea was "just plain funny"; any sensible person could tell that the problem was merely a few ghosts. But large numbers agreed with the columnist who saw the new interest in the Devil as a sign of a spiritual awakening.

Finally, in England this week the talk was not of writers or artists or devils but of the prospect of "a catastrophe unparalleled in our postwar industrial history," as one official put it. The coal miners had voted to strike, a general election had been called, and the economic life of the nation was grinding to a halt. In Britain, the simple life had given way to physical, not mental, collapse. They were calling it a new Dark Age.

MARCH 18, 1974

WE'VE just learned that Arab financiers are helping to put up a Hilton hotel in Atlanta. We've also heard rumors that the Arab nations are going to lift their oil embargo against the United States. Not long ago, of course, when the world was just waking up to some of the dire consequences that an oil shortage could have for the industrialized nations (among others), Arab leaders were touring the world threatening economic destruction of any nation that did not fall in with their political demands. Somewhere along the line, their mood seems to have softened, and the softening may have had something to do with that hotel in Atlanta. As the oil flows out of the Middle East at its new, exorbitant prices, astronomical sums of money are flowing in. Over the next several years, the amounts will rise into the hundreds of billions of dollars. The Arab nations will need places where they can spend the money and invest it. And money, like oil, it seems, must flow West in large amounts if it is to be worth much to the Arabs. According to one real-estate report, Arab investors will buy something like a billion dollars' worth of real estate in the United States alone in the course of the next two years. If the oil-producing nations use their power to destroy the economies of the industrialized nations, they will be destroying the base on which their power rests. If they should go as far as to expropriate American businesses, the United States can always expropriate the Atlanta Hilton. What all this suggests to us is a new economic law: the Interdependence Theory of Value. According to classical economics, the value of a thing varies with its scarcity. According to Marx, the value of a thing varies with the amount of labor that goes into making it. According to the Interdependence Theory of Value, the value of a thing varies with the manners of the nation that produces it. The goods of nations that blackmail other nations lose value. The goods of nations that get along well with other nations rise in value. Value, according to this law, is generated by steady, reliable associations with others. When such relationships are missing, even money loses its value, as the Arab governments may now be learning. They might as well fill up their bank vaults with oil.

MARCH 25, 1974

J AMES D. St. Clair, the new man at the White House, says that he is a counsellor to "the office of the Presidency," not a counsellor to the President. The title has a high-sounding ring to it. It puts a distance between St. Clair and such matters as the eighteen-and-a-half-minute gap and the "milk money." And it fits in with the President's description of his own role in the case. He is another defender of the Presidency. In fact, listening to both of them, one gets the distinct impression that the office has no occupant. This impression of an elusive Chief Executive is enhanced when one hears Richard Nixon talking about "the President" in the third person, as though he—the man speaking to us—were only a very illustrious press secretary. But if St. Clair is a counsellor to the Presidency, then the President needs a lawyer. After all, it was not the Presidency that talked over the various "options" that might be exercised in dealing with the Watergate defendants, or took questionable tax deductions, or brought the country's Constitutional system to the edge of ruin. In our opinion, the best way for Mr. St. Clair to defend the Presidency would be for him to work for the President's impeachment. Certainly it would not be for him to write letters to the House Judiciary Committee advising it to restrict its inquiry to matters he thinks are relevant and telling it what evidence it can and can't have. (We are particularly bemused by the suggestion that the large quantity of material already promised—"nineteen recorded Presidential conversations and more than seven hundred documents"—relieves the White House of the obligation to give up any more. In an investigation, of course, if the suspect has the power to withhold even one document the whole proceeding is rendered meaningless.) The real threat to the Presidency—and, what is more important, to the Constitution—comes from the President. If the "defense" of the Presidency put up by the President and St. Clair were to succeed, the office would be permanently damaged. It would be associated forever with the Watergate crimes. What that high office needs now is not a defense but respect. The Presidency doesn't need a lawyer. It needs a President.

APRIL 8, 1974

A couple of months ago, when we read that four leaders of the radical movement of the nineteen-sixties—Jerry Rubin, Abbie Hoffman, Tom Hayden, and Rennie Davis—were going to be interviewed on the "Dick Cavett Show," we tuned in at the appointed hour. We had been watching a lot of television lately—particularly anything to do with the impeachment proceedings in Washington. Much of what we had been seeing was bewildering to us. Sometimes the events in Washington seemed like the rites of an alien civilization. By our reckoning, for example, a leader whose Administration is in disgrace might be showing some public signs of regret or contrition, whereas others in the public realm might be showing some signs of anger and disgust. But just the opposite was happening. The President and his men were in a towering rage at their investigators in the Congress, and the congressmen, by comparison, were meek and silent. We wondered what Cavett's radical—or ex-radical, for all we knew—guests might be thinking about it all. We settled into our chair. The show was announced. Then came the familiar theme song. Then the list of Cavett's guests: Sally Struthers, Anthony Quinn, Ike and Tina Turner. Cavett came on. No word from him about what had happened to the radicals. Soon, an out-of-date reference made us realize that we were watching canned material. Cavett couldn't explain anything, because at the moment he was speaking there was nothing to explain. We felt annoyed, puzzled, and a little frightened. What was more disturbing than the fact that we weren't being allowed to see the show was the fact that it had disappeared without any explanation. We tried calling A.B.C., but the line was busy for several hours. Somebody, somewhere, didn't want us to see that show, and we had no way of finding out who it was.

Later, we read that the management at A.B.C. had decided that the show wasn't "balanced" enough for its viewers. Our thoughts went back to a memo that came out during the Watergate investigation and that had to do with "balance" on television programs. We got hold of a copy and read it with new interest. Charles W. Colson had been reporting to H. R. Haldeman on a meeting he had had in September of 1970 with the top executives of all three of the big networks. At the time, of course, the public had no idea that network executives were having meetings with political advisers to the President. Colson had been pleased with the meeting. He wrote, "They were startled by how thoroughly we were doing our homework—both from the standpoint of knowledge of the law, as I discussed it, but, more importantly, from the way in which we have so thoroughly monitored their coverage and our analysis of it. . . . They are terribly concerned with being able to work out their own policies with respect to balanced coverage and not to have policies imposed on them by either the Commission [the Federal Communications Commission] or the Congress. . . . In short, they are very much afraid of us and are trying hard to prove they are 'good guys.' "

Not long after our unpleasant experience with A.B.C., we picked up an issue of *TV Guide* and got another jolt. There, in the pages of that previously unpolitical publication, was an article by Patrick Buchanan attacking television news. Later, we learned that *TV Guide* had just hired five regular contributors to comment on the news in a column called "News Watch." One is Buchanan, who is one of the President's chief speechwriters, and who was one of the drafters of ex-Vice-President Agnew's attacks on the press in 1969. We had seen Buchanan on TV recently, too. He had been interviewed by Bill Moyers on the Public Broadcasting Service, and we had been surprised to hear him say that even if the President were guilty of "a technical obstruction of justice," he should be allowed to remain as President, because of his achievements in foreign policy. Did we want to throw out a great President merely because he might have "sat on it [the evidence] too long," he asked. Buchanan had been on during what had turned out to be a wild period in our television-watching. The President had recently been in Nashville playing with a yo-yo, and shortly afterward, in another public appearance, he had said, "I am suggesting that the House follow the Constitution. If they do, I will." It was the first time we had ever heard a President paraphrase his oath of office on a conditional basis. And since he had already said that the House Judiciary Committee had gone outside the bounds of the Constitution in asking for too much evidence, he seemed, in fact, to be making a declaration of independence from the Constitution. His audience, as it happened, was made up partly of the owners of the television stations on which the networks depend for their survival. The audience applauded the President's remarks.

Another of the columnists that *TV Guide* had just hired is John D. Lofton, Jr., the former editor of *Monday*, which is a propaganda organ published by the Republican National Committee. Lofton had worked with Buchanan in bringing the Administration line to the public. In a memo to Haldeman, Buchanan had recommended Lofton as a member of a committee that would work on the "Assault Strategy" against McGovern during the election. Another of the columnists is Edith Efron, the author of *The News Twisters*, which attacks network news from a right-wing point of view. In *The News Twisters*, Miss Efron adds up the number of words she considers anti-Nixon in a given news program and then adds up the words she considers pro-Nixon, and compares the results. Usually, she arrives at the conclusion that there were more anti-Nixon words. Another of the columnists is Kevin P. Phillips, the author of *The Emerging Republican Majority* and a onetime aide to former Attorney General Mitchell. Phillips is now getting out a publication called *Media Report*, which purports to have discovered the "beginnings of public interest in breaking up the television networks." The fifth of the *TV Guide* columnists is John P. Roche, a Democrat who describes himself as a liberal but whom some liberals describe as a conservative. He had been added, the editors of *TV Guide* said, to provide "balance." This lineup of columnists recalled to our mind another memo we heard about a few months ago—a memo from Mr. Buchanan to the President. In it Mr. Buchanan had proposed setting up a foundation that would seem to be independent but would actually be run by and for the Administration. Describing the foundation as "a countervailing power outside the federal government," Buchanan suggested that one of its aims would be to "bring together experts—on the networks, for example—to discuss and produce a book of papers on their lack of objectivity and need for reform." Of how it would be run, Buchanan wrote, "We would have to lock it into the White House with probably two individuals at the top level—who had the ear of the President at all times. . . . The board of directors would run from right to center of the political spectrum, no kooks but unquestioned pro-Nixon people would have to have a complete lock on it, we would have to have people there who knew what was up and agreed to it; and then let the handpicked staff run the thing." *TV Guide* happens to be owned by Triangle Publications, the president of which is Walter H. Annenberg, President Nixon's Ambassador to England. *TV Guide* has the largest circulation of any weekly in the country and reaches a third of the adult population of the United States each week.

A couple of weeks ago, A.B.C. decided to let us see the four radical leaders after all, but in a changed format. After their hour-and-a-half show, two conservatives would come on for half an hour, presumably to right the "balance" of any minds that had been tipped too far to the left during the first part of the show. We tuned in again, interested now to see what it was we had been protected against on the first occasion. Jerry Rubin said that he and many others were getting in touch with their bodies. There was a "revolution" of getting in touch with one's body, he said. When enough people got in touch with their bodies, capitalism would collapse. Asked what it meant to be out of touch with your body, Rubin said that President Nixon was a good example of someone who was out of touch with his body. Abbie Hoffman said that he had been doing "quiet things" recently. Hayden said that he had been lobbying in Congress against continued American support for the South Vietnamese government. Rennie Davis displayed the nonstop, glowing smile and the glazed eyes of one who is "blissed out." He is now a follower of Guru Maharaj Ji, the sixteen-year-old spiritual leader from India, and he described his belief that the Guru was God. (This was enough "balance" for us.) Toward the end of the show, Cavett asked what any of them would do if someone came up to them and announced his intention of throwing a bomb at a munitions plant. Hayden dodged the question, and said it was more important now to "blow up what's in people's heads." Hoffman suggested that it might be more productive now to bomb an oil-refinery office than a munitions plant, but we were not allowed to hear this. (We learned it later.) His voice was momentarily silenced, and we were allowed only to see his lips move. Suddenly, we lost our appetite for the show, and we turned it off. It seemed to us that the screen was radiating fear into our living room and into other living rooms across the country. The show had become a public display of fear: of the networks' fear of the government, of the government's fear of the left wing, and of the fear all of us now seem to have—the *embarrassment* we feel—when *any* political views are expressed without inhibition by anyone but the President. We remembered the staggering power that, Watergate or no Watergate, lies coiled in the White House—power that is veiled for the moment but can be used any day by the incumbent or by a successor to lash out at those who he decides are his foes. Our thoughts went back to the men in Washington—the leaders of the Judiciary Committee (Representative Pete Rodino and Representative Edward Hutchinson); their counsel (John Doar and Albert Jenner); Special Prosecutor Leon Jaworski; and their colleagues on the Judiciary Committee and in the Special Prosecutor's office—who are approaching, in their gingerly way, the wrathful presence in the White House, and we wished them whatever strength and courage they can find for the time of danger that lies ahead.

APRIL 15, 1974

FOUR hundred and thirty-two thousand seven hundred and eighty-seven dollars and thirteen cents. A hefty figure. The kind that announcers read with automatic added emphasis. A figure that seems to explain a lot. To many, it suggests some answers to the whys and wherefores of the White House scandals: plain human greed. Wilbur Mills thinks that it will go further than anything else we've learned recently to force the President from office. The people understand taxes, he says. They are preparing their own returns at the moment. To our mind, however, the whole tale of the President's finances, as it has unfolded so far, only deepens the mystery. What surprises us is not the largeness of the benefits the President had arranged for himself but their smallness. The Presidency is the highest honor in the gift of the American people. In the view of most Americans, it is, among other things, the place where the climbing stops. From that pinnacle, half a million dollars, or a million dollars, or a hundred million dollars—any sum of money, for that matter—fades into insignificance. But President Nixon's financial maneuverings suggest a different perspective. It is a shrunken view of the Presidency. Some statesmen overreach themselves. President Nixon underreached. At some point, it seems, the honors bestowed on him outran his capacity for grasping or appreciating them. Apparently, he always found something to be missing: more appreciation, more pomp and splendor, more money. Not content with one White House, he bought two more. He was twice elected President, and yet the Presidency eluded him. There is no surprise when the humble dream of greater things. But what are we to make of it when the already great dream of meaner things?

MAY 6, 1974

I N recent months, a spirited debate has arisen over whether the President should resign or be impeached. Some of those ranged on the side of resignation are *Time* and our own Senator James Buckley. Some of those ranged on the side of impeachment are the Washington *Post* and Tom Wicker. The argument in favor of resignation is that it would cause less turmoil in the nation. Senator Buckley has painted a particularly vivid picture of the turmoil that impeachment might bring. "The [Senate] Chamber," he says, "would become a twentieth-century Roman Colosseum, as the performers are thrown to the electronic lions." And he adds, "The most sordid dregs dug up by the Watergate miners would inflame the passions of the domestic audience." Moreover, "History would come to a stop." In the light of all this, he believes, it is the President's patriotic duty to resign. The argument for impeachment is that impeachment is the proper Constitutional procedure for removing a President, and that resignation would be an irregular procedure (although the Constitution does specify that a President may resign). It is further pointed out that if the President were to resign, he might then portray himself as a martyr, and go about the country stirring up trouble, whereas if he were impeached, convicted, and removed from office, the charges against him would be fully proved, and he would sink into harmless obscurity. One proponent of impeachment proceedings as a method of legal inquiry, Representative Walter Flowers, of Alabama, has even begged the President not to resign. "So, Mr. President, do not resign—you may be impeached, even convicted. But do not resign," he has said.

It seems to us that a misconception lies somewhere near the heart of this debate. It has to do with the fact that each of the opposing pieces of advice is addressed to a different protagonist. Those who favor resignation are talking primarily to the President. He can resign, but he cannot impeach himself. He no doubt has many reasons for refusing to resign, but it seems unlikely that the arguments in favor of impeachment are among them. The thought that he should really leave office but that his impeachment and conviction would be better for the country than his resignation—because they would give the country a marvellous civics lesson in Constitutional procedures—is not, we would think, likely to be uppermost in his mind. Those who favor impeachment are talking primarily to Congress. Congress cannot prevent the President from resigning in order that it may impeach him. To be sure, individual congressmen can call on the President to resign, but even such calls gain their force from the existence of the Congress's real power in the matter—the power to impeach, try, and convict. There is no choice between resignation and impeachment, because there is no one in a position to choose. The real issue, of course, is whether the President is guilty of whatever it is that constitutes "high crimes and misdemeanors." If he is not, then he should neither resign nor be removed by the Congress. If he is guilty, then the important thing is that, one way or another, he leave office. In that case, resignation becomes his responsibility, impeachment and conviction ours.

MAY 13, 1974

THE master of concealment, in a sudden reversal, has stunned the nation with an avalanche of garbled disclosure. Although President Nixon may stand lower in the public's esteem than any Chief Executive before him, he has, in an exercise of seemingly unimpaired power, brushed aside the House Judiciary Committee, stupefied the Congress as a whole, and tied the judiciary in knots. And through the sheer volume of the release he has accomplished a takeover of our daily lives. The good citizen who reads it all finds himself leading Richard Nixon's life instead of his own. The new strategy was born of a new peril. It was that material already in the hands of the committee contained, as we can now see, everything that the nation needs to know about President Nixon. The President had asked us all to believe that he learned of the Watergate cover-up for the first time on March 21st. But would an innocent President, upon learning that he had been betrayed by his closest aides, and that the White House was being blackmailed, say to one of those aides, "It seems to me we have to keep the cap on the bottle that much [by paying the blackmail money] or we don't have any options"? And would he, speaking of his aides' potential appearance before a grand jury, advise, "But you can say I don't remember. You can say I can't recall. I can't give any answer to that that I can recall"? To ask these questions is to answer them. The President's most pressing need, therefore, was not to conceal anything more, although there may be a lot more to conceal, but somehow to neutralize what was about to be put on the record. It is important to bear in mind that it is not really the President who has released the March 21st tape. Archibald Cox saw to that last fall, at the cost of his job. What the President has done is to pre-empt the Judiciary Committee's inevitable release of that same information to the public by making it public himself in a self-serving manner. His method is something new in the history of propaganda: it is to use an apparent confession of crime as a means of establishing innocence. He hopes that we will draw such a powerful inference of his innocence from the fact that he is releasing the evidence that we will be blinded to the proof of guilt that the evidence contains. We are meant to think, "How can this be the proof of his guilt when he has released it himself?" His method requires him to put out two opposing versions of the facts at the same time: first the "interpretation" of the facts, then the facts. For example, in his speech introducing the transcripts, he said that he rejected the notion of paying money to buy E. Howard Hunt's silence about White House crimes. But in the transcript he tells his legal counsel that they have "no choice" but to pay Hunt. Likewise, in the speech, the President described an instruction he gave to John Dean to write a report about the Watergate cover-up as one measure he had taken to "find the truth." But the transcript shows that he planned to use Dean's report as a means of thwarting the Ervin investigation, which was coming up soon. As the President put it on March 21st, "Then I offer the Ervin committee [the] report this way, I say, 'Dear Senator Ervin. Here is the report before your hearings. You have the report, and as I have said previously, any questions that are not answered here, you can call the White House staff member and they will be directed to answer any questions on an informal basis.'" Or as John Ehrlichman said to the President, "Assuming that some corner of this thing comes unstuck, you are then in a position to say, 'Look, that document I published is the document I relied on . . .'" In these and in a thousand other details, the President invites us all to set aside the reports of our own eyes and ears and brains as we read the transcripts and to let his "interpretation" take their place. He shows us thirteen hundred pages of what in tone and substance is apparently a record of criminals planning their crimes and tells us it is a record of the police trying to crack a case. He unveils a swamp and instructs us to see a garden of flowers. With the old method of concealment, he tried to tamper with the public record. With the new method of disclosure and contradiction, he tampers with the public's sanity. Having failed to conceal the evidence of crime, he has launched a campaign to destroy the country's capacity to recognize what crime is. He has contrived to use the full power of his office to drive the nation out of its mind.

MAY 27, 1974

A FTER spending a year or so virtually in hiding, the Democratic Party has finally hit upon a position to take on the question of the President's fitness to continue in office. The denunciations of the President by such men as Senator Hugh Scott, the minority leader, and the calls for the President's resignation by other prominent Republicans gave the Democrats their opportunity to take a stand. In a rare show of unanimity, the Democrats raised objections to the Republicans' show of concern. Senator Robert Byrd, the Democratic whip, warned of "capitulation to emotionalism, which takes so little to deteriorate into mass hysteria." And Robert Strauss, the chairman of the Democratic National Committee, criticized the "terrible hue and cry by Republicans running for office trying to put some distance between themselves and the President." Among the many strange developments in the story of impeachment, this is surely one of the strangest. The Democratic Party has, of all things, made a show of interposing itself between a besieged Republican President and the supposedly hysterical members of his own party. The way the Democrats tell it, they have had to protect the Constitution from hotheaded Republicans who want to railroad a Republican President out of office through mob action. There is even the implication that the Democrats are perhaps saving us from President Nixon's own possible impulse to resign, as though they had taken on the role of the eloquent officer of the law who persuades the would-be suicide on the ledge of an office building not to inflict his horrible display of self-destruction on the public.

We have scrutinized the scene carefully but have simply been unable to spot any sign of the mass hysteria that Senator Byrd is worried about. Nor have we heard any hue or any cry. Here in New York, at least, the usual sobriety of life remains undisturbed. And, reassuring as it may be to some people to know that if Senator Scott or some other Republican goes out of control Mr. Strauss will step in to restrain him, most people we've heard from were encouraged rather than frightened by the Republicans' rather normal human response—in the fad phrase of the moment, "moral revulsion"—to the White House transcripts. In fact, they wished it had come sooner. But wherever the country's best interests may lie, and however sincere some members of both parties may be in believing that they are serving those interests, the fact is that, politically, right now impeachment looks like the best course for the Democrats and resignation looks like the best course for the Republicans. And that seems to be why we see the sudden—and, we assume, temporary—alliance between the Democrats and the desperate men in the White House. Resignation would get things over with quickly and install another Republican President right away. Impeachment would be long and drawn out and would prolong the Republicans' humiliation. Resignation, insofar as it might be precipitated by people outside the White House, would mainly involve Republicans, and therefore would redound to their credit. Impeachment would involve the whole Congress, where the Democrats predominate, and would have more the look of a national judgment against a Republican President. Moreover, the Democrats, by staying safely in the background, remove themselves as objects of any backlash against the President's removal. At a solemn time in our history, when we dare to hope that politicians will rise above politics, we appear to be seeing one more example of the opposite.

There is another, perhaps more important, benefit for the Democrats in their new position. They have seized the political high ground of the "responsible," "restrained" position. Mr. Strauss says that he is proud of the Democrats' "remarkable restraint" in dealing with the matter of impeachment. There is, of course, more than a little poetic justice in the Democrats' assumption of the "responsible" position. For some five years now, they have been forced into the "irresponsible" position by President Nixon. Any form of opposition to the President was branded as irresponsible in those years. To oppose the war was irresponsible, to oppose repressive criminal legislation was irresponsible, to vote funds for social needs was irresponsible. What was responsible was to support the President. The Democratic Party, or a large part of it, was out in the political cold. Its numbers in the Congress increased somewhat, but its power to influence national affairs, like the power of the Congress itself, waned steadily. In a strange reversal of the traditional role of the loyal opposition, its power was reduced to whatever credit it could win by renouncing, with a show of "responsibility," its right to oppose. In this way, the idea grew that the role of the opposition was to line up with the President. Now it is the Republicans who have been forced, by the revelations in the transcripts, to abandon the "responsible" position, and to go into opposition to the President. And no sooner had they abandoned their advantageous position than the Democrats rushed in to occupy it. Senator Byrd has even suggested that the President's resignation under fire could do "serious and irreparable damage to our Constitutional system." (His position, paradoxically, represents a high point in the overawed respect for the Presidency which has grown up in our day. We have all just learned that the President can destroy the Constitution by seizing too much power. Now Senator Byrd tells us that he can also destroy it by relinquishing power.) But then it has always been the tactic of those in the "responsible" position to attack the "irresponsible" people for supposed "hysteria," "alarmism," "self-righteousness," "negativism," and the like. And this is what is discouraging about the Democrats' new tack. The roles have been reversed for the time being, but the old pattern has held. Senator Scott, by speaking up against official misconduct, and House Minority Leader John Rhodes, by merely stating that the President has the option to resign, are automatically placed in a position of weakness, while Mr. Strauss and Senator Byrd, by joining their voices with those of Patrick Buchanan, Dean Burch, and Julie Eisenhower, are in the position of strength. The Republicans are represented as hysterical as soon as they take notice that all is not well at the White House. Now, as before, those in opposition are attacked as "irresponsible" at exactly the moment when they begin to behave like responsible men.

JUNE 24, 1974

O N the day the President set out on his trip to Europe and the Middle East, he sent off two letters that are likely to loom far larger in the history books than any business he might transact abroad. One went to Judge Gerhard Gesell and declared that the President, rather than the courts, would be the final arbiter of what evidence from White House files could be presented in the criminal trial of one of his former aides, John Ehrlichman. The other went to Chairman Peter Rodino, of the House Judiciary Committee, and declared that the President, rather than a committee of Congress, would be the final arbiter of what evidence from White House files could be presented for use in the inquiry into his possible impeachment. The letters were of special importance because they outlined, for the first time, a comprehensive rationale, amounting to a declaration of fundamental political principle, of the President's position in relation both to the impeachment proceedings and to the legal proceedings against former members of his Administration. The letter to Judge Gesell, which was signed by the President's counsel, James St. Clair, was simple and to the point. It asserted that the President, by virtue of his right of "executive privilege," "shall determine whether or not it is in the public interest to produce the notes [from Ehrlichman's White House files] for use in the trial." The letter to Chairman Rodino, which was signed by the President, was more expansive. The President offered two broad justifications for his refusal to give up evidence subpoenaed by the Judiciary Committee. The first was legal, and the second was ad hoc. The President argued that, owing to the separation of powers under the Constitution, each of the three branches of government exercised sovereign control over any information it decided was "confidential." As he put it, "preserving the principle of separation of powers—and of the executive as a co-equal branch—requires that the executive, no less than the legislative or judicial branches, must be immune from unlimited search and seizure by the other co-equal branches." Having asserted his right to withhold information from the other branches (and from anyone else, for that matter), the President proceeded to exercise it. "The voluminous body of materials that the Committee already has . . . does give the full story of Watergate insofar as it relates to Presidential knowledge and Presidential actions," he stated. He went on to advise the committee to stop pursuing "the chimera" of more evidence on other tapes. Then, temporarily assuming the role of an objective third party stepping in to settle a quarrel between two strangers, he declared, "There would be no end unless a line were drawn somewhere by someone. Since it is clear that the Committee will not draw such a line, I have done so."

The President seems to describe a system in which the three branches of government are so well separated that they amount to three independent governments. In reality, of course, if the links that make the branches of government accountable to one another and to the public were to be broken, only one branch—the executive—would eventually survive, because it is only the executive that can both give and carry out orders. The other branches can only give them. Faced with a disobedient executive, the judiciary and legislative branches are as powerless as generals without troops. Two recent events have already foreshadowed their ineffectuality in a system like the one described in the President's letter. One is the decision of the Judiciary Committee not to ask the full House to cite the President for contempt of Congress after he refused to comply with several of their subpoenas for evidence, on the ground, according to one member of the committee, that the citation would be unenforceable. The other is the apparent hesitation of Judge Gesell to cite the President for contempt after his apparent refusal to supply evidence for the trial, because, according to at least one report, that citation, too, would be unenforceable. In these cases, "unenforceable" simply means that, whatever the legal merits may be, the President, in the real world, commands superior forces: the people with the guns obey him rather than judges or congressmen. The truth of the matter is that nothing but the President's directives is "enforceable" when the executive stops co-operating with the other branches of government.

One of the links between the branches which the President's letter to Chairman Rodino leaves out altogether is the provision of the Constitution which the letter ostensibly sets out to discuss: impeachment. At the close of the letter, the President argues, "Whenever one branch attempts to press too hard in intruding on the Constitutional prerogatives of another, that balance [the balance of power among the three branches] is threatened." And, of course, it is true that impeachment cannot be used to diminish the power of the office of the Presidency by one jot. What impeachment, if it is followed by conviction, will do is to strip a particular President not just of any power of executive privilege that he may hold but of all the powers of his office. Any privileges arising out of the separation of powers fall before the impeachment power, because impeachment and conviction are precisely a total and final judgment of the conduct of one branch of government by the members of another. To raise the doctrine of the separation of powers against impeachment is to nullify impeachment. Nor is the power of impeachment an incidental or marginal power. It is the foundation on which every other provision of the Constitution rests, for it is the remedy for usurpation: only when the Chief Executive, or any other civil officer of the United States, gives the appearance of violating in a grievous way his Constitutional oath of office by seeming to commit "treason, bribery, or other high crimes and misdemeanors" does the House of Representatives have recourse to impeachment.

The President's two letters, therefore, are not just one more set of legal arguments. They are briefs against Constitutional government. They are a proposal for a new form of government, in which a President, once elected, is beyond any restraint. They put in writing what the President's actions over the last year or so have been leading up to: suspension of the law insofar as it applies to the President.

JULY 1, 1974

JUST about everything that is happening in Washington these days is of such startling strangeness that it seems to be happening for the first time anywhere. Now the White House has hit upon still another unheard-of tactic in the President's defense strategy. It is to beat the public senseless with more news of Presidential wrongdoing than it can endure. The President's release of his transcripts is a case in point. Recently, two White House aides spelled out the new White House thinking for Philip Shabecoff, of the *Times*. After it had been made known that the President had been named unanimously by a grand jury as an unindicted co-conspirator in the Watergate cover-up, and after the President had sent off his letter defying the House Judiciary Committee's subpoena of more tapes, Raymond Price, a speechwriter for the President, said, "These recent disclosures are not damaging," and added, apparently approvingly, that the public was now "anesthetized." Operation Candor had given way to Operation Anesthesia. Ken W. Clawson, the President's communications director, observed that "the impact isn't there anymore," and he explained, "Last fall, we used to talk about what the next bombshell would be. But now there aren't any more bombshells." If there aren't, the reason, of course, is not that no more bombs are being dropped but that the public's sensibilities have been bombed out. In the new White House strategy, everything that once hurt the President can now be used to help him. Revelations that were once damaging serve only to promote the supposed public unconsciousness on which the White House is now relying as the President's best protection. (Recent polls, however, seem to show that the unconsciousness is to be found more in the Congress than in the country at large.) What stands between the President and impeachment is not a scarcity of evidence but a mountainous superfluity of it. The evidence is all around us, in the wreckage of our institutions as well as in the Judiciary Committee's thirty-six volumes. The evidence is so pervasive that many of us can barely remember what innocence is. It is as though we had too much evidence to convict, and had been condemned to eternal impeachment. Once, the bombshells harmed the President's cause. For the moment, it seems that the more wrong he does, the safer he becomes.

Not long ago, it was reported that the Democratic Party, by making a show of opposition to calls for the President's resignation which had come from within the Republican Party, was trying to use the issue of impeachment for political advantage. Now, as the House Judiciary Committee moves toward a vote on whether or not to recommend articles of impeachment to the full House, there have been reports that some of the Republicans on the Committee may, for political reasons of their own, vote against any articles of impeachment. If all these reports are correct, it means that both parties are maneuvering around the issue of impeachment purely for short-term political gain. There is another school of thought in the matter, however. It holds that the members of the House Judiciary Committee will rise above petty political interest, because they know that the eye of history is on them. According to this school, the members will reflect that whereas everything they have done as representatives so far is likely to be forgotten, this one vote will surely be remembered. And since on this single occasion the spotlight of history will penetrate the convenient obscurity in which representatives normally act, the committee members will be on their best behavior. This school of thought, no less than the school holding that the vote will reflect political calculation, belittles the members of the Judiciary Committee. "History," in this connection, is nothing more than the future's image of the present. By invoking the judgment of history—a judgment that, in any case, is unknowable to us—we rely on a deferred form of public relations in which the images are merely more lasting than contemporary images. In doing so, we pass the buck to the future. We mentally remove ourselves to a point outside the corrupt present, as though by this operation we could gain access to a fund of wisdom unavailable to us in our time and could use the future to gain moral leverage on the politicians of the present. But in performing this trick we overlook the fact that the representatives in our era have mental and moral equipment, too. The men and women of the House Judiciary Committee, who will have to cast the first votes on the question of impeachment, have minds and consciences of their own to consult, and need not try to peer into unwritten history books. The evidence is spread out before them, the vastness of the stakes is inescapably plain, and the decision is theirs—to be made not in remote periods by persons unknown but here and now by the thirty-eight members of the Judiciary Committee.

JULY 8, 1974

I T is not often that one is tempted to date precisely the opening of an era. A remarkable article in the *Times* by Marvin and Bernard Kalb, however, tempts us to name Saturday, October 20, 1973, as the day when the political era that mankind is now living in began. It is an era characterized, if one is to judge from such a brief glimpse of it, by a nearly all-pervading and bottomless uncertainty—an uncertainty that includes doubts about the continuance of constitutional democracy in the United States, doubts about the fundamental health of the world economy, and the abiding, ever-present doubts about the survival of humanity in the nuclear age. On October 20th, the human race was in the opening stages of one of its periodic brushes with its collective mortality: four days later the United States would begin a worldwide alert of its armed forces, including its nuclear forces. In the Middle East, the Yom Kippur war was under way. The Israelis had gone on the offensive, and the situation on the battlefield was fluid. In Washington, President Nixon was preparing to dismiss Special Prosecutor Archibald Cox. Secretary of State Henry Kissinger, who apparently had no inkling of the imminent dismissal of Cox and the resultant "firestorm" that was about to engulf the domestic scene, was airborne on his way to Russia, where he planned to talk over the situation in the Middle East with Secretary-General Leonid Brezhnev. One of Kissinger's hopes, certainly, was to forestall the possibility of a non-metaphorical firestorm that might engulf the whole world if things in the Middle East went further awry. While he was aloft, the Kalb brothers report, he received two messages of great importance. Each, in its own way, was like a warning shot signalling the advent of the new era. One was a message from the President, entrusting Kissinger with what the Kalbs call a "power of attorney" to make agreements with Brezhnev in the President's name. The President, preoccupied with his own survival, had temporarily handed the world's survival over to Kissinger: later it would be Kissinger who, acting under an even more sweeping grant of authority, would order the nuclear alert while the President remained virtually incommunicado on another floor of the White House. The second message was that Saudi Arabia had decided to impose an oil embargo on the United States. The oil crisis, which has threatened ever since to throw the world economy out of whack, was upon us, but for the moment, according to the Kalbs, Kissinger didn't give the matter much thought. Whether he knew it or not, the airborne Secretary of State, who now literally held the fate of the earth in his hands, had been buffeted in mid-flight by shock waves spreading out from two historical events of the first magnitude: the dismissal of the Special Prosecutor, which would precipitate impeachment proceedings by the House Judiciary Committee against the President; and the energy crisis, which would force the world to recognize that there were global limits to certain key resources. Yet the Secretary was probably in a worse position than most American newspaper readers to grasp the meaning of the events. He was puzzled by the President's sudden grant of authority. Not until he had left the Soviet Union and arrived in England (where there is a free press) did he see the enormous headlines from Washington and understand the gravity of the crisis at home and the extent of the President's preoccupation with it. And not until some time after that was he able to turn his attention to the question of energy. The Secretary had been making decisions having a bearing on the future of the world, but at the time he did so he had been all but out of touch with the world.

The scene of Secretary of State Kissinger at thirty thousand feet on his way to Moscow receiving messages of tremendous but partly obscure import is one more vivid illustration, if any were needed, of the merging of all major events that confront the United States, whether they occur at home or abroad, into a single political field, which turns out, the impeachment inquiry notwithstanding, to be increasingly dominated by the executive branch. Not even a President is required for executive supremacy. When he is incapacitated for some reason, the Secretary of State can take charge. It is not the man that counts but the centralized machinery for making decisions and then carrying them out. If Secretary Kissinger's predicament on his way to Moscow shows who makes the decisions in our country, it also shows how they are made. The political structure within which we confront our uncertain future presents us with the anomalous fact that unimportant decisions are weighed carefully and at great length in open, democratic forums while the important decisions are made by a few men in secret. The Congress fully debates this or that detail of policy before taking any action—and the action is often overridden by a veto or by Presidential impoundment. The President and his men, acting in virtual isolation, weave the broad pattern of national and global affairs. Each of these branches of government has become distorted. On the fringes of power, Congress sits like a bank of spectators. The pressure is low, the debate is close to frivolous, the actions taken are futile. At the center, the President and his men try to cope with an onslaught of events too vast for them to handle. The pressure is crushingly intense, the debate is often perfunctory, and the actions taken are sometimes reckless. We Americans have now organized things in such a way that our control is greatest where it matters least and is least where it matters most. The route of the school bus and the price of beef we deliberate with ponderous care and hedge about with restrictions. The survival of the world we suspend from a thread.

JULY 29, 1974

A Republican member of the House Judiciary Committee predicted last week that he and his fellow Party members would vote in a bloc against recommending articles of impeachment to the full House, and, in a burst of determination, he added, "We're going to win this goddam thing." His remarks were out of keeping with the spirit of the impeachment inquiry as it has been conducted so far. At no time is the Constitutional responsibility of any branch of the government heavier than that of the Congress during impeachment proceedings. It has often been said that the courts are the final arbiters of the greatest issues in American politics. But the impeachment of a President, once it is under way, with the Congress constituting itself the "grand inquest of the nation," reminds us that, when all is said and done, it is the Congress that is the final repository of the sovereignty of the people.

During any impeachment, the Congress is transformed. The separation of powers is partly suspended, and the Congress reaches into the other branches of government to investigate and try men, and sometimes to remove them from power. When a full-scale Constitutional crisis exists, as it does now, not the President or the Supreme Court Justices but the members of Congress are ultimately entrusted with the survival of the American form of government. They have the last, unreviewable word. (It is a measure of how far we have strayed from the Constitution that in the matter of compelling the President to produce evidence the rulings of the courts have appeared to carry more weight with the public than the subpoenas of the House of Representatives.) During Presidential impeachment proceedings, the members hold the integrity of the whole government temporarily in trust. Having taken on a quasi-judicial function, they must act with the fairness and thoroughness of the judiciary. Having placed the power of the Chief Executive in limbo, they must act with the efficiency and dispatch of the executive. They not only must decide whether to remove the President from office but must conduct themselves in a manner so scrupulously lawful and fair that the public's confidence in the government, if it has been shaken by the President, is restored by his judges. Having temporarily taken on duties associated with all the branches of the government, they must assume the virtues of all the branches. When affairs reach this point, and the future of the country is at stake, any announcement by a member of Congress that "we're going to win" is simply out of order. The issue is not one that shapes up as a contest between two sides, in which one side's gain is the other's loss; rather, everyone wins or everyone loses. In this situation, the only "we" with any standing is the entire people of the United States.

AUGUST 5, 1974

L AST week, in the days leading up to the House Judiciary Committee's votes on impeachment, there seemed to be a change in the American air. It was not that—as the thought is often expressed—"the tide was moving against the President." Another tide appeared to be running in our affairs, and that tide had remarkably little to do with the President. Indeed, it was a part of the new atmosphere that suddenly the President seemed almost a peripheral figure in the proceedings. The fusillades of charges coming out of the White House—that the Judiciary Committee was a "lynch mob," that it was a "kangaroo court"—were not so much opposed as ignored. A shift in the country's attention seemed to have occurred. The nation's gaze was moving away from the one, omnipresent man whose angry statements and restless travels about the country and the world had held us spellbound for so long—as though it were he, and not we, who held the key to our future—and was focussing on scores of other men, justices and congressmen, who now occupied the center of the stage for the first time. Suddenly our affairs seemed to be in the hands of "reasonable men, acting reasonably"— in the phrase of John Doar, special counsel of the Committee. The shift in attention was a sign of recuperation in the body politic. Observers had been on the lookout for one more "firestorm" to resolve the issue; instead, they found themselves in the midst of this quiet mending. The fortunes of Richard Nixon were never the main issue of the impeachment proceedings. "Our judgment is not concerned with an individual but with a system of Constitutional government" is how House Judiciary Committee Chairman Peter Rodino put it in his statement opening the impeachment debate. In fact, it had been the President's blurring of his own interests with the nation's interests, and his use of government power to "get" his own political opponents, that had led to some of the offenses under examination by the Committee. The change in atmosphere was anticipated by the moving words of counsellor Doar, when, in recommending the President's impeachment, he said, "As an individual, I have not the slightest bias against President Nixon. I would hope that I would not do him the smallest, slightest injury." Doar's words were a signal that the President would be judged by new standards. This was not a case of the "enemies" taking revenge. The new judges, perhaps bearing in mind that the way we now handle a President may set the standard for the way future Presidents will handle all of us, were steering clear of vengeance. The intemperate accusations levelled by the President's aides seemed to invite a response in kind. But the Committee left all that aside. They were not hitting back. They were starting over.

AUGUST 12, 1974

I N Greece, a military dictatorship has yielded in favor of a democratic civilian regime. Performing an act that we think is without precedent, a general who was serving on the military junta put through a call to a civilian in exile and invited him to come home and form a government. There was jubilation throughout the country. Thousands of people poured into the streets of Athens, holding candles aloft and shouting "Democracy!" Immediately, newspapers began to publish uncensored news. Political prisoners were released, to joyous welcomes. A composer and an actress returning from exile were mobbed by well-wishers at the airport. In Portugal, meanwhile, military leaders have deposed a civilian dictatorship and are apparently moving the country in the direction of democratic government. In Thailand, a military junta has been replaced by a civilian government. In France, where Valéry Giscard D'Estaing, a conservative, has recently been elected President, one of the new government's first acts was to ban wiretapping. In Spain, Generalissimo Franco has handed power over to Juan Carlos de Borbón, a man of more moderate persuasion, and an ad hoc coalition of civilian leaders is reported to have announced its willingness to form a new government and restore full democratic freedom. The unbroken succession of coups of recent years has now been interrupted, in a manner of speaking, by a series of reverse coups, in which power reverts to the people. For reasons unknown, a shift in the political climate of the world has occurred, and it seems to favor liberty. Here in the United States, of course, the House Judiciary Committee has met and cast its votes. No regime fell, no one was out in the streets with candles. But some invisible equivalent of these celebrations was quietly taking place. And when it was all over, everything was changed. Here, too, freedom had somehow won the day.

AUGUST 19, 1974

ON Thursday night, when President Nixon announced his resignation, his demeanor was hardly different from the demeanor we had grown accustomed to in the last five years. His face was a mask; his words were cold and unreal. But on Friday morning, when he appeared before his Cabinet and staff to bid them farewell, everything was changed. The mask was gone, and the man was before us. Human feeling played across his face: grief, regret, humor, anger, affection. He spoke of his parents. His father, he said, had failed at many things he had undertaken, but he "did his job" and had been "a great man." His mother "was a saint," he said simply. However, no books would be written about her, he said, weeping now. All at once, he was reading what Theodore Roosevelt had written when his first wife had died: "She was beautiful in face and form, and lovelier still in spirit. . . . Her life had always been in the sunshine. There had never come to her a single great sorrow. . . . Then, by a strange and terrible fate, death came to her." We hardly knew why President Nixon was telling us these things, and it

seemed to us that he hardly knew, either. Yet there was more warmth and
feeling in these chaotic, uncontrolled words than in all the other words of
his Presidency put together. A few hours later, President Ford addressed the
nation. He, too, spoke movingly and with feeling. Three times in his remarks
he spoke of love. Hearing the word gave us a small start. Love was something
we had not looked for in any of its shapes or forms in the public sphere for
a very long time. The America of the last ten or twelve years was a loveless
place. "Nobody is a friend of ours," Richard Nixon had told his young legal
counsel John Dean. Of the 1972 election, he had said, "This is a war." For
lawbreakers, his world had been one, as he put it, "without pity." The wretched
of the earth had been out of luck in his scheme of things, whether they were
the peasants of Vietnam and Bangladesh or the poor at home. His had been
a cold universe. Listening to President Ford speak of love, we thought back
to President Nixon's incoherent remarks shortly before. For the first time in
several years, he had been talking like a free man. Something in the new
atmosphere had dissolved the walls of reserve and released a torrent of
emotion. Richard Nixon, freed, like the rest of us, from the oppression of
his rule, was pouring his heart out to the whole nation.

AUGUST 26, 1974

A S the Nixon Administration approached its end, the President's supporters dwindled to a mere handful. They were an odd but interesting
assortment. One was Representative Earl Landgrebe, of Indiana, who
said, "I'm sticking by my President even if he and I have to be taken out of
this building and shot." (The building in question was the Capitol.) Landgrebe
also said, "Don't confuse me with the facts. I have a closed mind." Asked for
his explanation of what was going on, he said that the President was being
driven from office by a conspiracy that included "the national media." He
suspected, he added, that it just might be run by the Communists. He apparently did not know that the Russian Communists, at least, were in close
agreement with his interpretation of events. Another of the President's un-
shaken supporters was Leonid Zamyatin, director general of the Tass news
agency. He, too, saw malicious propaganda by "the mass media" as responsible
for the President's downfall. "The impulse for this affair came after the Democratic Party suffered defeat," he told the Russian public; it might have been
Patrick Buchanan or Ronald Ziegler talking. "A very definite brainwashing of
public opinion was taking place on both radio and television, and it certainly

was not in favor of President Nixon," he went on, engaging in a bit of brainwashing himself. Zamyatin and his colleagues had adopted the Nixon line down to its smallest details; Valentin Zorin, a prominent Soviet television commentator, said that the American public was more interested in inflation than in Watergate. Missing from their explanation was any reference to any misbehavior on the part of the Nixon Administration. Here was an entire government built on the pattern of Earl Landgrebe's mind. The Soviet authorities didn't want to be confused by the facts.

In the early days of the Watergate scandal, some of the President's supporters argued that the scandal should be suppressed because our foes would make use of it in their propaganda. Then, when the Russians instead blacked out the impeachment story, it seemed for a while that they might be trying to curry favor with the President in the hope of winning concessions at the bargaining table. But now that the President has fallen and the Soviet leaders are suppressing any true account of why, it is plain that their reasons ran deeper than any hope of gaining an advantage over the American government. The paramount consideration was evidently the effect that such a story might have on their own affairs. Unquestionably, the spectacle of a head of government and his aides being driven from office for involvement in crimes such as illegal wiretapping, breaking and entering, and the use of government agencies to punish political opponents was extremely dangerous to them. They were quick to realize that their real affinity was not with the President's opposition—as they had thought in the days of the anti-war protesters—but with the President himself. The interpretation of events in the United States which was offered by the President's supporters suited their needs perfectly. It allowed them to portray what was actually a victory for justice over illegitimate rule—such a dangerous process for their people to observe—as a mere "interparty struggle," in Zamyatin's words.

At the same time, it gave the Russian authorities an opportunity to denigrate the American press. For they understood that, with the American government maintaining silence on the Soviet Union's treatment of its dissidents in the name of preserving détente, a free press was the one remaining major forum in the world where the truth about the Soviet regime could be made known. If President Nixon had been able to put an end to press freedom in the United States, no tears would have been shed in Moscow. For, secure as the Soviet regime appears to be, its own slight experience with truth-telling has given it some inkling of the power of "the facts." No less a figure than Alexander Solzhenitsyn put them on notice about that. During the period of "de-Stalinization" under Premier Khrushchev, *One Day in the Life of Ivan Denisovich*, Solzhenitsyn's account of life in a Soviet concentration camp, was published in Russia, and, to his amazement, he was invited to appear before officials of the Military Collegium to elaborate on his views. "It was like a dream," he writes in *The Gulag Archipelago*. The officials "stepped onto the rostrum and talked about *Ivan Denisovich*," he continues. "They said happily that the book had eased their consciences. . . . They admitted that the picture I painted was decidedly on the bright side, that *every one of them* knew of camps worse than that. (Ah, so they did know?) Of the seventy people seated around that horseshoe, several turned out to be knowledgeable in literature, even to be readers of *Novy Mir* [the Soviet literary magazine]. They were eager for reform. They spoke forcefully about our social ulcers, about our neglect of our rural areas. And I sat there and thought: If the first tiny droplet of Truth has exploded like a psychological bomb, what then will happen in our country when whole waterfalls of Truth burst forth? And they will burst forth. It has to happen."

SEPTEMBER 2, 1974

MOST of the changes our new President has made so far have been of the kind that are generally described as "atmospheric." We're told that he sometimes gets his own breakfast in the morning, and the news is somehow full of portent. He and the First Lady are reported to have returned to a White House party after seeing off the guests of honor, and to have danced on into the night. Democrats and newsmen—people considered "enemies" by the last Administration—were there applauding. And, in a move that perhaps has done as much as anything else to establish the new atmosphere, the President has broken the ice on the subject of amnesty. "In my first words as President of all the people, I acknowledged a power higher than the people, who commands not only righteousness but love, not only justice but mercy," he told the Veterans of Foreign Wars in Chicago. And he said, "I am throwing the weight of my Presidency into the scales of justice on the side of leniency." "Love," "mercy," "leniency"—these sentiments have been out of favor at the White House in recent years. Leniency, in particular, was shunned. It was too close to another quality despised by the Nixon White House—"softness." The thing to be in those days was hard. "Hardheaded," "hard-line," "hard-nosed," "tough" were the words in fashion. We were taught to keep our eyes rigidly trained on the "realities" of self-interest. If a single crack appeared in America's emotional armor, we were told, the whole structure of our power might crumble.

Many people who have observed the changed atmosphere in Washington go on to point out that dancing in the White House isn't going to do much to solve inflation or anything else on the formidable agenda of concrete difficulties facing the country. It may not. But we do know where the old atmosphere of hardheaded realism got us. It got us into Indo-China and then into impeachment—into the suppression of imaginary threats abroad and the pursuit of imaginary enemies at home. Hardheaded realism led us straight into a world of fantasy. Self-interest turned out to be the path to self-mutilation. The walls of toughness that shut out love and mercy and leniency shut out much, much more, until, in the end, the White House was wandering blind in a world it found wholly incomprehensible. One lesson of this experience may be that if you willfully close down your heart, your mind cannot stay open for very long. The changes we now see in the White House seem to be signs of mental and moral wholeness in our new leaders. If this is what is called atmospheric, then atmosphere may be more important than we think. The President should decide soon how to deal with inflation, but as he does so, let him go on getting his own breakfast for a while. Let the dancing continue.

SEPTEMBER 30, 1974

G ERALD Ford is still the thirty-eighth President of the United States, and he still seems the same agreeable man he seemed during his first days in office, yet as we listened to him at his press conference last week explaining his decision to pardon ex-President Nixon, and reflected on what has happened to his Administration following the pardon, we came to feel that, for the fourth time in not much more than a decade, the nation has suffered what amounts to the untimely loss of its President. Watching President Ford during this period has been like watching someone come down with a familiar virus. We have no name for it, but its symptoms, which have now attacked at least three of our Presidents, are all too well known. Among them are a tendency to consult only with a few anonymous White House advisers on the most important decisions, a penchant for secrecy and surprise, a willingness to ignore or contradict one's own recent public statements, and an inability to read the country's mood or anticipate the public's reactions. The nation has spent the better part of its political energy in the last few years seeking a cure for this affliction, but clearly it hasn't yet found one. And it is no comfort to note that, by the look of things, President Ford is as bewildered as we are by what has happened to him.

The magnitude of the loss, which seems at a glance so disproportionate to the single decision that precipitated it, was determined by both the peculiar nature of the Ford Administration and the peculiar nature of the pardon. The legitimacy of past Administrations has been grounded in an electoral mandate. The legitimacy of the Ford Administration, however, was grounded in the repudiation of an electoral mandate—the one given to Richard Nixon and Spiro Agnew in 1972. President Ford's Administration was born out of the pure workings of the law, and his mandate, if he can be said to have had one, was the legal system itself. The people's respect for the Constitutional arrangements that put him in office, rather than any respect for Ford personally, formed the basis for the broad support he immediately received when, unelected, and all but unknown to the country, he assumed the Presidency of the United States. When he suddenly intervened in the continuation of the legal process by pardoning President Nixon, therefore, he was doing a great deal more than disposing of just another difficult issue facing his Administration. He was playing with the foundations of his own authority as President. This particular pardon, which has virtually no precedent in the history of executive clemency, was uniquely suited to the undoing of his Administration. It attacked the taproot of his legitimacy. President Ford, by declining to wait for the Watergate Special Prosecutor to bring charges, and by declining to enumerate any offenses himself in his proclamation, was obliged to pardon Mr. Nixon for crimes he "may have committed"—or, by implication, may not have committed—while in office. Such a sweeping pardon, which manages to grant boundless absolution without levelling a single accusation, is fully commensurate with the sweeping claims of privilege that were made by President Nixon when he was seeking to use the power of his office to escape accountability for his actions, and gives unexpected new life to the Nixonian philosophy of government. It grants to ex-President Nixon the immunity he was denied as President, and fully associates Ford with the conception of limitless executive power whose rejection by the country was the reason for his Presidency. Once again, the holder of more power than any other man in the world seems to look with a benevolent eye on every conceivable abuse of power.

By embracing the Nixonian philosophy, Ford joined himself to the disgraced Administration that preceded his, and disconnected himself from the nation. He established a political continuity that no one wanted, and broke the continuity of legal procedure that was the origin of his Presidency and the sole basis of his authority. We are left with something new in our experience: a rootless President, whose power is intact but who apparently does not know where it came from or what to do with it. The first man to gain the highest office in the land without running for President or Vice-President now truly governs without a mandate. At a time when the nation needs the strongest leadership it can get, its President has disabled himself. The loss to him and to the country is beyond calculation.

JANUARY 6, 1975

T HE other day, as we were reading that the figures on crime in the United States had gone up once again, we were reminded of a phrase that we had not heard for quite a while: law and order. We could clearly remember the time, not so very long ago, when we had heard about almost nothing else. Candidates for office, in particular, had been preoccupied with the subject. Each one had said that if he was not elected crime rates would rise. In Congress, one "tough" measure after another was passed, in many instances by overwhelming majorities. The measures included provisions for "no-knock" entry into private homes by the police, provisions for the "preventive detention" of certain criminal suspects, and other seemingly un-Constitutional measures. President Nixon promised to alter the complexion of the Supreme Court; "softheaded" justices were to be replaced by "strict constructionists." The President also asserted that criminals should be treated "without pity" and proposed the restoration of the death penalty for some offenses—a penalty that the Supreme Court had struck down only a few months earlier. The mood of the public grew panicky, too. We remember that in our city an atmosphere of fear—almost of terror—developed. The streets emptied at night. People stopped going to the theatre, because they were afraid of being mugged on the way home. Our taxis came to be equipped with grimy transparent plastic shields between the rider and the driver.

But none of the measures taken by the politicians or anyone else worked. All were false cures, as many of the men who proposed them and voted for them well knew even as they did so. Then, rather suddenly, in the months following Richard Nixon's fall, the atmosphere changed. The scare words vanished from the lips of the politicians. The no-knock law was repealed. The theatres filled up again. But it was *only* the atmosphere that changed. As far as anyone has been able to tell, the fall of President Nixon had no measurable effect on the crime rate. In the last decade or so, a wave of fear swept over the nation and then subsided. Politicians, the press, and television took up the issue of crime for a few years and then dropped it. The spread of crime was a real and enduring affliction, but the campaign to cope with it turned out to be illusory and evanescent, and vanished like last year's fad. What it left behind is what we see around us now: a collection of damaged institutions; a deeper suspicion than ever among citizens that what they hear from public men has nothing at all to do with the conditions of their daily lives; and a rising rate of crime.

JANUARY 13, 1975

SHORTLY after the jury in the Watergate trial handed down its verdicts, John Ehrlichman, H. R. Haldeman, and John Mitchell emerged briefly from the courtroom to say a few words to the press. Their pictures were in the paper the next morning, and we scrutinized the faces closely. Ehrlichman, insisting that he had been convinced even before the trial began that it would not be a fair one, and butting against all known facts in his customary way, declared, "Nothing that has happened today has changed my mind." Yet something in Ehrlichman's face, at least, had changed. Something on the inside, it seemed to us, was beginning to erode and rearrange that "stone wall" the country had looked at for so long. We were reminded that in his defense at the trial Ehrlichman had at least admitted the *existence* of a cover-up, though he had attempted to shift the blame for it onto his former colleague, Haldeman, and his former employer, Nixon. A measure of the truth had penetrated Ehrlichman's world, if only for reasons of self-protection. For Haldeman, there were no such ambiguities. His mind was clear. When he emerged, he did not merely drop a few casual remarks to reporters but stepped right up to the microphone with a statement to make. "There's only one human being in the world who knows to an absolute moral certainty the truth of my innocence or guilt," he said. "That person is me, and I know that, legally and morally, I'm totally and absolutely innocent." Of all the defendants, Haldeman had been the most consistent throughout the Watergate affair. He had maintained his and the President's innocence from the beginning to the end. He had also been the remotest from reality. As far as he was concerned, the thousands of pages of documents and the hundreds of hours of television we had all seen in the last two years had uncovered nothing that was unseemly or culpable in the White House. His proclamation of innocence brought to mind once again the inverted moral order that prevailed in the Nixon White House. There a strong man was one who succumbed to White House pressure to commit crimes. A trustworthy man was one who could be relied on to lie to a grand jury. On one occasion, at least, ordinary moral standards were doubly inverted. In 1971, Patrick Buchanan, a speechwriter for President Nixon, noted in a memorandum that the plan to harass Daniel Ellsberg would be "good for the country" but "would not, it seems to me, be particularly helpful to the President politically." The idea that a piece of repression would be "good for the country" was already morally inverted, but Buchanan inverted morality again and decided that the benefit to the country should be forgone in favor of the President's political advantage. In Buchanan's world, idealism counselled repression, but pragmatism ruled against it. When Mitchell came out of the courtroom and was asked if he planned to take a vacation, he answered, "I think I'm going to the moon." From the look on his face, it seemed that inwardly he was on the moon already. In his expression was a world of weariness and woe. Yet we found that in the Watergate lineup Mitchell's face was somehow a relief. On his face alone did the entire story of the Nixon Administration's tremendous fall seem to be written. From his distant look one could guess that the ordeal had left its mark on his mind and spirit, and that he had long ago abandoned the faith that Haldeman was now championing with redoubled zeal. Here was at least veiled recognition of what we had all been through in the last few years. Mitchell, unlike the others, seemed to know everything we knew.

FEBRUARY 5, 1975

THE other day, we turned our television set on and heard New York State Assemblyman Andrew Stein, who has done much of the work in investigating the current nursing-home scandal, say, "This investigation, nationally, will turn out to be as big as, if not bigger than, the Watergate scandal." Not long afterward, we picked up our paper and found a two-column headline that announced, "BERGMAN CERTIFIED WORTH WAS ALMOST $24 MILLION." (Bernard Bergman is a nursing-home entrepreneur and the major target of Assemblyman Stein's investigations.) That afternoon, we saw a headline that read, "DISPUTE BERGMAN ON WEALTH DATA." On other recent front pages, we read of other investigations. At the national level, there was the investigation of the C.I.A. and the investigation of the F.B.I. Several existing committees of Congress would be looking into these, and senators were said to be competing vigorously for a place on the special committee that was being set up to look into the C.I.A. Closer to home, there was an investigation of a "major educational agency"—an outfit called the Institute for Educational Development—for mismanagement of funds, and there was a story on what was happening to New York State money for the arts. And in the *Wall Street Journal* we read a story about a journalism professor who had trained her entire class as "investigative" reporters by sending them out to "compile lists of the surrounding county's most reversed judges, its biggest slumlords, its heaviest political campaign contributors, and the business interests of its planning-and-zoning-board members."

There was something in all this that bothered us. It was not, as Senator John Stennis said in the debate on the makeup of the special Senate committee to investigate the C.I.A., that the inquiries now going forward were likely to destroy worthy institutions. Nor was it, as one columnist maintained, that a new wave of "McCarthyism" had been unleashed. The investigators had, on the whole, been scrupulous. We had not seen a single fact that we would not have wanted uncovered. What bothered us was not the stories themselves but the way they were being handled. In part, the problem was the idea— implicit in the big headlines, and explicit in Assemblyman Stein's remark that the nursing-home scandal might be "bigger" than Watergate—that the new headlines would fill a gap left by the tapering off of Watergate headlines. We wanted the investigations of scandals that have come to light more recently to go on, but perhaps with a little less fanfare. Watergate—the word we now use to refer to about three-quarters of what went on in the United States in the last five years or so—was many things. It was a nearly successful attempt to subvert constitutional democracy from within; it was a mass of governmental and corporate corruption; and it was one of the best stories ever to find its way into American journalism. It is this last, and least important, aspect of Watergate which seems to be emphasized by the prominence of the new investigative stories. It is as though the country, having developed an appetite for sordid secrets, now had to be fed a steady diet of them. At the moment, the mode of the journalism, rather than the content of the story, often seems to determine the place of a story on the front page or its prominence on the television news: if it's "investigative," it gets heavy play; if it's straight "reporting," it gets less play. Of course, in the time of Watergate it was the substance of the stories, and not the way in which they were uncovered, that gave them their importance. The prominence of the new investigative headlines has the odd effect of seeming to diminish the importance of the Watergate headlines by placing the Watergate story and the new stories on the same footing. And at the same time attention is drawn away from present stories that are of larger importance. These stories—the

economic predicament of the world, the energy predicament, the food predicament, the troubles in the Middle East, and the new difficulties in our
relations with the Soviet Union—are a mass of confusion, but they are out
in the open. They call for a new kind of news reporting, as yet undiscovered,
which will answer the special needs of our era as brilliantly and as daringly
as investigative reporting met the special needs of the era of Watergate.

FEBRUARY 10, 1975

WE were interested to read the other day that Richard Nixon is thinking about getting back into politics. Senator Barry Goldwater had
just had lunch with him, and reported that the former President
might like to be a Republican "Party spokesman." Goldwater thought it
sounded like a good idea. "My mail shows there's no lessening of interest in
him within the Party," he said. "After all, he had millions who voted for him."
That same day, we read that President Ford was asking Congress for a three-
hundred-million-dollar increase in American aid to South Vietnam. In Saigon,
President Thieu was granting "exclusive" interviews to quite a few American
newsmen and was telling them all that without the new aid the North Vietnamese might take over. Just a few weeks ago, of course, when Phuoc Binh,
the capital of South Vietnam's Phuoc Long Province, was falling, an American
naval task force was discovered heading toward Southeast Asian waters from
the Philippines, and there were rumors that the United States was contem-
plating a more active role in the war. We've been hearing it said that the
people in Washington haven't come up with enough new ideas recently. But
here are two: a new political career for Richard Nixon, and a new, expanded
role for the United States in Vietnam. Mr. Nixon's timing may be opportune.
If the United States is getting back into the war, we can't think of a better
man to lead the way.

MARCH 3, 1975

AS the Senate was voting to delay enactment of one of President Ford's
energy proposals last week, we sat down to try to puzzle out the logic
of the Administration's economic program as a whole. In purely economic terms, as many observers have argued, the policy cancels itself out,
or even has harmful effects. On the one hand, the tax rebate of some billions

of dollars would increase the public's spending power, while on the other hand the rise in oil prices caused by new taxes would decrease the public's spending power. The net result for the economy would be inflationary pressure without the stimulating effects of a rise in buying. The only beneficial aim is the conservation of energy: a reduction in the use of fuel, and a reduction in imports of oil. The President's "economic" policy seems to emerge as a conservation policy to be paid for with economic sacrifices. But that description, too, would be misleading. For, as many observers have also pointed out, the reduction attainable by the President's oil policy would fall far short of breaking America's dependency on imported oil. It is a long way from being anything like a Project Independence, or even the plausible beginning of one. In fact, government planners have yet to come up with any workable plan that would make the United States independent in energy in the near future. Pared down to its final consequences, then, the President's policy offers only a less tangible result: a display of resoluteness—the appearance, but not the substance, of effective conservationist action. As Secretary of State Henry Kissinger put it a few weeks ago in the course of arguing for an energy policy that would permanently prevent the price of imported oil from returning to its very low, pre-embargo level in order to encourage domestic investment in the search for alternative sources of energy, "It is the glory of our nation that when challenged we have always stepped forward with spirit and a will to dare great things. It is now time to do so again, and in so doing to reaffirm to ourselves and to the world that this generation of Americans has the integrity of character to carry on the noble experiment that began two centuries ago." Mr. Kissinger has frequently been a strong advocate of actions and statements that, while perhaps not attaining any concrete ends in themselves, demonstrate America's resolute intentions to its adversaries. His Vietnam policy was rooted in calculations of this sort, and recently we have had his mention of the possibility of using force in the Middle East, and the dispatch of the aircraft carrier *Enterprise* to the Indian Ocean. In a recent article in the Washington *Post*, titled "Force and Diplomacy," Barry Blechman, of the Brookings Institution, wrote, "Through an array of verbal, diplomatic, and military instruments, the United States sent a tough message to the Arab oil-producers: under certain circumstances, this nation would utilize its armed forces to end an oil-embargo." And he concluded, "By deterring a specific threat to the nation's security, a minor military and diplomatic demonstration may have preserved progress toward peace in the Middle East, thus helping to avoid contingencies with real dangers for wider conflict." If the Kissinger threat of force was a military and diplomatic "demonstration" of resoluteness—aimed at the Arabs—then it stands to reason that the President's energy policy may well be an economic demonstration of resoluteness aimed in the same direction. It may have been decided that just as a demonstration of force might obviate the use of force, so a demonstration of economic sacrifice might obviate the need for a full-fledged Project Independence. If this is the logic of the policy, then the policy was misnamed. It is not an economic policy but a foreign policy. In fact, in terms of the foreign-policy objective of letting the oil producers know just how serious we are, the unfortunate economic consequences we endure may be helpful, since a demonstration is more convincing when it is backed by sacrifices. In Vietnam, the sacrifice was tens of thousands of men and the nation's political health; today, it is the nation's economic health. The people who are losing their jobs and paying higher prices don't know it, but the whole new system proposed by the Ford Administration, with its fees and its rebates and its circular flow of billions of dollars throughout the American economy, may be not a program at all but a message—a move in the diplomatic, not the economic, game.

MARCH 17, 1975

SIMONE Weil, in describing the traits of character that the Romans brought to their conquests, once wrote, "With unswerving resolution, they always sacrificed everything to considerations of prestige; they were always inflexible in danger and impervious to pity or any human feeling." The United States, too, in its policy toward Indo-China, has sacrificed everything to considerations of prestige, and it, too, has been impervious to pity and human feeling. Today, after all that has happened, the Administration once again tells us that our prestige is at stake in Indo-China—this time in the battle between the government of Lon Nol and insurgent forces in Cambodia. At a press conference a week or so ago, President Ford spelled out the reasoning once again. His words were the ones we've been hearing for fifteen years. "If we abandon our allies," he said, "we will be saying to all the world that war pays. Aggression will not stop. Rather, it will increase. In Cambodia, the aggressors will have shown that if negotiations are resisted, the United States will weary, abandon its friends, and force will prevail." Secretary of Defense James Schlesinger went further, and said that the fall of the Phnom Penh government would be a "disaster" for the United States. Oddly, with all this at stake the Administration was asking for an appropriation of only two hundred and twenty-two million dollars in supplemental aid. The smallness of the sum is emblematic of a disparity that has grown up between what the United States is willing to expend in Cambodia and what it hopes to gain. Though the United States is barred by its own laws from fighting in Cambodia, the Administration asserts that our prestige is at stake there. The blood that is now flowing is Cambodian blood, but the credibility on the line is said to be American. The performers are Cambodian, but the "performance" remains ours. The stake seems to have been created by pure projection: American prestige is at stake in Cambodia because high United States officials have said that American prestige is at stake in Cambodia. The concern with prestige is of long standing, but the cheapness is new. Once, if the government believed American prestige to be at stake it was willing to pay billions of dollars and risk thousands of American lives to protect it; and if this decision led to tragedy, at least there was the dignity of sacrifice in what was thought by some to be a noble cause. Now things have changed. American officials still talk of prestige, but without seeming to believe what they are saying. Today, we seem to be dealing with a very low-grade sort of prestige. American prestige is up for sale at recession prices. Two hundred and twenty-two million dollars is all it costs, and unnumbered Cambodian lives.

APRIL 7, 1975

W ITH the military collapse in South Vietnam and the diplomatic collapse in the Middle East—two areas where American commitments have been heavy in recent years—the question of exactly what a "commitment" is when it is undertaken by a democratic country is suddenly being raised on all sides. A commitment consists of words: it is a promise. A commitment consists also of the wherewithal to take action in support of the words. And for a democracy a commitment consists, finally, of a determination among the people to use the wherewithal in support of the words. In Vietnam, the United States has never made more than two-thirds of a commitment. The government spoke the words and supplied the wherewithal, but it never fully obtained the support of the people. The people were, at best, tolerant of the government's adventure for a while. Later, they came to actively oppose it, and now, according to a recent poll, some seventy-five per cent of the public opposes further aid to South Vietnam. Nevertheless, spokesmen for the executive branch of our government continue to refer to a commitment to provide such aid. Dr. Kissinger, asked at his press conference the other day to describe its nature, asserted that although it was not legally binding, it was morally binding. The question remains, On whom was it binding? The public had not made it, and the Congress had not made it. According to Dr. Kissinger himself, only he and former President Nixon had made it. Earlier, on the basis of a "commitment" made by the executive branch alone, the United States had spent one hundred and fifty billion dollars and more than fifty-five thousand lives. Then, over the years, the Congress and the people removed the money and the troops from the exclusive control of the executive, in an assertion of their Constitutional prerogatives. In fact, so lacking in substance is the commitment that not even the Administration has dared to so much as suggest that practical steps be taken to make the commitment real. Dr. Kissinger has described the possible fall of Saigon as an event of potentially "cataclysmic" significance for the United States, but not even he is willing to recommend the dispatch of a single American soldier to Vietnam. All that remains is the word "commitment"—spoken by American officials. Never has the gap between word and deed in American foreign policy been greater than it is at this moment. Policy now seems to be a matter of talismanic phrases and pure theory. Meanwhile, history takes its course in Vietnam, this time without any supervision from us.

APRIL 14, 1975

THE victory of the revolutionary forces in Vietnam has been something like a certainty for years now; indeed, to speak the awful whole truth about this matter, it has been something like a certainty for more than a quarter of a century, and all the efforts that the French and we ourselves have made to prevent it—the thirty years of forced evacuation, massacre, and carpet-bombing—have been a waste and a crime of measureless proportions. If this endeavor has had any redeeming features, they have yet to be discovered. Certainly none have appeared in recent days, as the war has moved toward its end. Events have unfolded more swiftly than thought could follow. At the heart of the South Vietnamese collapse there seems to have been a vacuum: the Saigon government. One moment, it was there, with its 1,100,000 men under arms and its gigantic Air Force—the third largest in the world—and the next moment it was gone. Reporters used words like "juggernaut" and "blitzkrieg," but observers on the scene had a different story to tell. "There is no war," one American eyewitness said. Speaking of the fall of Danang, a French eyewitness said, "There never was a last battle for

Danang." And an American intelligence official said, "There's a complete lack of communication, a breakdown in the chain of command. Colonels aren't following orders. No one cares. It's become every man for himself. There's paralysis in the government [brought on] by worry and panic. And there's silence at the top." City after city was falling without a battle. The North Vietnamese invasion, swift as it was, could not keep pace with the South Vietnamese collapse. Cities fell; days later, the foe approached. So rapidly did the territory of South Vietnam change hands that many Vietnamese were convinced that President Thieu had made a deal with the Communists. Others maintained that the deal was between the Americans and the Russians. Few seemed to doubt that their fate had been bartered in one manner or another. If at the top there was silence, at the bottom there was something for which there is no adequate word—something described in news reports as "breakdown of law and order," "chaos," and "panic." The South Vietnamese troops were not only fleeing the enemy but attacking the civilian population and each other. As the Army disintegrated, directionless rage burst out on all sides. In Danang, a mob sacked the deserted United States Consulate. Lieutenant General Ngo Quang Truong, the commander of the troops in the area, removed himself to a "command post" on a boat offshore, and his soldiers proceeded to go on a rampage. They fired randomly and for no reason at passers-by, including children. The bodies of their victims littered the streets. An American reporter on the scene wrote, "People are jogging crazily and pointlessly down the streets. Others are taking houses apart, piece by piece. A young man walks outside carrying a wooden door, wrenched from its hinges, atop his head. Another is carrying bits of broken glass in his hands." At the end, the soldiers went down to the beach, where some threw away their weapons and their uniforms and dived into the sea to swim out to waiting American ships, while others commandeered boats and then began firing at one another on the open water. Americans had long spoken a great deal about bloodbaths in Vietnam. Those who favored the war effort had spoken of a bloodbath that might be perpetrated by the Communists if they should take control of the South. Those who opposed the war effort had spoken of the bloodbath of war itself. But no one had foreseen this bloodbath: the massacre of civilians by the disintegrating South Vietnamese Army. Soon the scenes in Danang were repeated in cities through most of South Vietnam. In one city, the renegade soldiers were shooting at the owners of the restaurants where they ate. Something deeper than the collapse of an army's discipline—deeper, even, than the collapse of a body politic—was taking place. It was the disintegration of a society that had been pulverized by war and corrupted by foreign invaders for thirty years. A society that had lost all sense of self-respect and that despised itself for its subservience to one foreign master after another—a society that had been turned into a literal brothel for millions of soldiers from foreign countries—was tearing itself apart in a frenzy of self-destruction. Naturally, the soldiers' anger, insofar as it was not directed at themselves, was directed at the American oppressor/ protector, rather than at the foe. On several occasions, South Vietnamese troops fired on American aircraft. And President Thieu summed up the general feeling when, as a visitor has reported, he said, "Many Vietnamese now have the feeling that they actually have been lured into all this and then abandoned." And so they had. For more than a decade, the United States had imposed an American fantasy on Vietnamese reality. Then we had left, and now the South Vietnamese government was fading like the mirage it had in fact always been.

Faced with the disappearance of the world that America had built up over the years, the American authorities had two ideas. One was to send in "spare parts" and similar supplies, and the other was to "rescue" South Vietnamese refugees from the North Vietnamese by transporting them to "safe" parts of the south. The spare-parts debate in the United States was attended by a great deal of military analysis of the kind that crops up whenever war is being waged anywhere. There was discussion of the strategic strengths and weaknesses of the South Vietnamese Army and the North Vietnamese Army. Command structures were compared. The decentralized structure of the South Vietnamese Air Force command was noted and deplored. The unified structure of the North Vietnamese Army command was noted and admired. The merits of a Russian anti-aircraft rocket—the SA-7—were weighed. The performance of both armies, and even of individual units, was predicted. But in the event there was "no war." The SA-7s never had to be fired. The units never met in combat. Instead, there was the sudden dissolution of the South Vietnamese side. It was not spare parts that had been missing. Even when all the parts are available, weapons cannot fire themselves. And no number of troops is of any use if the troops attack civilians and each other instead of attacking the foe. Rarely has there been a clearer illustration of the lesson, never grasped by the United States in Vietnam, that the foundations of power are political, not military. With the fall of Danang, the full irony of the spare-parts debate was driven home. In their flight southward, the South Vietnamese abandoned some three hundred aircraft and other American-made military equipment, altogether worth as much as a billion dollars. At a glance, it appeared that the North Vietnamese would be greatly aided by their capture of so many planes. But then it appeared that they might not. They would lack spare parts.

The rescue mission was announced in the early days of the collapse. Army Colonel Robert Burke, a Pentagon spokesman, said, "We have all kinds of contingency plans." In the minds of the Americans, the aim of the mission was to bring people to "safety." But, as has so often been true of American ideas for Vietnam, noble intentions led to horrific results. There were the boats. Thousands of refugees crowded onto barges that were to take them out to ships that, in turn, were to take them to points south. But the ships were slow in coming, and hundreds perished of thirst, starvation, and exposure. Often, children would fall overboard and their mothers would dive in after them, and both would drown. On the American ship *Pioneer Commander*, renegade South Vietnamese Marines murdered twenty-five refugees for no apparent reason. The rapings, robbings, and random brutality that had begun in Danang continued on the ships. Many civilians were thrown overboard by soldiers. By the time the boats arrived at Nha Trang and Cam Ranh Bay, down the coast, with their cargo of the suffering, the dying, and the dead, these cities, too, had come under attack by renegade South Vietnamese soldiers. Meanwhile, it was reported, the revolutionary authorities had restored order in Danang. The trip to "safety," as it was usually put in the newscasts, turned out to be a trip to danger, or to death.

A few planes were made available, too. An airlift from Danang that would carry as many as three hundred and fifty thousand people to "safety" had been announced, but the collapse proceeded too swiftly, and the airlift was abandoned. At the last minute, the president of an outfit called World Airways, Edward Daly, shortly to be known to newsmen as Ed, took it upon himself to fly into Danang in a Boeing 727 to evacuate refugees. But when he arrived his plane was mobbed—not by the expected "widows and children," as it was sometimes put, but by the Black Panthers, the remnants of a disintegrated unit of the South Vietnamese Army. Daly, the would-be savior of the Vietnamese, was soon throwing punches at soldiers and firing a pistol into the air. It was reported that as the plane took off, it ran over several people, and it was fired upon by berserk soldiers on the ground. Other soldiers clung to the jammed landing gear of the plane. Once the plane was aloft, several fell off. A reporter described the flight as "a flight out of hell," and it was, but it was also a flight into hell. And the flight itself was hell. A completely senseless movement of millions of people, encouraged and abetted by the United States, had started up all over South Vietnam. Some people were said to be fleeing the Communists, and others were said to be fleeing war. But wherever they went they found both. The United States was busy transferring people from one end of a sinking ship to the other, and it always seemed to choose the end where the danger was greater. These unfortunates were not the first

Vietnamese to be doomed by American efforts to "save" them. But they may have been some of the last.

If the unreal world that had been created by the Americans was collapsing last week in South Vietnam, it was still standing in America. In the momentous days when the northernmost two-thirds of South Vietnam was falling to the Communists, Americans were mechanically continuing to do the things that Americans had done throughout the war. Some were opposing the war; some were supporting the war. The debate over spare parts raged. A debate over "phase-out" aid intensified. Secretary of State Henry Kissinger, speaking as though America were still able to influence the situation, said we could not afford to "destroy an ally." To this, one was tempted to answer that it was the North Vietnamese, not the Americans, who were destroying our ally. But the truth was stranger still. Our ally was destroying itself. Many Americans were blaming one another for the fall of South Vietnam. But the one thing in South Vietnam that the United States was not responsible for was its fall. What the United States was responsible for was the death and devastation brought about by the futile prolongation of the war for some fifteen years.

At the White House, too, Americans were going on doing what they had been doing for years. They were sending ships; they were sending military observers; they were installing new telephone lines; they were sending military supplies. (A day or so after it became known that the South Vietnamese had abandoned hundreds of aircraft in their flight southward, an American C-5A arrived in Saigon and unloaded fourteen howitzers.) The South Vietnamese military machine had broken down, but the American support machine was grinding on, even though its reason for existing had disappeared. Where could the ships land? To whom could the telephone calls be made? Who would take delivery of the spare parts? The lines of communication and control stretched out from Washington as always, but now they connected with nothing. At times, the ships bobbed helplessly on the high seas, unable to find safe ports at which to land; the phones in Hué, Danang, and Cam Ranh Bay had gone dead; the supplies were being delivered to the North Vietnamese. The Administration policymakers were confronted with a situation that they could not fathom: there were no more "contingencies" for the United States in Vietnam. One project after another was stillborn, or recoiled upon itself. Ronald Nessen, the President's press secretary, announced that "diplomatic initiatives" were under way, and then he withdrew the announcement. The airlift was announced, and then it was abandoned. Even in their public statements, officials went on mouthing the old words, as though they were unaware that the world to which the words referred had dissolved. "I believe that if we support the people of South Vietnam, in the way that they deserve, that no enemy can ever defeat them," Army Chief of Staff Frederick Weyand said after the inspection tour he made for the White House.

In the United States, as in Saigon, there was silence at the top. The President was playing golf in Palm Springs. Correctly anticipating a question about Vietnam at an airport, he laughed playfully and broke into a run. When his press secretary was asked if it was proper for the President to play golf at a time of such great suffering for the Vietnamese, he answered, "Would it prevent anything from happening in Vietnam if he didn't play golf?" Meanwhile, the nation, seeing that its military efforts were futile, turned its attention to the projects for shifting civilians about, which now came to be known everywhere as "humanitarian" projects. A large part of the nation, including the Administration, repaired to this cause as though to safe high ground. At the close of the most inhuman war in our history, American officialdom was suddenly turning sentimental. In the midst of moral confusion, the "humanitarian" projects seemed to offer moral simplicity. In the midst of boundless shame, they seemed to offer reasons for pride. Could anyone fail to be moved by the plight of the refugees? But this was Vietnam. This was the war where the "good" intentions had consistently led to the grotesque consequences. Already corpses were piling up on the "rescue" ships, and soldiers were falling to their death off Ed Daly's plane. But Daly had one more idea. He would rescue orphans. Soon the government took up the idea. As one reporter observed, many children had lost their parents in the war or "had been separated" from their parents. Now Ed Daly and the government would fly those children to America. Suddenly, the news was filled with babies. These were not, at first, wounded babies or dead babies or babies falling into the South China Sea, like the ones we had been seeing all week; they were live, happy, well babies. Smiling prospective American parents were interviewed. "It's fantastic," one delighted American mother said. (As it happens, there is a shortage of children up for adoption in the United States at the moment.) Unable to do anything else in Vietnam, the United States was now making off with planeloads of Vietnamese babies. Somehow, a conviction seemed to have grown up that their lives were being saved. If the Vietnamese authorities did not allow them to go to America, one correspondent reported, then they would have a difficult time growing up in South Vietnam, "and perhaps will never grow up at all." Similarly, a reporter on Daly's flight from Danang who had seen an old woman try to get on the plane and fail had written that "life itself" had slipped out of her hands. However, there was no reason to think that orphans or old women would be endangered by a North Vietnamese takeover. Yet there were many Vietnamese—perhaps tens of thousands— who from having worked with us might well be in danger. We were "saving" people who didn't need saving, and we were leaving behind people who did. And then, in an accident that no one could have foreseen, an American Air Force plane carrying orphans crashed, and the "baby-lift," ill-conceived from the start, also turned to tragedy.

The Vietnam war was coming to a close, and at the end, by chance, there was only Ed Daly—compassionate millionaire, adventurer, and, according to a friend, "an outgoing good party guy who will gather up a planeload of friends and fly off to Europe for a weekend." On our television screens, there was Ed Daly in Danang waving his pistol and socking a South Vietnamese soldier in the jaw; there was Ed Daly getting fired at as his plane took off; there was Ed Daly in Saigon giving news conferences; there was Ed Daly stopping over in Tokyo with his babies. Despised by those on whom his compassion had fastened, attacked by the people he wanted to help, Ed Daly was rushing all over South Vietnam, as though he really were what to all of us at home he seemed to have become: the last American in Vietnam.

MAY 12, 1975

I N Vietnam last week, there was desperation and there was exultation. Some people were running for their lives, and other people were cheering in the streets. Here in America, the emotions were different. We stood apart now. The victory in Vietnam was not ours, and neither, for that matter, was the defeat. We could only sit before our television sets, watching old scenes being replayed, and trying to make a certain sense of what had happened. Our emotions had to be reflective ones: regret at the irredeemable waste of our efforts; relief that it was all over. Fifteen years or so ago, the stream of American history and the stream of Vietnamese history flowed together. Nothing but grief ever came of it. Last week, the two streams flowed apart again, and the two peoples were free to pursue their separate thoughts, their separate emotions, and their separate destinies.

It seems worth noting, just for the record, that April 30, 1975, the day the war ended, was, as far as we can tell, the first day since September 1, 1939, when the Second World War began, that something like peace reigned throughout the world.

AFTERWORD

THE purpose of a nation's political activities, presumably, is to make the best of whatever historical circumstances it may find itself in—to head off any calamities that are looming, to seize opportunities, and (if only rarely) to create political forms that express a people's beliefs in some new way. Measured by this standard, the crisis of the American republic that arose out of the Vietnam war and culminated in the resignation of Richard Nixon emerges as a turbulent, far-flung, feverish, at times dreamlike and absurd distraction of the nation's energies from its real tasks. It is true that in this crisis the nation overcame great difficulties and saved itself from great disasters, but all of these difficulties were self-created ones. We extricated ourselves from a pointless and ruinous war, but we had travelled to the other side of the earth to get ourselves into it. We forced a lawless President from office, but we had twice elected him to the office. We rescued our Constitutional system from breakdown, but we had propelled it toward that breakdown. Such troubles as these, no doubt, are mainly characteristic of nations that, like the United States in the nineteen-sixties, are at the pinnacle of wealth and power. Indeed, both the war, which was launched simultaneously with huge increases in expenditures on social programs, and the protests against the war, which were carried out in considerable part by young people who believed they could live indefinitely without employment, seemed to be based on an assumption that the wealth of the United States was inexhaustible. Today, only thirteen years after the war's end, the United States—burdened with debt, falling behind other nations in technical competition and in its standard of living, described by some as "in decline"—appears to lack the wherewithal to threaten itself again in this profligate way anytime soon. Our debt-strapped government would seem unlikely to embark on such

a war, and our career-minded youth unlikely to protest it. Whatever difficulties
the United States may next face seem likely to be of a more nearly necessary
kind.

A T the root of our self-created torments, certainly, was the war, and at
the root of the war was a picture of the world that was firmly entrenched
in the minds of the policymakers and others. Three Presidents—two
Democrats and one Republican—and the great majority of their foreign-
policy advisers, as well as most of the leaders of opinion in the society at
large, deeply believed that they lived in a world formed in such a way that
if the United States allowed the Communists to take over South Vietnam
(or any other non-Communist country) the floodgates of global Communism
would burst and inundate the free world. It is hard today, now that the fall
of South Vietnam is history, to recall the intense foreboding, bordering on
panic, that afflicted American policymakers when they contemplated the
possibility that South Vietnam would fall. A few quotes will serve as reminders
of their embattled state of mind. In a speech in April of 1961, President
Kennedy said:

> We dare not fail to grasp the new concepts, the new tools, the new sense
> of urgency we will need to combat [Communism]—whether in Cuba or
> South Vietnam. The message of Cuba, of Laos, of the rising din of Com-
> munist voices in Asia and Latin America—these messages are the same.
> The complacent, the self-indulgent, the soft societies are about to be swept
> away with the debris of history. Only the strong, only the industrious,
> only the determined, only the courageous, only the visionary who deter-
> mine the real nature of the struggle can possibly survive. No greater task
> faces this country or this Administration.

President Johnson warned in July of 1965 that if South Vietnam fell "no
nation can ever again have the same confidence in American promise or in
American protection." He said to a group of staff members, "Why, Ho Chi
Minh and the Communists in Southeast Asia are as much a threat to our
national security as Hitler." And after he left the White House (but while
the Vietnam war was still continuing) he told an interviewer:

> I honestly and truly believe that if we don't assert ourselves, and if Chinese
> communists and the Soviet Union take Laos, Vietnam, Cambodia, it se-
> riously endangers India, Pakistan, and the whole Pacific world. Then we'll
> really be up for grabs. We're the richest nation in the world and everybody
> wants what we've got. And the minute we look soft, the would-be aggressors

will go wild. We'll lose all of Asia and then Europe and then we'll be a rich little island all by ourselves. That means World War Three.

President Nixon warned, on April 30, 1970, when he announced the invasion of Cambodia,

> . . . if when the chips are down, the world's most powerful nation, the United States of America, acts like a pitiful helpless giant, the forces of totalitarianism and anarchy will threaten free nations and free institutions throughout the world. . . . We will not react to this [North Vietnamese] threat to American lives merely by plaintive diplomatic protests. If we did, the credibility of the United States would be destroyed.

And Nixon said privately to Kissinger, in April of 1972, as a North Vietnamese offensive was being launched, that (in Kissinger's paraphrase) if the regime in the south was toppled "not only South Vietnam but the whole free world would be lost."

These statements, which are only a few of hundreds that could be cited, reflect, of course, the famed "domino theory," according to which the fall of South Vietnam to Communism would cause the fall of its neighbors, which would cause the fall of *its* neighbors, and so forth, until, at last, the United States was directly threatened. The domino theory was powerfully supported in the minds of the policymakers by a historical lesson often known as the lesson of Munich, in reference to the meeting in that city, in September, 1938, of Allied leaders with Hitler in which they acceded to Hitler's demands for territories in Czechoslovakia. Just as acquiescence to Hitler had only led to Nazi aggression, and to the Second World War, the policymakers believed, so acquiescence to the Communists in Vietnam would lead to more Communist aggression, and, perhaps, to a third world war. To the simple, mechanical imagery of the domino theory was later added a more supple, psychological variant of the theory, which can be called the doctrine of credibility. It taught that the fall of a country to Communism could do more than affect its neighbors; it could act at a distance to undermine and topple countries far from the scene by destroying their confidence in the United States' capacity or will to protect them—that is, by destroying the United States' credibility. By losing its credibility, the United States also would forfeit the "respect" (as Nixon liked to put it) of the Soviet Union and China, who would be emboldened to challenge us. In the words of Kissinger, a strong believer in the crucial importance of credibility, "I continue to believe that those initiatives at the summit meetings of the Nixon years [with Peking and Moscow] would have been impossible had we simply collapsed in Vietnam."

History rarely gives direct, unequivocal answers to our questions, but in this case it has given them. We live in the future about which the credibility theorists made their predictions. The disaster they strove so mightily to prevent—the fall of the government in South Vietnam—occurred. Worse, the protracted downfall of South Vietnam was accompanied by the downfall of two Presidents—events that, if the theory meant anything, could only hugely magnify the harm to American credibility. After all, if the American public threw out Presidents who tried to defend other countries against Communism, how much confidence would these countries place in the United States? Nevertheless, the dire consequences foreseen by the theorists did not occur. Southeast Asia did not fall to Communism. Its neighbors did not fall. Countries around the world far from the scene did not fall. The Soviet Union and China showed no sign of having lost "respect" for the United States. "Free institutions" all over the world remained standing. The free world did not collapse. The credibility doctrine was tested, and it was wrong. It might be logically compelling, or it might be historically sound, or it might prove right in some future place or time. But in this place and this time it was wrong.

STRICTLY speaking, the doctrine of credibility, which ruled policy throughout the Vietnam war, had little to say about Vietnam per se. It offered no counsel regarding the history or politics of that country and no judgment regarding the question of whether it could defend itself or be defended by the United States. Nor did the doctrine have any wisdom to offer regarding the history or politics of the United States, nor any light to shed on the question of whether this country had the ability or will to fight a war like the one in Vietnam. Rather, this doctrine applied to the rest of the world. It predicted that *if* the United States proved unable to prop up the South Vietnamese government, and *if* the South Vietnamese government therefore fell, then *other* countries would lose confidence in the United States and fall in their turn. Thus it is precise to call the doctrine of credibility a picture of the *world*. The theory pertained, you might say, to events in almost any country but the United States and Vietnam—to say, Egypt, or the Congo, or Mexico. It was a proposition about how the world worked in our time, and it was this proposition that was disproved by events in the world since the end of the war in Vietnam.

In the hours and days after his landslide re-election in 1972, Richard Nixon displayed behavior that his colleagues found odd. This was "the strangest period" of that strange presidency, Henry Kissinger tells us in his memoirs. The morning after the election, Nixon summoned the White House staff to a meeting. "He was grim and remote, as if the more fateful period of his life still lay ahead," Kissinger reports. The President briefly and unemotionally thanked the group, and left. Haldeman then stepped forward and instructed everyone to offer his resignation, immediately. There followed wholesale firings, not only in the White House but throughout the executive branch. Noting the "frenzied, almost maniacal sense of urgency about this political butchery," Kissinger speculates on the possible psychological reasons for it, and suggests that "Nixon, who thrived on crisis, also craved disasters." Nixon himself was mystified by his dark mood, and in his memoirs he writes, "I am at a loss to explain the melancholy that settled over me on that victorious night." He suggests that "perhaps it was caused by the painful tooth" he was suffering from at the time. But he adds, "To some extent, the marring effects of Watergate may have played a part."

And in truth there was no need to invoke any convoluted psychological drives or any toothaches to explain Nixon's truculent despondency. The landslide notwithstanding, his presidency was in deep crisis. He was by then far down the path of high crimes and misdemeanors that in eighteen months would cause the House of Representatives to vote articles of impeachment against him, and on some level of his being he surely knew this. "The more fateful period of his life" did indeed lie ahead. There was in fact not just one crisis, there were two crises, heading toward a climax. The first was the cluster of abuses of power later known as Watergate, and the second was the Vietnam war. They were inextricably entwined in their origins, but by now each had an independent life and momentum of its own. The Watergate burglars had been apprehended at the Democratic National Committee headquarters in June, and the White House had been laboring all summer and autumn to conceal their sponsorship by the Committee to Re-elect the President—to buy the burglars' silence, to short-circuit the law-enforcement agencies that were supposed to be looking into the crime, to head off or cripple congressional investigations, and to undermine and discredit news organizations that were working on the story. At the same time, the President, apparently aware that no limited cover-up could long conceal the mountain of his Administration's misdeeds, had sharply stepped up efforts to bring the agencies and departments of the executive branch under his personal and political control, the better to prevent them from investigating him and to use them to threaten, blackmail, pressure, and otherwise harass and intimidate his political opponents. A "diary" entry for September that he quotes in his memoirs reveals something of his mood and intentions at this time. John Dean, the legal counsel to the White House, had been put in charge of the cover-up, and had been performing well, and now Nixon had wider responsibilities in mind for him:

> I had a good talk with John Dean and was enormously impressed with him. . . . He had the kind of steel and really mean instinct that we need to clean house after the election in various departments and to put the IRS and the Justice Department on the kind of basis that it should be on. There simply has to be a line drawn at times with those who are against us, and then we have to take action to deal with them effectively. Otherwise, they will be around to deal with us when their opportunity comes to them.

That opportunity was coming soon, as Nixon well knew, and the political "butchery" that followed the election was one of Nixon's preparations for the struggle.

In retrospect, we can see that the months just after the election—months in which Nixon was moving at top speed to get into a position to "deal with" his investigators so that they would no longer "be around" to deal with him, but in which neither those investigators nor the public showed much awareness of this growing threat or was doing anything about it—were the most dangerous for the country of the Watergate crisis. If the Administration was in any doubt as to the extent of its peril, a letter from James McCord, one of the Watergate burglars, to his White House contact was available in December to set it straight. McCord, a former employee of the C.I.A. who was afraid the White House would seek to pin the blame for the burglary on his old employer, warned that if the White House pursued such a course "it will be a scorched desert," and "every tree in the forest will fall." The reach of Nixon's power at this point was formidable. In the fall, a House Committee formed to look into campaign abuses had effectively been disabled. Owing in part to White House pressure, a majority of the members voted to deny its chairman, Representative Wright Patman, the power to subpoena witnesses, and he was reduced to asking questions of an empty chair. But the task before Nixon was formidable, too. It was not just the executive and legislative that had to be brought to heel, it was the judicial branch and the press as well, for all of them were involved in investigations of the White House. Nixon was sometimes accused of paranoia, but at this moment his

fears were not exaggerated; nor were the measures he was taking disproportionate. What his investigators could do to him now was remove him from
the political scene once and for all, and what he meant to do to them—and
do it first—was the same. The difference was that while they, in pursuing
him, would be carrying out the law, he, in stopping them, would have to
overthrow it.

While the Watergate story was about to burst into public view, the Vietnam
story, now having continued for more than a decade, was proceeding inex-
orably to its conclusion. In his Vietnam policy, Nixon had pursued two goals
that appeared to be ultimately irreconcilable. The pursuit of each had a
historical development reaching back long before Nixon's arrival in office.
The first goal was the withdrawal of American forces from Vietnam. It had
originated in the peace movement in the nineteen-sixties, been adopted by
mainstream politicians after the Tet offensive in early 1968, when the candidacy of Senator Eugene McCarthy and other circumstances had led President Johnson to quit the Democratic Presidential primaries and open
negotiations with the North Vietnamese and the National Liberation Front,
and it had been embraced by Richard Nixon, who, accepting the public's
clearly expressed will, had promised in his campaign to end the war, and
then, as President, had, while continuing to promise to end the war, in fact
withdrawn most of the American ground forces from Vietnam. The second
goal was guaranteeing the survival of the South Vietnamese government. This
goal had an even longer lineage, having been actively pursued by both
President Kennedy and President Johnson. It became clear only gradually
during Nixon's first term that he intended, even as he withdrew the troops,
to guarantee the survival of the Saigon regime. Indeed, as soon became
evident, there was no goal he believed in more fervently than this one.
Withdrawing the troops was a matter of political necessity. Preserving the
Saigon regime was a matter of deepest conviction. For of all the Presidents
of the postwar period Nixon was probably the one who believed most deeply
in the doctrine of credibility and its teaching that a defeat for American
power anywhere would undermine it everywhere. In this belief he was fervently supported by his national security adviser, Henry Kissinger. If there
is a single dominant theme of the Nixon Administration (and, one might
add, of both Nixon's and Kissinger's memoirs) it is that the credibility of the
United States—or the "honor" of the United States, or "respect for the presidency of the United States," as it was variously put—must never be compromised, and above all not by a defeat in Vietnam.

The great dilemma of the Nixon Administration was how to maneuver to
protect American credibility in Vietnam within the tight constraints of the

public's demand for a troop withdrawal. Herein lay also the roots of Nixon's secretive, high-handed, and eventually illegal behavior, for he believed national security required him to do many things that the public would not countenance. Unable to secure public approval for the measures he thought necessary, he acted alone—either secretly or in open defiance of the other branches of government—and came to believe himself besieged by domestic enemies. The origin of the particular Watergate abuses of power in particular abuses related to the Vietnam war has often been mentioned, but of much greater importance was the geopolitical philosophy that, by endowing the war in Vietnam with an apocalyptic importance, trapped the government in the war for so many years after the public had turned against it.

Nixon sought to bridge the gap between the two goals in his policy by what he called "Vietnamization"—seeking to equip and train South Vietnamese soldiers to take over the role played by the departing Americans. However, nothing the Saigon regime or military (which were in essence one and the same) had done in Nixon's first term suggested that they were in any way prepared either to fight the war on their own or to govern the country on their own. On the contrary, whenever they had been left to their own devices (as they had, for example, in the invasion of Laos in the spring of 1971) they had proved almost ludicrously incompetent. Nixon's other hope, as we know now but did not know at the time, was that the Soviet Union or China would help us by restraining the North Vietnamese, but that hope had also come to nothing. In his memoirs, Kissinger—a master of the oblique acknowledgment—refers indirectly to the crucial contradiction in the Administration's Vietnam policy. He writes that at a meeting in February of 1970, Le Duc Tho, his opposite number in the Vietnam peace negotiations, "cut to the heart of the dilemma of Vietnamization. All too acutely, he pointed out that our strategy was to withdraw enough forces to make the war bearable for the American people while simultaneously strengthening the Saigon forces so that they could stand on their own. He then asked a question that was tormenting me: 'Before, there were over a million U.S. and puppet troops, and you failed. How can you succeed when you let the puppet troops do the fighting?' " Kissinger, an acute and realistic observer of the situation on the ground in Vietnam, never gives a satisfactory answer to this question, and we are left to guess what he thought might really happen. Some observers suggested that the goal was to leave a "decent interval" between the American withdrawal and the collapse of the South. Kissinger denies this in some passages of his memoirs, but in others seems to come close to confirming it. For example, at one point he acknowledges that Vietnamization was "precarious" and would lead to "a delicate point . . . where our withdrawals would create uncertainty about South Vietnam's political future, jeopardizing the whole enterprise in the final hour," but then defends a negotiated withdrawal on the ground that it would give South Vietnam "a fair chance to survive," and would "end the war with an act of policy and leave the future of South Vietnam to an historical process." A "fair chance," in this context, sounds suspiciously like a "decent interval." (And the phrase "historical process" seems a particularly ingenious euphemism for the predictable onslaught of the North Vietnamese divisions.)

Now, in late 1972, the final hour was approaching. At a press conference on October 26th, after successful negotiations with the North Vietnamese on a peace accord, Kissinger had announced that "peace is at hand," and the public fully expected this promise to be fulfilled. However, in the agreement with the North Vietnamese, the United States had dropped a key demand— that the North Vietnamese troops in the South be required to withdraw— and no one with any knowledge of the war could doubt that North Vietnam had ever abandoned its intention of persisting in its historic quest to take over the south. Nor was it possible to doubt that, barring the re-entry of American forces into the war, the North Vietnamese would soon succeed (as of course they did). The question hanging in the air after Nixon's re-election was which of the two opposing goals Nixon would pursue to its conclusion when the moment of decision came. Would he hold to the path of withdrawal, and let South Vietnam collapse, even though, in his judgment, the free world might collapse with it? Or, defying the public's expectation of a withdrawal, and banking on the public support for him demonstrated by his landslide re-election, would he instead try to save South Vietnam by re-introducing American forces into the war, even though this would certainly provoke a domestic political crisis on an unprecedented scale?

Some actions taken by the Administration and some statements made later by Kissinger and Nixon in their memoirs have a bearing on this question. On November 14th, in a secret letter to President Thieu of South Vietnam asking him to sign the peace accord that Kissinger had negotiated in October with the North Vietnamese, Nixon wrote, "You have my absolute assurance that if Hanoi fails to abide by the terms of this agreement it is my intention to take swift and severe retaliatory action." On January 5th, he wrote to Thieu, "We will respond with full force should the settlement be violated by North Vietnam." And Kissinger wrote to Nixon in a cable on December 6th, "We will probably have little chance of maintaining the agreement without evident hair-trigger U.S. readiness, which may in fact be challenged at any time, to enforce its provisions." The touchiness of the hair-trigger was demonstrated in December, when Nixon, without public explanation or warning, ordered the heaviest bombing of North Vietnam of the war, including the use, for the first time, of B-52s against targets in Hanoi. The reasons for this bombing have never been fully explained. Nixon and Kissinger have said that it was to pressure the North Vietnamese into improving the terms of the peace accord, but this may be doubted, inasmuch as the terms of the final accords, signed that January, are substantially the same as those negotiated by Kissinger in October. Another explanation is that Nixon ordered the bombing to reassure Thieu of the genuineness of his will to re-enter the war if the North Vietnamese violated the agreement. Notwithstanding Nixon's letters of assurance, Thieu had refused to sign the accords in October, forcing the cancellation of a plan agreed to by both Nixon and the North Vietnamese to sign the accords before the Presidential election. It may have been that Nixon hoped that by bombing North Vietnam he could induce the south to sign the accords. A further possible explanation is that Nixon wished to demonstrate to the North Vietnamese that he had the will and the ability, at his discretion and without consultation with Congress or anyone else, to send American forces back into the war if North Vietnam violated the agreement.

Kissinger has defended the accords as sustainable (if he did not, he could not claim that the four years of continued American involvement during Nixon's first term had served to protect America's "honor"), but Thieu, who did not agree to sign the accords until the very day of the signing ceremony, saw the situation in a clearer light. In an interview with the Italian journalist Oriana Fallaci a few months after the signing, he described his negotiations with Kissinger in vivid terms. " 'You are a giant,' Thieu told Kissinger, referring to the United States. 'You weigh two hundred pounds, and if you swallow the wrong pill you don't even notice it . . . But I'm just a little man, maybe a little sick. I weigh hardly a hundred pounds, and if I swallow the same pill, I can die of it. . . . For me, it's not a question of choosing between Moscow and Peking. It's a question of choosing between life and death.' "

No one can know, of course, whether, if Nixon had been President when the North Vietnamese attacked, he would have sent American forces back into Vietnam, but the evidence points to an affirmative answer. Had he done so, his action would have precipitated a Constitutional crisis—one that would almost certainly have put the Watergate crisis in the shade. A passage from Kissinger's memoirs points to the form that this crisis might have taken:

As to the American response to violations, I reiterated Nixon's assurance that in the event of massive North Vietnamese violations the United States would act to enforce the agreement. The argument was later advanced that it was not within the President's power to give such assurances without explicit authorization by the Congress. This idea not only did not occur to us; it would have struck us as inconceivable that the United States should fight for years and lose 45,000 men in an honorable cause, and then stand by while the peace treaty, the achievement of their sacrifice, was flagrantly violated. Diplomacy could not survive such casuistry. Negotiations would become exercises in cynicism; no agreement would ever be maintained. In Vietnam this meant the agreement would have been a blatant subterfuge for surrender. We could have done that earlier and with much less pain. Honor, decency, credibility, and international law all combined to make it seem beyond controversy that we should promise to observe the treaty and see it enforced. What else could be the meaning of a solemn compact ending a war, ratified by an international conference? The point was made privately to Thieu and his associates. It was also made publicly by Nixon, Elliot Richardson (when he was Secretary of Defense), me, and other officials. . . . We thought we would be in a better moral and political position to assist Saigon to maintain its freedom in the name of a peace program in which the American people could take pride than in the context of open-ended warfare tearing our country apart. Whether the judgment would have been vindicated in normal times will remain forever unknown. Soon after the agreement was signed, Watergate undermined Nixon's authority, and the dam holding back Congressional antiwar resolutions burst.

In a meticulous, razor-sharp essay in *Foreign Affairs*, McGeorge Bundy has subjected several of the assertions here to intense examination. Searching through the public record, he finds that Nixon, Kissinger, and the other members of the Administration by no means announced to the world their commitment to Thieu to re-enter the Vietnam war with "full force" if the North Vietnamese violated the agreement. Rather, thoroughly mindful of the public's exhaustion with the war and of its firm expectation that the fighting was over, Administration spokesmen steered the country's attention away from thoughts of such dread actions. (For example, when Kissinger was asked in an interview with Marvin Kalb in February what "the nature and depth of the American commitment to Saigon" was, he mentioned economic assistance and the replacement of expended military equipment but made no mention of any promise to unleash "full force" if the agreement were broken.)

Bundy goes on to argue that Kissinger is wrong in claiming that it was the Watergate crisis that broke the dam holding back congressional action to stop the war. He points out that it was congressional debate about the bombing of Cambodia, which continued after the American withdrawal from Vietnam, that led to the passage, in July of 1973, of legislation prohibiting the use of force in Indo-China after August 15th. He finds that the Congress was heading toward such a resolution for reasons having to do with the war alone, and that "there is no evidence at all that this result was caused by Watergate." This judgment can be questioned. By June, the tables had turned in the Watergate crisis, and it was clear to all that Nixon's drive to concentrate power in the White House had been checked and that he was on the defensive. The turnabout came, in fact, on a particular day—April 17, 1973—when Nixon, unable any longer to keep the lid on the cover-up from within, lost the cooperation of its organizer, the White House counsel John Dean, and was forced to announce to the public that "major developments" had occurred. The Washington political community understood immediately that a watershed had been reached. Just as Nixon's bid for unconstitutional power had been all of a piece, so the rebuff to it by the Congress and other centers of power was all of a piece, and the disposition of many matters that had nothing to do with the burglary at the Watergate hotel was altered or reversed. Congress, in particular, was emboldened, across the board, to re-claim powers it had lost to the executive. There can be no doubt that after the reversal, Nixon's ability to take *any* action of doubtful constitutionality was sharply restricted.

One may further ask whether, if Nixon had been triumphing in the Wa-tergate struggle, he would have respected the congressional ban in the event that one had been passed anyway. Or, believing as he did that the survival of the free world was at stake, would he have overridden the ban and re-entered the war—while perhaps simultaneously challenging the legality of the ban in court, or asking Congress for some sort of retroactive sanction? It is even conceivable that Nixon would have seized on a crisis in Vietnam as an opportunity. Given a choice, he might well have preferred to battle his opponents over questions of supposedly supreme national interest in a foreign war—an area in which the country's reflexive reaction is to "support the President"—rather than to tangle with them in court over the question of whether he was using his office to obstruct justice at home. Another question is what forces Nixon would have used had he decided to make good on his pledge to re-introduce "full force" into the war. Air forces are an obvious candidate—especially for "hair-trigger" response. But if, as seems likely, these had failed to turn the tide, would he then, in order to avoid what now would be a direct defeat of American arms, have re-introduced ground forces? (Kissinger wanted to "enforce" the agreement, not just retal-iate.) Would not "honor, decency, credibility, and international law" all combine to require this? And wouldn't anything less make the agreement a "blatant subterfuge for surrender"? Indeed, "What else could be the meaning of a solemn compact ending a war, ratified by an international conference?" But if Nixon had re-introduced American ground forces—and introduced them in numbers sufficient to defeat a full-scale North Vietnamese invasion of the south—how would the Congress have responded? And how would the public at large have responded? Would Nixon, in these undoubtedly stormy circumstances, have respected the rights of demonstrators, or would he have suspended their rights wholesale, as he did in the much less menacing circumstances in May of 1971, when thousands of demonstrators in Washington were rounded up without benefit of due process? Might he have reached for emergency powers? Might these steps have appealed to him as a way of "dealing" with his opponents before they dealt with him?

The question of policy was whether the United States should re-enter the war. The Constitutional question was who should make that decision. In the passage just quoted from his memoirs, Kissinger raises the latter question ("The argument was later advanced that it was not within the President's power to give such assurances without explicit authorization by the Congress") but then ducks away from it by immediately answering the former question ("This idea not only did not occur to us; it would have struck us as inconceivable that the United States should fight for years and lose 45,000 men in an honorable cause, and then stand by while the peace treaty, the achievement of their sacrifice, was flagrantly violated"). The question he asks is *who* was to decide, but the question he answers is *what* should have been decided. In another passage he remarks that "in 1972 we had every intention of carrying out" the threats to re-enter the war. The question left unaddressed was who this "we" was. Was it the American people? Was it their elected representatives in the Congress? Was it the executive branch of the government? Was it Nixon and Kissinger, deciding alone, and in secrecy? The Constitution gives the power to declare war to the Congress, and the power to wage it to the executive. Nixon and Kissinger had a different understanding. They located the power to go to war, as well as the power to wage it, in the presidency. A startling passage in Kissinger's memoirs in which the issue of war and peace was raised suggests how far he and Nixon had gone in the direction of taking such decisions into their own hands. Kissinger reports that at the very beginning of the Administration Nixon and he had decided that if the Soviet Union attacked China the United States would come to China's aid. With evident pride, he states, "From the beginning, Nixon and I were convinced—alone among senior policymakers—that the United States could not accept a Soviet military assault on China. We had held this view before there was any contact [with China] of any sort; we imposed contingency planning on a reluctant bureaucracy as early as the summer of 1969." In 1969, a year in which the Soviet Union and China clashed repeatedly on their border, the possibility of a large-scale Soviet attack on China was real, and so, therefore, was the possibility that the United States would go to the aid of the latter in a confrontation that, by its very nature, would have threatened global nuclear war. As Kissinger notes, the United States at that time not only had no defense treaty with China (it still doesn't), it had no contact of any sort with that country, and in fact was engaged in a war in Vietnam whose aim, in part, was to "contain China." Yet without a word to the Congress or the public, he and the President had determined that in certain circumstances the United States should go to the defense of China, in a war in which the very existence of the United States—not to mention the rest of the world—would be threatened. To men used to making such decisions as these, in secret and at their sole discretion, a decision to re-enter the Vietnam war on their own authority may have seemed comparatively minor, and we can begin to believe Kissinger when he says that doubts on this point "not only did not occur to us" but were "inconceivable."

Ordinarily, speculation on the ifs of history is a dubious business; what actually happens is mysterious enough to us without wondering about what might have happened. In 1973, however, the United States was in the final stages of a crisis—the Vietnam war—which unexpectedly was resolved by another crisis—Watergate. A central part of the significance of Watergate, therefore, lies in the nature of the crisis that it headed off. For throughout the Vietnam war, the United States had labored under a great burden—the burden of believing that the credibility of the United States, and thus the survival of the free world, depended on the survival of the regime in Saigon. It was perhaps the greatest of the many great benefits of the successful resolution of the Watergate crisis that it permitted the country to relieve itself of this burden without a final crisis in the Vietnam war—without, that is, the re-entry into the war that Nixon promised Thieu, and without the domestic tumult that would have ensued. The underlying question—whether South Vietnam was really as important to the free world as not only Nixon but also the two Presidents before him had said—was not faced and settled; it was simply sidestepped. The attention of the country was drawn away from Vietnam to the story of Watergate. To be sure, the legal issues raised by Watergate were at bottom the ones also raised by the war. They were the questions that must arise in any full-scale Constitutional crisis: What are the powers of the President and of the other branches of government? Are government officials bound by the law? What are the rights of the people?

However, Watergate permitted these questions to be answered in the comparative calm of courtrooms and congressional committee rooms rather than in the streets or on foreign battlefields, as they would have been had the final struggle over Vietnam ever been joined. When the Watergate story reached its conclusion, it turned out to have removed from the picture the figure—Richard Nixon—who also was the central protagonist of the Vietnam story. In some mysterious way, his departure from the presidency lifted from the country the burden of protecting its credibility in Vietnam, as if he carried that burden away with him to San Clemente. The day Richard Nixon left office, but not one day earlier, the American withdrawal from Vietnam became irrevocable, and the decade-long crisis of the American intervention in Vietnam was at last resolved.

After all the years of dire warnings, the fall of South Vietnam, when it came, was barely noticed in the United States. The President—President Gerald Ford—made a point of playing golf at the height of the debacle. The nation as a whole went quietly about its business, as if it had never occurred to any American that some special importance might attach to the fate of the small half of a country which was now being settled on the other side of the world.

O F all the major political figures of recent years, the one whose reputation is least deserved is George McGovern. His party shuns him. The philosophy that bears his name—"McGovernism"—is a term of opprobrium, invented by the Republicans to discredit the Democrats. In every election since 1972, the Republicans have sought to portray the Democratic candidate as "another McGovern." Even the generic word for his political views—"liberal"—has been turned into an epithet: the "l-word." As late as the election of 1988, the principal strategy of the Republicans was to affix the liberal label on the Democratic candidate while the Democrats' principal strategy was to try to evade this, even at the price of seeming not to have any philosophy at all. They wanted to escape the designation because it was stained with the mud of political defeat—above all, the defeat of McGovern at the hands of Nixon in 1972, but also the defeat of Carter in 1980 and of Walter Mondale in 1984.

All of this would be perfectly comprehensible (considering how politicians feel about electoral defeat) if it were not for the fact that the election of 1972 was the one whose results were nullified by the impeachment proceedings of 1974. It's a thought-provoking fact about American political life that McGovern's electoral defeat has proven to be heavier political baggage for the Democrats than Nixon's indictment for high crimes and misdemeanors and resignation from the presidency has been for the Republicans. Today, while McGovern wanders in political exile, Nixon, staging yet another of his legendary "comebacks," returns to the limelight. His books are best-sellers; his advice is sought by the White House. This curious inversion of reputations, in which the disgraced President is honored and the unblemished candidate who opposed him and warned the country of his abuses of power is held in disrepute, points to one of the central mysteries of American political life in the post–Vietnam war period. McGovern, after all, was right, as the country soon came to believe, about the two great issues of his day: Vietnam and Watergate. But he was something more than right. He—or his message, at any rate—was heeded. In 1972 his voice cried in the wilderness; in 1974 he was heard: the nation did demand an end to the war, and the war ended; the nation did understand that Nixon threatened Constitutional rule, and Nixon was forced from office. The mystery goes beyond the fact that the prophet was not honored, for while he was losing the battle for public opinion, and has gone on losing it to this day, he was winning the battle for policy— for the decisions he wanted on the matters that were the most fateful ones of his time. The deeper paradox, therefore, lies not in the fact that the country reveres Nixon and rejects McGovern but in the fact that in doing so it seems to turn its back on its own choices and decisions of the early 1970s.

W HEN facts contradict theories, we are told, the theories should be discarded. It was not so with the theories that led the United States into the war in Vietnam. There is a large hole in the literature on foreign policy of recent years: the hole left by the absence of self-examination on the part of those who mistakenly advised three Presidents that the fall of South Vietnam would be catastrophic for the United States and the free world. How did they arrive at their mistaken theory, one would like to know? Which elements in the world scene did they overemphasize? Which did they overlook? Not only are the self-examinations of these men lacking but other men soon stepped forward to describe Vietnam—the obsession of the nation for a decade—as if it had been some freakish exception to a general rule that remained valid. No "lessons," these people argued, should be drawn from the experience, and any attempt to do so was a sort of mental aberration—the "Vietnam syndrome." The war had ended, but the picture of the world—the one sketched out by the domino theory and the credibility doctrine—survived. To be sure, in a sort of domestic version of the "decent interval," there was a period, lasting until about half-way through the presidency of Jimmy

Carter, in which this picture of the world was in eclipse; but soon it was advanced again, now teaching its lessons about Latin America, Africa, and other parts of the world. Once again, the government interpreted internal events in small countries simply as moves in the spread of World Communism. Once again it regarded the "loss" of any country as the leading edge of overall collapse of the forces of freedom. Once again it saw the power of the United States as the principal or sole bulwark against this drastic eventuality. And once again it saw credibility as the critical element in American power.

Yet there were differences. At first, it seemed likely that the Reagan Administration, which had derided the Carter Administration for weakness, would revive an interventionist policy; but as the years went by the intervention never came. In the Vietnam years, belligerent words were accompanied by belligerent deeds. That was what credibility was thought to require. In the Reagan years, the world of words and the world of deeds drifted apart, as if belligerent words had become an end in themselves. To be sure, whenever apparent toughness could be demonstrated without paying a high cost—as it could be, for example, in the invasion of the tiny nation of Grenada, or in the bombing of Libya, in response to terrorist attacks—the Administration acted, and the public applauded. But when intervention clearly had a high cost attached, as it would have, for example, in any intervention by American forces in Nicaragua, or, after a certain point, in stepped-up intervention in Lebanon, the Administration held back, and the public made no complaint. The line that the public did not wish to cross was clearly, if not nobly, drawn: the expenditure of the lives of people from other countries was acceptable; the expenditure of American lives was not. (The combination of tough words and weak action appeared in other areas of policy, too. The Administration was in theory opposed to high budget deficits but in practice opposed to the increased taxes that were needed to reduce them. This performance, too, was popular with the public.) The Administration proved skillful at cutting losses in situations in which the costs of intervention threatened to get out of hand. In July of 1973, for example, Secretary of Defense Caspar Weinberger defended the presence of American Marines in Lebanon on the grounds that "a force" (presumably the Soviet Union) otherwise might take over the Mid-East, and therefore the "credibility on a global scale" of American power was at stake; yet shortly afterward the Administration quietly withdrew the Marines from Lebanon. And in May of 1983, United Nations Ambassador Jeane Kirkpatrick told of "a plan" she knew of "to create a Communist Central America," but no American forces were ever dispatched to prevent this. (Instead, the C.I.A. organized the contras, and Colonel Oliver North was sent in secret to deliver the Ayatollah Khomeini's money to them. These policies have kept Nicaragua in a state of war for eight years; whether they will prove sufficient to topple the Nicaraguan government has yet to be seen.)

The public, it seemed, was philosophically in favor of intervention but viscerally opposed. Thanks to Watergate, the Vietnam war ended while the nation's back was turned, and this was certainly fortunate, inasmuch as it spared the country a crisis that its Constitutional system might not have survived. Yet it may be that just because that crisis never took place, and therefore no final debate on the theories that underlay the war ever took place, those theories were left unaffected by the debacle, and survived to guide policy statements (if not policy) again. Strangely, after ten years of fighting in Vietnam and political turmoil at home, the war remained undigested in public opinion, which was left in its state of unresolved ambivalence—repelled by the tangible prospect of any more Vietnams, yet still attracted to the policies that had led the United States into Vietnam. McGovern's political mistake had been to begin to articulate a picture of the world that reflected only one side of the public's ambivalence. President Carter, straying further down this path, won a McGovern-like reputation for weakness, and was rewarded with defeat in the 1980 Presidential election. The Reagan Administration was politically wiser. Reagan followed to the letter the public preferences revealed in the latter days of the Vietnam war: he gave the public McGovernite decisions accompanied by Nixonian talk, and the public returned him to office in a landslide.

I N the Reagan years, the debate between those who wanted to learn "lessons" from the war in Vietnam and those who regarded these lessons as an illness underwent a generalization into other issues of policy. The process by which this occurred showed the remarkable power of analogy in the nation's political thinking. The rationale for the Vietnam war, of course, was based on the Munich analogy, which insisted that the challenge to the United States posed by a North Vietnam or a Cuba was essentially the same as the challenge posed to the democracies by Hitler in the years before the Second World War. Now a new analogy, based on Vietnam, was put forward by many of those who had opposed the war. At its heart was the idea of the limits of power. Just as the United States, in spite of its military might, had failed to have its way in Vietnam, they argued, so it would fail in other countries it might intervene in. Furthermore, they said, revolutionaries in small countries now represented chiefly themselves, not World Communism; therefore it was unnecessary for the United States to oppose them. Soon, the idea of limits was extended to cover matters that had nothing to do with military intervention. Just as there were limits to the use of military power, so there were limits, it was said, to oil and other energy resources (the Arab oil embargo of 1973 was fresh in people's memory), to the resiliency of the natural environment, to the capacity of the earth to sustain population growth, and, perhaps, to economic growth. These limits were spelled out and projected into the future in a bleak volume called "Global Report 2000" that President Carter had ordered written.

The Republicans seized on the theme of limits—but only to reject it wholesale. The limits were all imaginary, they proclaimed, beginning with the supposed limits of the usefulness of military force. What was even worse, they said, the belief in limits was in actuality a symptom of a dangerous "loss of nerve" afflicting the West—a collapse of will that, if not reversed, would send the West into a needless, self-inflicted decline. In opposition to the Vietnam analogy, they raised again the banner of the Munich analogy. The only limit on the usefulness of force, they argued, was the limit on the Democrats' willingness to use it. (The capture of American hostages by Iranians and the failure of the Carter Administration somehow to compel their release promptly was held up as an object lesson.) The Republicans, too, generalized their new theme. Just as the limits on the usefulness of military power were self-created, they said, so were the various limits on growth. Against the Democrats' "pessimism," they offered a generalized "optimism"— optimism regarding the military power and economic potential of the United States. The Democrats were "mesmerized by defeat," and had lost "the confidence and optimism about the future that has made us unique in the world," as President Reagan put it at the Republican Convention in 1984. The nation's turnabout since ending the war in Vietnam was now complete. The "lesson" of the war was to *not* learn any lesson from it, and this wisdom had been enlarged to encompass not just military intervention but virtually any matter whatever.

I T'S a commonplace, and a well-founded one, that American politics in recent decades has been based more on public-relations images than on substance, and many explanations of a technical nature, including the rise of television and the rise of public-opinion polling, have been offered as explanations. However, there may also be an explanation stemming from the political events of the period. In the early nineteen-seventies, the nation made two momentous decisions: it left—and "lost"—South Vietnam, suffering its first military defeat of this century; and it forced Richard Nixon from the presidency, in the first forced departure of a President from office in its history. The nation made these decisions in anguish, after long delay, and by circuitous paths, but it did make them. Neither decision was in any way casual or accidental: the Vietnam war ended and Richard Nixon left office in mid-term because that was the will of the American people. In 1980, this same American people elected to office a man who, to judge by his record of support for both the war and President Nixon up to the last minute, favored neither of these decisions, who had learned nothing from them, and who conducted himself thereafter as if neither had ever occurred. The public, however, did not extend any permission to him to repeat either intervention of the Vietnam variety or abuses of the Watergate variety, as the public's unfavorable reaction to the prospect of intervention in Nicaragua and to the fact of the Iran-contra scandal showed. Attorney General John Mitchell once advised unhappy civil rights leaders to "watch what we do, not what we say," and in the nineteen-eighties the American public as a whole seemed to adopt the motto as its own. Now not just the government but the people apparently wanted to say one thing while doing another—to talk belligerently but act with restraint. The techniques of public relations permit one to say one thing while doing another, and in the nineteen-eighties the need for such an ability was there. It went back to the final days of the Vietnam war, when it became clear that the nation's capacities (for fighting and winning wars like the one in Vietnam) could not achieve its goals (controlling the internal events of nations all over the world). Unwilling either to continue its exertions or to give up the goals, the country embarked on the bifurcated course of rhetorical toughness and practical restraint. There followed, in the Reagan years, the most spectacular flowering of the techniques of public relations ever seen in the United States—a flowering in which the world of images was offered not just to prettify policy but to supplant it. An election is meant to express the will of the people, and in 1980, and again in 1984, that will may have been not to come to grips with the world's problems but to take a vacation from them.

I N the years since the end of the Vietnam war, the United States has been at peace, and this is to the credit of Presidents Carter, Ford, and Reagan. (History is likely to judge them more on what they did than on what they said.) One reason, certainly, was the public's reluctance to support a policy of intervention. Another, which may have been more important, was the nature of events in this period. The struggle in Vietnam was crucial in the eyes of the policymakers because it was supposed to be a "test-case" of

Communist insurgencies that were primed to erupt in innumerable countries. The Russians, it seems, shared this expectation, and in 1961 Khrushchev announced his support for "wars of national liberation." Che Guevara, the Cuban revolutionary, looked forward to "one, two, three . . . many Vietnams." They never came. In the post–Vietnam war years, the world simply failed to provide a long succession of wars of the kind predicted by the credibility theory, which would have tempted the United States into repeated intervention. No doubt doves were primed to point out that the United States could not prevail in this or that situation, and hawks were ready to answer that such views were symptoms of the Vietnam syndrome, and that this time intervention would work. (And in fact these arguments were heard in a lower key in the debate over the use of the contra proxies in Nicaragua.) If, in the second term of the Reagan Administration, the doctrine of credibility began to lose its grip to some extent on people's minds, the reason was not that the argument against it had been won but that events did not supply sufficient grist for its continuation. The theory was at last beginning to starve for want of facts to keep it alive.

And what *was* happening in those years? Many things: a fundamentalist Islamic movement, as divorced from American capitalism as it was from Soviet Communism; a return to democratic government in many countries that had been run by military dictatorships (no need here for the United States to uphold dictatorial regimes against left-wing insurgents); a powerful, non-violent rebellion against Soviet totalitarian domination in Poland; a far-reaching, if unpredictable, movement for reform in official circles throughout the Communist world. These events—the events that were actually redrawing the map of the world—did not directly refute the domino/credibility theory; they were simply irrelevant to it. One event, however, did have a direct bearing on the theory, though in an unexpected way—the Soviet invasion of Afghanistan. Seeming at first to offer confirmation of the notion that World Communism was on the march, it later offered the first example, since Hitler's invasion of the Soviet Union, of Soviet armies retreating under fire and in failure from a country they had occupied. This spectacle seemed to confirm one of the principal lessons of the war in Vietnam: that in the contemporary world Great Powers would find it either impossible or profitless to try to extend their domination over small countries.

If in the political climate of today's world another Vietnam seems unlikely, so does another Constitutional crisis of the kind that grew out of Vietnam. What the United States might have done to its Constitution and its liberties had history handed it "one, two, three . . . many Vietnams" we cannot say, although the record of what we did to ourselves with just the one does not support optimism. As it was, the policymakers' predictions were wrong, and we can afford to be more hopeful. The Constitutional crisis of the Vietnam period belongs to a day that has passed. The world, unmindful of our theories, went its own variegated way, and we were spared.

ABOUT THE AUTHOR

Jonathan Schell was born in 1943 in New York City, where he still lives. He attended the Dalton School, the Putney School, and Harvard College. From 1967 until 1988, he was a writer for *The New Yorker*. His previous books are *The Real War*, *History in Sherman Park*, *The Abolition*, *The Fate of the Earth*, and *The Time of Illusion*.